THE ARAB
UPRISING

THE ARAB UPRISING

THE UNFINISHED REVOLUTIONS
OF THE NEW MIDDLE EAST

MARC LYNCH

PUBLICAFFAIRS
NEW YORK

Published in the United States by PublicAffairs™,
a Member of the Perseus Books Group

PublicAffairs books are available at special discounts for bulk purchases in the
U.S. by corporations, institutions, and other organizations. For more information,
please contact the Special Markets Department at the Perseus Books Group,
2300 Chestnut Street, Suite 200, Philadelphia, PA 19103, call (800) 810-4145,
ext. 5000, or e-mail special.markets@perseusbooks.com.

Text design by Jill Shaffer
Set in 11-point Albertina by Eclipse Publishing Services

Library of Congress Cataloging-in-Publication Data
Lynch, Marc, 1969-
    The Arab uprising : the unfinished revolutions of the new Middle East /
Marc Lynch. — 1st ed.
        p. cm.
    Includes bibliographical references and index.
    ISBN 978-1-61039-084-2 (hardcover) — ISBN 978-1-61039-085-9
(electronic) 1. Democratization—Arab countries. 2.
Democratization—Middle East. 3. Democracy—Arab countries. 4.
Democracy—Middle East. 5. Protest movements—Arab countries—History—
21st century. 6. Protest movements—Middle East--History—21st century.
7. Arab countries—Politics and government—21st century. 8. Middle
East—Politics and government—21st century. 9. Protest movements—Arab
countries I.
Title.
    JQ1850.A91L928 2012
    956.05'4—dc23
                                        2011042999

First Edition
10 9 8 7 6 5 4 3 2 1

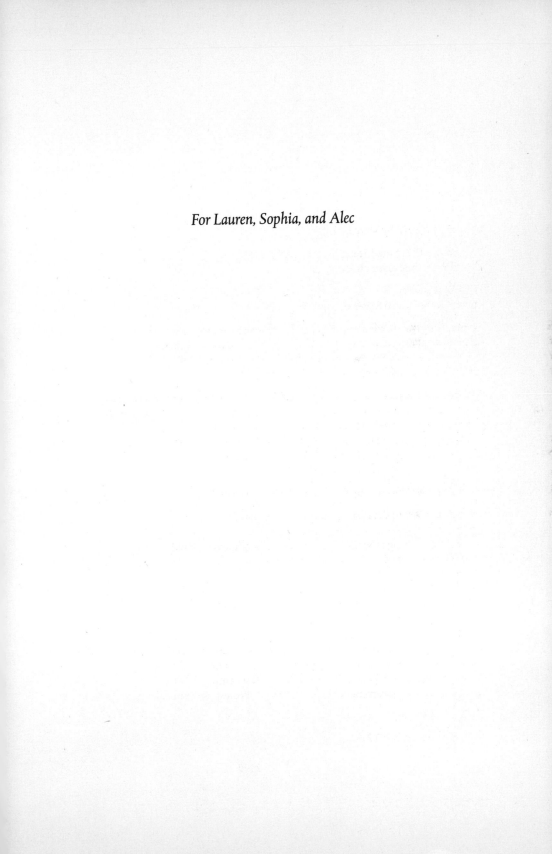

For Lauren, Sophia, and Alec

CONTENTS

INTRODUCTION 1

CHAPTER 1: THE ARAB UPRISINGS 7

CHAPTER 2: THE ARAB COLD WAR 29

CHAPTER 3: BUILDING TOWARD REVOLUTION 43

CHAPTER 4: A NEW HOPE 67

CHAPTER 5: THE TIDAL WAVE 101

CHAPTER 6: THE EMPIRE STRIKES BACK: 131
THE COUNTERREVOLUTION

CHAPTER 7: INTERVENTION AND CIVIL WAR 161

CHAPTER 8: AMERICA'S CHALLENGE 193

ACKNOWLEDGMENTS 237

NOTES 241

INDEX 257

INTRODUCTION

O N FEBRUARY 10, 2011, Egyptian President Hosni Mubarak stepped before the TV camera for the third time since the January 25 revolution began. Massive crowds in Tahrir Square quieted. President Barack Obama and his closest advisers turned up the television volume on al-Jazeera English. After weeks of escalating protests, tense clashes in the streets, turmoil in the ruling elite, and fierce international pressure, virtually everyone expected Mubarak to announce his resignation.

Instead, casting himself as "a father to his sons and daughters," he delivered a meandering, condescending address. He assured, paternalistically, that "as a president I find no shame in listening to my country's youth"—but showed no sign of having actually done so. He laid out a time line for a transition of power over seven months, which made clear that he had no intention of immediately stepping down. The hundreds of thousands of Egyptians gathered in central Cairo roared with rage.

Seconds after the speech ended, I received an e-mail from one of President Obama's top advisers on his way to a meeting in the Situation Room: "What do you make of that?" This book is in part my attempt to answer his question, and my own, about the dramatic changes that have unsettled so many assumptions and certainties in the Middle East.

It is commonly said that nobody predicted the upheavals in the Arab world that began in December 2010 and defined the following year.[1] But that does not mean that nobody saw them coming. The crumbling foundations of the Arab order were visible to all who cared to look. Political systems that had opened slightly in the mid-2000s were once again closing down, victim to regime manipulation and repression. Economies failed to produce jobs for an exploding population of young people. As the gap between rich and poor grew, so did corruption and escalating resentment of an out-of-touch and arrogant ruling class. Meanwhile, Islamist movements continued to transform public culture even as Arab regimes used the threat of al-Qaeda to justify harsh security crackdowns.

Regional politics was equally stalled. The Israeli-Palestinian peace process, which remained central to Arab political identity and discourse, had long since gone on life support. Arab states seemed indifferent to its collapse, though, and even cooperated openly with Israel on the enforcement of the blockade of Gaza. In the spring of 2010, the Arabs were unable to even organize a single Arab summit meeting to discuss the problems of Palestine and Lebanon due to the bickering of the competing regimes, as Egyptian and Saudi leaders declined to travel to Doha in support of Qatari initiatives. A debilitating "cold war" between America's autocratic allies and the forces of *muqawama* (resistance) such as Iran, Hamas, and Hezbollah dominated the official agenda of regional international relations, spreading in its wake a nasty Sunni-Shi'a sectarianism that divided many Arab societies. To many Arabs, the behavior of their leaders contributed to the perennial failures of the Arab order. The need for change had grown urgent and painfully obvious to frustrated youth who had long since given up any hope that their leaders might themselves change.

All of these frustrations festered at a time of radical, revolutionary change in the information environment. Perhaps the Arab regimes had always been bickering, incompetent, corrupt. But now, thanks to satellite televisions stations like al-Jazeera and the spreading presence of the Internet, their follies were on full display to a skeptical Arab public. Arab leaders could no longer go about their business in private while crushing any sign of discontent. Their people now had access to information and an ability to express their opinions publicly far beyond anything the region had ever before known. When Mohammed Bouazizi set himself on fire in Sidi Bouzid in protest over abusive police on December 17, 2010, the Arab world was ready to respond.

I have been deeply immersed in the evolution of what I call a "new Arab public sphere" for well over a decade. My 2006 book *Voices of the*

New Arab Public had focused on al-Jazeera and the satellite television revolution that had shattered the Arab regimes' ability to control the flow of information or the expression of opinion. Most of my academic writings have focused on the impact of new communications technologies and their effects on political and social action. I had written about Egyptian bloggers and their political activism, as well as how Internet activism was changing the perspectives of young members of the Muslim Brotherhood. I had written about how al-Qaeda and radical Islamists used the new media, including Internet forums, to spread their narratives and their propaganda. I had written about al-Jazeera's talk shows and news coverage, and how they spread both a pan-Arabist identity and a political orientation highly critical of the authoritarian status quo. All of these writings pointed toward the evolution of a new public sphere that would inevitably challenge the pillars of Arab authoritarian domination.

I also played an active role in the Arab public sphere through my own blog, "Abu Aardvark."[2] While written in English (like many of the more influential Arab political blogs), Abu Aardvark was deeply immersed in Arab political debates and discourse. I tried to translate the debates in Arabic for a Western audience, while engaging personally in the contentious debates that consumed Arab discourse. When political discourse moved onto Twitter, so did I (you can find me at @abuaardvark). In the spring of 2010, I helped to launch the Middle East Channel on ForeignPolicy.com, where I solicited and personally edited hundreds of essays by leading academic experts as well as commentators from the region. My dual personalities had never felt more intertwined than on January 25, 2011, as I watched the Egyptian revolution unfold in real time on Twitter, while sitting on a stage moderating an academic panel discussion about the Tunisian revolution.

Through my own blogging and research, I got to know many of the leading Arab Internet activists personally, both through online engagement and during my travels to the region. I followed in real time over the course of a decade the struggles, travails, and successes of the new public. I saw them fail to force immediate political change, but argued repeatedly that they were nonetheless driving a generational revolution in expectations and attitudes. I struggled with the moral hazard inherent in encouraging their political activism while leaving them at the tender mercies of state security. And I struggled every day with the vast chasm that separated their views of America and the Middle East from what I heard every day in Washington.

I also became deeply involved in debates about American foreign policy. In the years following 9/11, I urged the Bush administration to take Arab opinion seriously and to engage more effectively with the emerging Arab public sphere through a reinvigorated public diplomacy. I challenged the neoconservatives aligned with the Bush administration to reconcile their avowed support for Arab democratization with their adoption of policies and rhetoric that infuriated exactly the people they claimed to want to empower. In the fall of 2008, I warned a congressional audience (and later, in private, the CENTCOM strategic review team tasked by General David Petraeus for the incoming Obama administration to review the foundations of America's strategic presence in the Middle East) that the crumbling Egyptian state and steadily closing political space would be unsustainable (a version of which I published on the blog).[3] My involvement with these policy debates sharpened my sense of urgency in translating academic expertise into real impact on these issues about which I cared so deeply.

I moved to Washington, D.C., in the summer of 2007 to join the new Institute for Middle East Studies at the George Washington University, and signed on as a Middle East policy adviser to the then long-shot presidential campaign of Barack Obama. I worked as one of the small core group of policy advisers to the campaign on Iraq and the Middle East until election day. I opted not to go into government service after the election, but remained close to many administration officials. When the Arab uprisings began, I found myself consulting frequently and intensely with administration officials from across the agencies. I attended dozens of off-the-record working groups and expert engagement sessions, spoke privately with administration officials at all levels, and debated Egypt policy with President Obama himself.

From these multiple vantage points, I can say from deep experience that many of us in the community of scholars warned of the crumbling foundations of Arab authoritarian rule. The canard that liberals or Middle East experts did not believe in Arab democracy could not be farther from the truth—if anything, these communities were too quick to identify with popular movements and too instinctively suspicious of the intentions of ruling elites. But I would not pretend to be anything other than stunned by the enormity or speed of the Arab uprising that finally came. I had anticipated a slower, generational transformation. It was the difference between seeing structural changes happening below the surface and watching the chaotic reality of politics.

The Tunisian uprising and its aftermath demonstrates the radical reality of contingency and randomness in politics. The course of events in each country could easily have gone differently at crucial moments: a panicked soldier in Tahrir Square could have opened fire and started a stampede; the Bahraini crown prince might have struck a reform deal before the Saudis lost patience and rolled in their troops; Syrian president Bashar al-Assad might have decided not to try to crush protests in Deraa. But beneath the random turbulence and human agency, there were deeper forces at work. The uprising would have been impossible without factors like generational change, new technologies, American leadership, and the regional military balance of power, all working together.

This book seeks to make sense of what happened and to offer a guide to what is to come. What we have seen in the first year of the uprisings, I argue, are only the very earliest manifestations of a deeper transformation. And understanding the implications of those changes will require us to move beyond stale ideological debates and outdated theories in order to grapple with the new realities of an empowered but far from triumphant Arab public.

CHAPTER 1

THE ARAB UPRISINGS

Why does every nation on Earth move to change their conditions except for us? Why do we always submit to the batons of the rulers and their repression? Didn't the Palestinians resist with stones and knives? Didn't Marcos and Suharto and Milosevic and Barri fall? Did the Georgian people wait for the Americans to liberate them from their corrupt President? How long will Arabs wait for foreign saviors?

—TALK SHOW HOST FAISAL AL-QASSEM,
AL-JAZEERA, DECEMBER 23, 2003[1]

THE UPRISINGS that have profoundly shaped the Middle East began in a remote outpost of southern Tunisia on December 17, 2010, with the self-immolation of an unknown young man named Mohammed Bouazizi in protest against abusive and corrupt police. His act could have been yet another well-meant but meaningless protest in an obscure region, accomplishing little. Yet something was different this time.

Within a month of this event and the first, small Tunisian protests, hundreds of thousands of youth protestors had taken to the streets in almost every Arab country. Protestors in different nations chanted the same slogans—"The people want to overthrow the regime!"—and waved the same banners. They fed off each others' momentum and felt the pain of each others' reversals. Within less than a year, three Arab leaders, long in power, had fallen and others faced mortal challenges.

The rapid spread of protests across the entire region transformed what had begun as a fairly typical bout of turmoil on the periphery of the Arab world into a revolutionary moment—a fully-fledged Arab uprising. Even before Tunisian President Zine el-Abidine Ben Ali's flight from his country on January 14, 2011, almost everyone with a stake in Arab politics was already focused on who was next. Every government declared that it was not another Tunisia. Every citizen in the Arab world seemed to hope that it was. Over the next few months, protests did indeed break out in most Arab countries—attracting very different responses from regimes and from outside powers, and producing very different outcomes.

Protests spread so quickly and powerfully from the margins of Tunis because they took place within a radically new Arab political space. A new generation of Arabs had come of age watching al-Jazeera, the Qatari satellite television station; connecting with each other through social media; and internalizing a new kind of pan-Arabist identity. They had protested together virtually in real time in support of the Palestinian Al-Aqsa Intifada in 2000 and against the American invasion of Iraq in 2003. They had watched together as Lebanese rose up against Syrian occupation in 2005 and then suffered Israeli bombardment in 2006. They had complained publicly about their leaders, stalled economies, and stagnant politics after long decades of keeping quiet—and had noticed the common concerns across the region. Virtually every Arab anywhere in the region could imagine herself in the shoes of these suddenly mobilized Tunisians.

The Arab uprising unfolded as a single, unified narrative of protest with shared heroes and villains, common stakes, and a deeply felt sense of shared destiny. Many of the upheavals after the one in Tunisia became known by the date of their home country's first protest or else of a pivotal moment of escalation or repression, used as a hashtag on Twitter or a promotional spot on al-Jazeera. The rhythm of revolt synchronized across the entire region, with each Friday's "day of rage" seeming to bring the region closer to fundamental transformation. At that moment, anything seemed possible and every Arab population could hope for immediate, peaceful change. The unified Arab world of which generations of pan-Arab ideologues had dreamed had never felt more real.

Then the tight interconnections of regional politics worked in the opposite direction. After the relatively peaceful departure of Egypt's president, Hosni Mubarak, and Ben Ali, the other Arab dictators refused to go peacefully. Brutal attacks on peaceful protestors in Bahrain, Yemen, Libya, and Syria signaled the beginning of the play's second, darker act. An empowered Arab public could force itself onto the stage, but it could not always survive when suddenly threatened dictators unleashed the full force of their violence. The magical images of a unified people peacefully forcing Mubarak from power gave way to gut-churning videos of unarmed protestors gunned down in the streets.

After intervening to prevent an impending massacre by Libyan president Moammar Qaddafi's forces, American and NATO warplanes were bombing Libya by March. A harsh sectarian crackdown against protestors in Bahrain risked sparking a new regional proxy war between Saudi Arabia and Iran. Yemen's regime teetered between peaceful protest and renewed insurgency with nobody able to find a path out of stalemate. Syria's incredibly courageous protestors were met with horrifying massacres and a paralyzed international community. Saudi Arabia emerged as the center of counterrevolution, spreading wealth and political support to conservative regimes across the region. Meanwhile, even the supposedly triumphant revolutionaries in Egypt and Tunisia found their own victories incomplete as they struggled with resurgent Islamist movements and opaque interim military regimes. Through it all, traditional rivals Israel and Iran sat nervously on the sidelines, and the United States struggled to balance its hopes for democratic change with fears for its vital interests.

What are the Arab uprisings? Clearly the events of 2011 in the Middle East are not yet a story of democratic transitions. Nor are they yet clearly revolutions. *Arab Spring*—a term that I may have unintentionally coined in a January 6, 2011, article—does not do justice to the nature of the change.[2] The uprisings are an exceptionally rapid, intense, and nearly simultaneous explosion of popular protest across an Arab world united by a shared transnational media and bound by a common identity. Those uprisings are playing out very differently across the region and are likely to produce new, very mixed regional politics—some new democracies, some retrenched dictatorships, some reformed monarchies, some collapsed states, and some civil wars. They will likely intensify regional competition, drive new alliances and rivalries, and change the nature of power politics.

I believe that these world-shaking events, from the peaceful revolutions in Tunisia and Egypt to the brutal, grinding battles in Bahrain, Libya, Syria, and Yemen, are but the first, early manifestations of changes still to come. They are driven in part by a generational change, as a frustrated youth population confronts hopeless economies, rampant corruption, blocked politics, and indifferent, abusive state institutions. Their grievances took form within a genuinely structural change in the very nature of regional politics: the rise of what for over a decade I have referred to as the rise of the "new Arab public sphere."[3] This change will fundamentally challenge the power of Arab states and force the demands, interests, and concerns of an engaged public onto every political agenda. That challenge will sometimes be peaceful, but will too often be bloody as regimes jealously cling to their accustomed power.

The fate of particular dictators is therefore the least interesting part of a much bigger story. The Arab uprisings are only the very earliest manifestations of a powerful change in the basic stuff of the region's politics. Regional and foreign powers alike will continue their competition within these more turbulent arenas, intervening where it suits their interests and turning a blind eye when it does not. New rules and norms will emerge to govern regional interactions. Perhaps, if things go well, it will become commonly accepted that rulers who massacre their own people will lose their legitimacy; perhaps, if they do not, more cynical patterns will take hold in which humanitarian interventions target enemies while the same infractions by friends go unremarked. The Palestinian issue will continue to occupy a central place in Arab identity but, with the fading hopes of a two-state solution, may adopt very different forms. The Arab people have been empowered. From now on, they will play an ever greater role in regional politics. And everyone with a stake in the region's future will be forced to adapt.

The transformation that led to the Arab uprising starts with new information and communications technologies, including satellite television, the Internet, and cheap mobile phones. The widespread dissemination and use of such technology has radically reshaped the way information, ideas, and opinions flow through Arab society. The role of social media and the Internet in the Arab uprisings has often been exaggerated, with too much emphasis on Facebook or Twitter rather than on the underlying political struggles. But this generational, structural change in the nature of political communication represents the most fundamental and significant real effect of these new media.

There were three great effects of this new media environment. First, the free flow of information and the explosion of public discourse and open debate have shattered one of the core pillars of the authoritarian Arab systems that evolved over the 1970s and 1980s: their ability to control the flow of ideas and to enforce public conformity. Second, it has given today's activists and ordinary citizens new skills, expectations, and abilities. They operate within a radically new information environment, expect different things from their states and societies, and are able to act in new ways to demand them. Finally, it has unified the Arab political space, bringing together all regional issues into a common narrative of a shared fate and struggle. This new Arab public sphere is highly critical of most ruling regimes, extremely pan-Arabist in its orientation, and self-consciously celebratory of the power of a long-denied Arab street.

These effects of the new public sphere matter more in the Middle East than in other parts of the world because Arab regimes depended so heavily on their ability to dominate and control the public sphere. Today, it is difficult to recall what a black hole the Arab media was only two decades ago. Arab information ministries tightly and ruthlessly controlled the flow of information and opinion. State television stations offered a monotonous, toxic brew of official pronouncements and glorification of presidents and kings. Editorials were often written directly by intelligence agencies or were rigorously censored so as to uphold the government's talking points. Many Arab state media outlets, from Egypt to Saudi Arabia, became so good at managing the media that in 1990, they were able to suppress information about the Iraqi invasion of Kuwait for days while regimes struggled to formulate a response. Today, such an invasion would be televised, blogged, tweeted, and posted to YouTube within minutes of the troops crossing the border.

Arab authoritarianism depended on iron control of the public sphere. The regimes ultimately rested on violence and fear, smoothed by patronage, but even the most brutal of them made some effort to legitimize their rule.[4] These systems depended on near-total public conformity, with extensive networks of intelligence services and oppressive policing of what Arabs typically call "the red lines" governing politically safe public discourse. As Middle East scholar Lisa Wedeen demonstrates in her brilliant dissection of the Syrian cult of personality surrounding then-president Hafez al-Assad, the operation of state power can be seem most thoroughly in its ability to enforce public compliance with ideas and rhetoric that almost all know to be false. In Wedeen's classic example, educated Syrian professionals would agree to pretend in public that their president was the country's greatest dentist—not because they believed it, but because the regime demonstrated its power by compelling them to say so.[5]

The new generation instead openly mocked their leaders. Al-Jazeera talk shows in the early 2000s made sport of the 99 percent electoral victories that once symbolized the unchallengeable power of the "presidents for life." Online forums circulated wickedly funny cartoons of the formerly infallible leaders. Before anyone could even remark on the changes, the most fundamental pillar of Arab authoritarianism in its deepest form had simply collapsed. But even as the information environment changed in such fundamental ways, as governing institutions crumbled and publics raged, the authoritarian regimes of the Arab world attempted to maintain their absolute control. After limited political openings in the middle of the 2000s, many Arab regimes became more repressive in the last years of the decade, even as their people grew more impatient and more capable of expressing dissent.

There was something else unique about the Arab world. More so than in any other part of the world, the Arabs were integrated within a shared political space, united by a common identity, a shared narrative, and a coherent set of debates, issues, and concerns. The Arab world had always been more tightly connected than any other region in world politics, linked by a common language and a politically constructed but very real sense of shared fate. In the 1950s, thousands of Arabs had poured into the streets to protest Western imperialism and demand Arab unification at the behest of incendiary Egyptian radio broadcasts. This had faded in the 1970s and 1980s. But in the early 2000s, driven in large part by al-Jazeera and the new media, the Arab space began to reunify. In this emerging reality, all Arabs cared about Palestine or about Iraq—and, indeed, caring about such things was part of what defined them as

"Arab." Satellite television and the Internet made those connections more intense and more intimate, faster and more focused than ever before.

This was a generational change. This rising generation of young people had spent their formative years on the Internet, plotting their next protest rather than hiding from politics. Most could not even conceive of the world of the 1970s and 1980s, when authoritarian regimes dominated every aspect of public life and citizens bowed down to personality cults. As one older pundit marveled over the summer, "I feel optimistic when I see the youth speaking on the satellite television programs . . . surpassing their elders in their thoughts and analyses, for they are liberated from the censor whose knife was at the throat of their elders."[6] The Arab public was transforming into something much more participatory, much less deferential to authority, much less patient, much less susceptible to regime propaganda, and much more able to connect and communicate across distances and to acquire information of all sorts. But their political systems failed to evolve to accommodate their new demands, even as economic hardship and a litany of political failures fueled popular alienation.

The combination of rising public challenge and a unified Arab public sphere rapidly rewired the game of regional politics. Over the first decade of the 2000s, the rhythms of televised and wired protest almost imperceptibly became the normal state of regional affairs. When massive protests marched simultaneously through Cairo, Rabat, and Sanaa in 2000 over the Palestinian-Israeli war and in 2003 over the American invasion of Iraq, al-Jazeera almost single-handedly united these disparate protests into a single coherent narrative of regional rage. Lebanon's "Cedar Revolution," following the assassination of Prime Minister Rafik Hariri in 2005, offered the spectacle of a single country's mass protests dominating the political agenda of an entire region. Egypt's Kefaya movement demanding political reform through the middle of the decade became the regional template for wired networks of online and offline youth activists. Meanwhile, the spirit of protest and challenge spread far beyond these highly visible youth activists. In Egypt alone, the last few years of the 2000s saw thousands of labor strikes as well as protests by pillars of society such as judges and lawyers. Tribes marched against the government in Jordan and Kuwait, workplace strikes proliferated through Tunisia and Algeria, and Palestinians experimented with new forms of nonviolent protest against Israeli occupation. This was a wide and deep wave of popular mobilization.

The new public sphere shaped the generation now rising to positions of leadership in their societies and changed the nature of Arab national identity. In the 1950s, Arabs had been energized by the urgent popular appeal to erase colonial borders and unite as a single great nation. In those days, even mentioning a concern for one's own country might be taken as treason to the higher cause of Arab unity. But by the 1980s, increasingly entrenched authoritarian regimes had made great headway in promoting a narrower state-centric patriotism. Where President Gamal Abdel Nasser told all Arabs to unify in the pursuit of a common good, two decades later President Anwar Sadat told Egyptians to revel in the return of the Sinai peninsula as the reward for making peace with Israel. In that moment, Fouad Ajami, a Lebanese-American scholar, decisively informed a generation of analysts that pan-Arabism had died.

But this new Arab public sphere simply sees no contradiction between their quest for freedom at home and their support for Palestinians. They saw Mubarak's support for the blockade of Gaza as part and parcel of the contemptuous autocracy he exercised at home in Egypt. They are not looking for a new Nasser, a powerful state to lead them; instead, they judge all regimes by whether or not they effectively serve causes that they themselves define and lead. They see the fates of Palestinians, Yemenis, and Egyptians as deeply, necessarily intertwined. As one Twitter activist explained, "Media should focus on every Arab revolution equally, martyrs should never fall unnoticed #Yemen #Syria #Libya #Bahrain #Egypt #Tunisia."[7] Upon receiving the Nobel Peace Prize, Yemeni protest leader Tawakul Karman declared: "This is a message that the era of Arab dictatorships is over. This is a message to this regime and all the despotic regimes that no voice can drown out the voice of freedom and dignity. This is a victory for the Arab spring in Tunis, Egypt, Libya, Syria, and Yemen."[8]

The new Arab public sphere is driven by a generation that has gained the platforms and the mechanisms to engage in sustained argument, debate, and discussions about their common concerns. For some, that took the form of political activism, but for many, it simply transformed the way they experienced their lives. That engagement radically expanded their competencies to organize outside and against the state as well as their expectations from politics, themselves, and others. And they gained those new horizons, expectations, and skills precisely as economic opportunities disappeared, corruption escalated, the Israeli-Palestinian conflict festered, and democratic channels of participation closed. The rise of this generation, with all of those new hopes and capabilities, is what makes the regional status quo finally unsustainable. When Bouazizi's act of desperation started the region's cascade, they were ready.

Many will want to reduce this vibrant new public to easy stereotypes—whether a rising Islamist menace or a liberal youth rejecting their elders. Making such generalizations about an Arab public that spans dozens of countries is dangerous. There are extremely significant variations in national political cultures, political histories, ethnic and sectarian distributions, and orientations toward key issues. We must be *attentive to internal debates and contestations*. There is no essence of Islam or of Arab culture that will provide a key to the elusive Arab street. Arabs are people. They are internally divided, sometimes confused, often brilliant, and always capable of holding more than one thought at the same time. Karman, the Nobel Laureate, could without difficulty be simultaneously a leading member of the Islamist party al-Islah, a feminist icon, and a tireless advocate for democracy and human rights. Any attempt to reduce such restless energy to a single stereotype, or to appropriate it for a political cause, will fail.

This is especially the case for Americans, who too often project their own prejudices, fears, and hopes onto the Middle East rather than being willing to take it on its own terms. September 11 created an American audience conditioned to accept the most absurd claims about Islam and the Arab world. Many quickly succumbed to the fear that Osama bin Laden commanded the allegiances of a wide swath of the Arab and Muslim world. He did not. But only a few years later, many Americans—indeed, often the same ones—allowed themselves to believe that "silent majorities" of Iraq and the Arab world secretly supported the United States and secular-liberal values. Neither the fears nor the hopes were helpful guides. Too often Americans take one side in a hotly debated internal issue—whether the definition of jihad or the nature of the Egypt-ian revolution—as the authentic, authoritative statement of the entire community. This is wrong. As publics become ever more strategically important, we can no longer afford lazy generalizations, ill-informed speculation, or misleading polemics. Nor can we afford to treat Arab publics as a barely relevant nuisance, as an object to be manipulated, or as a tool to be wielded or discarded as our political needs of the moment merit.

We should remember that as we try to discern who now speaks for the Arab public. Articulate liberals may not speak for the Arab world any more than does al-Qaeda. The people who are the most fun at bars in tony areas of town or who have 20,000 followers on Twitter are not neces-sarily the ones with influence over or a firm understanding of their own societies. The test of the ballot box may prove cruel to those who emerged from revolution claiming to represent their people. Within weeks of the success of the Tunisian and Egyptian revolutions, analysts were warning of attempts to monopolize revolutionary legitimacy.[9] Often, leading activists are far out of touch with the mainstream views in their society—a reality that has deeply shaped the postrevolutionary political drama in Egypt, especially, as impatient youth activists have confronted the limits of their sway and have struggled to retain popular support for their activism. Many of the conventional narratives about the Arab upheaval neglect the role of more traditional actors such as labor and trade unions, working class and poor neighborhoods, and Islamists of various stripes. If Muslim Brothers, trade unionists, and angry football fans fought in Tahrir Square alongside liberal and leftist online activists, why should the latter monopolize claims to speak for the Egyptian revolution? As postrevolu-tionary politics revolve around claiming the mantle of revolutionary legit-imacy, these narrative battles have real political stakes.

Understanding this newly empowered public and its effects on the region's power politics will be one of the major challenges for policy and scholarship in the coming years. The best guides to the emerging era in the Middle East may have actually been written decades ago: *The Arab Cold War*, by Malcolm Kerr, and *The Struggle for Syria*, by Patrick Seale. Both recount an era in the 1950s in Arab politics in which ideologically powerful states competed by jockeying for influence in the domestic politics of their weaker neighbors. Syria in those days was not a regional power, in large part because of how open its politics were to these competitive mobilizations. Egypt amassed power through incendiary broadcasting and masterful ideological appeals to Arab unity, while conservative regimes sought foreign support and tried to counter with appeals to Islam. The emerging Arab order may have a lot in common with the classic days of the Arab Cold War.

The intense power politics of the 1950s, in which powerful states sought to exploit and capture genuinely popular movements, has many echoes today. The Arab uprisings erupted within the context of a decade-long cold war that polarized the region into a "resistance axis" led by Iran and including Syria, Hezbollah, and Hamas as well as a broad swath of public opinion, and a "moderate axis" aligning the United States with Israel and most of the other Arab states. That new cold war came to define all regional interactions in classic bipolar fashion, giving regional strategic meaning to local events and bringing together unlikely coalitions.

The early Arab uprisings clearly hoped to transcend that regional cold war. Yemeni and Bahraini protestors challenging Saudi-backed regimes angrily denied accusations of Iranian support, while Egyptians in Tahrir pointedly rejected Iranian claims to be leading an Islamic Awakening. Arab activists have simply dismissed the appeals of Syrian President Bashar al-Assad to ignore his domestic repression because of the value of his country's resistance to Israel. Iran has been almost invisible, despite the best efforts of Saudi Arabia, Bahrain, and their allies to blame their problems on Tehran's meddling. Its 2009 crushing of the Green Movement protesting a fraudulent presidential election badly harmed Iran's image with the new Arab public regardless of its "resistance" credentials. Instead, new lines of division have appeared that do not neatly map onto the previous ones: "revolution against counterrevolution" rather than "resistance and moderation." But the turbulent environment created new opportunities for all would-be regional powers to advance their interests, and it would be deeply out of character for them to decline such openings. Competitive meddling, from Egyptian elections to Syrian insurgency, would become the new normal.

The regional cold war found the United States in an awkward position of trying to be on what the Obama administration considered the right side of history, aligning with the Arab public in demands for democratic transformation, while also attempting to mollify traditional allies such as Israel and Saudi Arabia that feared and detested the revolutionary wave. The Obama administration genuinely wanted to support the Arab uprisings as an irresistible, inevitable change driven by the fact that "the people of the Middle East and North Africa had taken their future into their own hands." President Obama had placed the U.S. firmly on the side of democratic transitions, declaring "that America values the dignity of the street vendor in Tunisia more than the raw power of the dictator."[10]

But at the same time, strategic realities imposed ever more heavily. Israel worried about its peace treaties with Egypt and Jordan and feared that the turbulence would reach the Palestinian areas. Iran sought to take advantage of the turmoil to break the tight containment built by the Obama administration in the previous two years, and to exploit the weaknesses of its recent adversaries such as Egypt. Saudi Arabia raged at American infidelity, complaining to all who would listen that Obama had discarded Mubarak "like a used Kleenex" at the first sign of trouble.[11] And even as its traditional friends fumed, the U.S. gained few friends with the newly empowered Arab public, which always saw U.S. efforts as too little and too late, and which refused to overlook American support for Israel and favor its efforts on behalf of democratic change.

How will this all end? Conventional accounts explain the end of the original Arab Cold War through the discrediting of the key pan-Arabist powers such as Egypt after the 1967 war exposed their military weakness and political failures. But that was only part of the story. The key structural change came with the oil-fueled growth of the smothering internal power of Arab states. Indeed, the Arab authoritarianism being challenged today was in many ways a direct product of the turbulence and ideological meddling prevalent during the Arab Cold War of the 1950s and 1960s. The massive state security institutions that came to dominate these states existed in large part to block that kind of competitive mobilization of domestic forces and inciting of military coups. The leaders who survived the Arab Cold War were determined to never again face such threats from within, and shaped their domestic regimes and foreign policies toward that overriding goal of staying on their thrones. It would be tragic if this wave or turbulence ends in the same sort of dictatorial retrenchment.

The Arab uprisings have loosened that control, at least temporarily, and opened more countries to such competitive meddling. That, alongside the independent mobilization of the activists and the unification of the Arab political space, is going to change the way regional power politics operates. In the emerging system, states will of course still derive power from their military capabilities, size, and wealth (especially the last). But three other dimensions matter more than the traditional realist focused on guns, bombs, and dollars would acknowledge.

First, the *ability to credibly align with the Arab public on its core issues and to shape those convictions will become an ever greater source of power and influence.* Put simply, real strength flows from being associated with popular ideas in such an environment. The appeal of the "resistance bloc" in the 2000s derived in large part from Iran's championing of the Palestinian cause and its presentation of itself as the chief rival to a widely unpopular American hegemony. The Islamic system of government in Tehran commanded little admiration, but Iran could credibly claim to be resisting a broadly despised regional order. In the newly emerging Middle East, "swing states," such as Qatar and Turkey, that enjoy decent relations with the U.S. but have in recent years become more independent in their foreign policy in order to appeal to the new Arab public will be well positioned. Thus, after long years of Turkish-Israeli alliance (and Turkey's irrelevance to the politics of the Middle East), Turkey's Prime Minister Recep Erdoğan shrewdly played to this new public by challenging Israel over its actions in Gaza and, for his efforts, was received as a hero in Egypt and Tunisia in the fall of 2011.

Those political movements and regimes that hope to survive and prosper will be more responsive to public attitudes. For instance, Egypt's then-foreign minister Nabil al-Araby quickly signaled shortly after the revolution that his government wanted to normalize relations with Iran, downgrade but not sever ties with Israel, and ease the Gaza blockade— all popular positions that the Mubarak regime had rejected to its own ultimate detriment. But memories may be short. Egypt's new military rulers did not follow through on these (and many other) promises, and soon lost public confidence. When Erdoğan, with a half-hearted Syria policy, failed to live up to the expectations of the public, it felt no qualms about turning on him. Libyans grateful for extensive Qatari support during their war against the Qaddafi regime quickly grew resentful of perceived meddling in their postliberation politics.

Finally, there will be far less room for rulers to play a double game of saying one thing to their own people and then doing the opposite abroad. The new public sphere relentlessly hunts down information about such transgressions and spreads it through all channels to hold the regimes accountable. Leaders accustomed to quietly cooperating with the U.S. and Israel while saying the opposite in public will find their room for such maneuvering considerably reduced. It won't stop them from doing so, of course, but it will make it more difficult. This will inevitably impose at least short-term costs for the United States, Israel, and other status quo powers.

The intense competition to capture the mantle of the Arab public and to shape the trends in Arab public opinion of the last decade will become even more intense as the stakes go up. Qatar's media empire, especially al-Jazeera, has become an ever more potent instrument of power. When Qatar was a minor player in regional affairs in the late 1990s and early 2000s, al-Jazeera's claims to simply represent the Arab street rang true. But as Qatari clout grew, so did the temptation in the palace to use its popular television station in the service of its foreign policy. As the regional cold war polarized, with a Saudi-fueled media campaign promoting a "moderate" bloc against an alleged Iranian-led "resistance bloc," al-Jazeera found it harder to carve out a position as a neutral voice of the Arab public. It became increasingly identified with the resistance bloc because of its refusal to sign on to the Saudi-led campaigns and because of its sympathetic coverage of Hezbollah's war with Israel in 2006 and of Gaza in 2008—even if that reflected the views of the vast majority of the Arab public with which it identified.

Over the course of the 2011 upheavals, al-Jazeera unabashedly supported some rebellions (Syria, Libya) while ignoring others (Bahrain). In 2011, for the first time since the 2003 U.S. invasion of Iraq, it suspended its trademark talk shows in favor of round-the-clock news coverage. Where the suspension in 2003 had lasted only six weeks, this one extended for more than six months—abdicating al-Jazeera's role as the central node for public discourse and debate at arguably the most crucial moment for such discussions in recent Arab history. Many complained that it had veered from journalism into advocacy, and from independence into openly serving the Qatari interest. Such moves likely served Qatari foreign policy goals in the short term, but undermined al-Jazeera's status over the longer term. Other states will likely stand up additional competing Arab television stations in pursuit of such power.

Second, *the unified political space will increase the linkage between issues across the region.* The unification of Arab political space is certainly not new; indeed, the shared identity and political references have for many decades been a distinctive characteristic of Arab politics.[12] Palestine has long been a common concern for almost all Arabs, of course, and Iraq became a similarly shared issue over the 1990s and 2000s. But the growing power of the transnational media makes this even more intense and more politically salient. This generation of Arabs sees all of the region's revolutions as part of a single, shared narrative, with a common set of heroes and villains. Crowds came out into the street in almost every Arab country in response to the successful revolutions in Tunisia and Egypt. Moroccans and Yemenis shared a common response to events in Tunisia, while the brutal violence in Libya captured on al-Jazeera generated a historically unprecedented Arab demand for Western intervention. When Qaddafi lost control of Tripoli, Yemeni protestors surged. Common arguments against "linkage" between, say, the Israeli-Palestinian issue and Iran's influence in the Gulf will become ever harder to sustain as the role of publics and the unification of political space increase.

Issues such as Palestine will be that much more difficult for regimes to shunt to the margins in such an environment. Such linkage is of course not new. The Palestinian Intifada that broke out at the end of 1987 offered one of the most comprehensive examples of popular social mobilization anywhere, inspiring Arabs across the region. But the regional interactions are far more intense this time, with every national challenge taking its place within a common narrative. This is why in March 2011, the Obama administration was right to take seriously the demonstration effect of a successful military response by Qaddafi in Libya, and why its failure to push forcefully for serious reforms in Bahrain hurt it far more than it anticipated. Linkage across issues, diffusion, and demonstration effects, and a regionally integrated narrative are likely therefore to be long-lasting characteristics of regional politics.

Third, *the ability to intervene in the domestic politics of rivals and to prevent penetration of one's own domestic arena will determine whether the state is a player or an arena within which the great powers wage their proxy wars.* Just as Syria's domestic weakness in the 1950s made it a playing field for the great powers of the day, so will certain kinds of regimes be more or less vulnerable. Iraq, Yemen, and Lebanon, for instance, have been arenas for competition between the regional powers in the 2000s and will likely remain so. The Arab uprisings will open more and more states to such external involvement—as has already been seen from Saudi and Iranian competition in Bahrain to Qatari arming of rebels in Libya. As the columnist Mustafa al-Zayn put it in March 2011, "every large Arab country is now acting in its close neighbors, Egypt is busy in Sudan and Libya, Syria is busy in Lebanon, Saudi is busy in Bahrain."[13]

The weakening of states at home has clear consequences for their external power. Syria, Libya, Yemen, and Bahrain join Lebanon and Iraq as arenas rather than actors, despite their size, wealth, or material power. Calculating the balance of power will therefore require looking deep inside states. Will a more diverse range of regime types have predictable and systematic effects on power? Will those countries that evolve democratic systems, such as Egypt, prove to be highly susceptible to external penetration by way of covert support to political parties and movements? Or will they be largely immune to such manipulation as voters focus on domestic issues? Will monarchies continue to be more resilient in the face of popular challenges than nonmonarchical regimes?

This is true entirely independently of the question of whether or not the uprisings lead to democracy or true revolution. The rise of publics does not mean that the state has faded away or that democracy will inevitably follow. During the dark days of Arab authoritarianism, a robust literature developed that explained the failures of democracy in the region. Those arguments focused upon "the strength, coherence and effectiveness of the state's coercive apparatus"—core competencies that remain potent, even in the face of turbulent popular protests.[14] The rising body counts in Libya, Syria, Bahrain, and Yemen should put paid to any thought that Arab states would easily relinquish their power. Should democratic transitions stall, or economic problems not be dealt with effectively, the Arab liberation may give birth to a resurgent populism focused on identity, resentment, and externally directed rage. Such an outcome would likely please the remnants of the old order, which would find a comfortable place in a recast authoritarian hybrid.

Nor should we assume that the forces behind the uprisings will always push toward liberal or democratic outcomes. The passions of an empowered public could even prove destructive, particularly if effectively institutionalized democracies do not quickly emerge. The episodic outbursts of virulent Sunni-Shi'a sectarianism are only one example of the dangerous directions an empowered public might pursue. The turn from relatively peaceful uprisings to the violent civil war environments of Syria and Libya increases the risk of sectarian or ethnic polarization. And even in countries where regimes have already fallen, such as Tunisia, Egypt, and Libya, empowered publics may quickly lose patience with the compromises and uncertainties of democratic political life. Angry protestors will likely still be trying to seize Tahrir Square ten years from now, regardless of whether Egypt has successful democratic elections or remains under military rule.

Empowered publics will reduce the *predictability* of regional politics, as new faces replace old leaders and domestic considerations trump the demands of the status quo. This will have particularly important consequences for Israel, which has seen its carefully constructed regional security architecture crumble. Protests against the Israeli Embassy in Cairo and in Amman in September 2011 demonstrated clearly the continued potency of Arab anger with Israel, the United States, and their own governments. Arab regimes will have to take this more into account than in the past. The very real hostility toward Israel could force governments into dangerous, provocative rhetoric and behavior that could trigger the kind of spiral toward war that took place in 1967—even if nobody sets out intending such a war.

The uprisings corresponded with the looming end of the decades-long peace process between Israel and Palestinians aimed at achieving a two-state solution. While it is of course conceivable that these fortunes could be reversed, it does not seem likely. The steady shift of Israeli politics to the right, its growing international isolation, and its lack of confidence in the Palestinian leadership have reduced its willingness to push for peace with the Palestinians. The division between the West Bank and Gaza has become ever more entrenched, leaving no Palestinian entity actually capable of negotiating on behalf of Palestinians. The steady expansion of Israeli settlements makes a territorially unified, viable Palestinian state more distant than ever. The Palestinian push for recognition in the United Nations and other international institutions, along with spectacular challenges such as the flotillas to Gaza, might have had little impact on the ground, but did refocus attention on the issue even as it further poisoned Palestinian relations with the United States and Israel. The rise of a Palestinian nonviolent protest movement self-consciously aligned with broader regional trends will force the U.S. and others to directly confront contradictions they would prefer to blur. The ever more intense interconnections among issues, and the centrality of Palestine to Arab identity, ensure that these will have significant regional fallout.

The spiraling conflict in Syria that began in March 2011, should be ample evidence of the possibility of sudden, highly significant, and unpredictable change. The Syrian regime considered itself—and was seen by most outsiders—as immune to the kinds of popular challenges faced by Mubarak or Ben Ali. The initial protests were small and received little media coverage. But a series of poor decisions, including the massive use of violence against small protests and a badly received offer of minimal reforms by President Assad, gave life to protests that soon consumed the country. Soon, al-Jazeera was heavily covering the violence and regional powers became increasingly involved. Syria's collapse into civil war or the emergence of a new regime aligned against rather than with Iran would fundamentally change the regional balance of power. Such a change would be as dramatic, if not as sudden, as the Iraqi revolution of 1958, which at a stroke toppled the most powerful member of the conservative alliance system in the region. The changes sweeping the Middle East today make such sudden, massive shocks far more likely.

This does not mean that we should panic. The uncertainty and passions associated with empowered publics are not unfamiliar terrain outside the Middle East. In most of the world, the U.S. has long had to deal with complex domestic politics in other important countries. America became far too comfortable dealing primarily with Arab dictators, though. And this all takes place at a time of global rebalancing, with America in relative decline, especially since the 2008 financial crisis. America has less appetite for the projection of military power after the wars in Iraq and Afghanistan; even the humanitarian intervention in Libya was a painfully negotiated and often politically tenuous multilateral affair. Instead, there is a more crowded strategic landscape of consequential players—not only Europe, Russia, and China but new rising regional powers such as India, Turkey, and Brazil. These realities constrain America's response to the changes, while creating new opportunities for an effective international response.

There has already been meaningful change, not only within individual states such as Egypt, Libya, and Tunisia but in the Arab regional order itself. For instance, the simple idea that Arab regimes should not kill their own people has taken root in profoundly new ways. In decades past, Arab regimes routinely resorted to brutal violence to crush their domestic opponents. The Charter of the League of Arab States, agreed upon in 1945, protected state sovereignty and national independence and allowed no exceptions by which regimes might lose their legitimacy through their internal behavior. And that is easy to understand, given how horrifically most of them treated their people. But over the last year, the Arab League suspended not one but two of its members—Libya and Syria—for the excessive use of violence against protestors, and the Gulf Cooperation Council involved itself in Yemen's crisis over the escalating violence. The core norms of the Arab regional order are changing then, in response to the outcry of the empowered public sphere, the ambitions of leading states such as Qatar, and the prodding of international actors such as the United Nations, the International Criminal Court, and the United States.

We are all struggling to understand these changes. Their historical novelty, dizzying pace, and rapid reversals have proven challenging to Arabs and outside observers alike. This book aims to lay out a pragmatic but theoretically and historically informed framework for understanding what really matters in the rush of events. It cannot hope to capture every nuance of individual countries, or to anticipate every twist and turn to come. At the time of this writing, major events loom on the horizon, such as the first parliamentary elections in Egypt and the Syrian response to its suspension from the Arab League, where different outcomes could

tip the regional dynamics in very different directions. But I believe that
the underlying structural changes associated with an empowered Arab
public sphere and the changing nature of power in regional politics are
clear enough.

Some of the most prominent interpretations of the changes in the
Arab world do not hold up well to scrutiny. Early enthusiasts for the Arab
revolutions, for instance, hoped that the absence of anti-American slogans in Tahrir Square meant that Arab publics would now focus on their
own domestic affairs and leave regional issues such as Palestine behind.
This has already proven to be shortsighted. These Arab publics see such
regional issues as intimately related to their own struggles at home.
America's role in maintaining the old Arab status quo has not been forgotten and will not be ignored in the coming era.

Many others have complained that the Obama administration has
not demonstrated sufficient leadership during these unfolding crises, that
it has been "leading from behind," in the unfortunate phrase popularized
by *The New Yorker*. Such critics insist that Arabs yearn for a more aggressive, vocal American role in supporting the revolutions and that Obama
has missed key opportunities. This too is almost certainly mistaken.
Obama correctly saw from the start that these Arab revolutions neither
wanted nor needed American leadership. They were truly authentic
forces from within and would look poorly on American attempts to
claim ownership. As detailed throughout this book, the low American
profile served an important political and strategic purpose, even during
the military intervention in Libya, where the U.S. intentionally took a
backseat to NATO, Britain, and France. Had Obama tried to stamp the
Arab uprisings with an American label, it would have provoked a fierce
backlash.

On the other side of the debate, many observers have gloomily concluded that the Arab uprisings have been largely detrimental to American (and Israeli) interests. They mourn the loss of cooperative autocrats,
who fought terrorists and cooperated with Israel against Iran. How, they
demand, could Obama have thrown these longtime allies under the bus
and "lost" the Middle East? Again, this badly misreads the situation. The
U.S. did not create these uprisings and could not have stopped them had
it so desired. The best that any U.S. leadership could have done was to

shape the new environment in ways conducive to American interests and values—which, I argue, the administration has tried to do.

The fiercest denunciations of the Arab uprisings come from those who see them not simply as compromising friends but as actively empowering Islamist enemies. These critics see the rise of Islamist forces in Tunisia, Egypt, and Libya as a sign of the rapid advance of radical Islam. While it is true that Islamists will do well in more open political spaces, this critique is almost completely mistaken. It wrongly conflates different strands of Islamism, imputing to them a unity of purpose that they simply do not possess. The Muslim Brotherhood in Egypt or el-Nahda in Tunisia cannot be equated with al-Qaeda. Their inclusion in emerging democracies will be necessary to create genuinely stable, representative political systems. What is more, Islamist-dominated regimes are not likely to form a unified Islamist regional bloc any more than pan-Arabist regimes cooperated in the 1950s; they are more likely to become fierce competitors as they bid for the leadership of the Islamist camp. Turning against Arab democracy out of a misguided fear of Islamists would be a tragic error for America.

THE BOOK THAT FOLLOWS attempts to put all of these tumultuous events into perspective. It begins by returning to history, since we cannot understand the current uprising without looking at those that have come before—namely, the Arab Cold War of the 1950s and 1960s, the aborted democratization of the late 1980s and early 1990s, and the turbulence and change of the 2000s. Particularly in the immediate antecedents of the Arab uprising, the mobilization and potential of the emerging regional public sphere become visible.

A narrative of the Tunisian and Egyptian revolutions kicks off the uprising in its most familiar form. Chapters 5 and 6 capture the highs and the lows: the dizzying days following those revolutions, when anything seemed possible, and then, immediately afterward, the grim days of counterrevolution that launched in the middle of March. Chapter 7 looks at the new era of intervention and civil wars, most clearly embodied by Libya to Syria. And then, in a final chapter, I step back from the region to consider the implications for America's place in the region. Understanding the forces behind these uprisings and how they intersect with other powerful factors in regional politics will be vital for effectively responding to the rush of events to come. That will often mean discerning when to ignore bad advice to act boldly in the name of leadership and when it is time to take a firm stand. It will mean distinguishing between rash, snap judgments about winners and losers and credible forecasts about important trends. And it means having no illusions about the challenges to come—or about the real opportunities that might still be seized.

CHAPTER 2

THE ARAB COLD WAR

W E CAN EASILY FORGET that 2011 was not the first time Arab politics have been driven by mass mobilization and protest. Massive numbers of Arabs have risen up before. During the Arab Cold War of the 1950s, millions routinely flooded the streets to protest against their regimes, instigated by radio broadcasts and political agitation from abroad. Broadcasts on Gamal Abdel Nasser's Voice of the Arabs radio station nearly brought down governments in Beirut and Amman, put constant pressure on Damascus and Riyadh, and contributed to the bloody revolution that toppled the pro-Western regime in Baghdad. During these decades, governments routinely fell, through military coups or popular uprisings, while all political actors engaged fiercely in a political battle that crossed national boundaries.

The wave of massive popular mobilization that took place between 1954 and 1963 has come to be known as the "Arab Cold War." Crowds demanding Arab unity (or militaries sympathetic to the idea) overthrew the Iraqi monarchy (at the time, the strongest force for counterrevolution), destabilized key American allies, and seized power in Syria and drove its short-lived unification with Egypt. The competition among Arabists such as Nasser and the Ba'ath Party seeking the political unification of the Arab world and conservative regimes aligned with the West led to a debilitating proxy war in the mountains of Yemen. Power lay in the ability to mobilize the street, to wield the rhetorical weapons of pan-Arabism, and to navigate the treacherous field of factional and conspiratorial politics.[1] The period ended only with the 1967 war between Israel and Egypt, Jordan, and Syria, and with the death of Nasser in the midst of

the "Black September" crisis when the Arabs stood by passively as
Jordanian troops slaughtered Palestinians and expelled the Palestinian
Liberation Organization from the kingdom. Afterward, the Arabs ended
up not with democracy but with the most brutally repressive regimes
they had ever faced, with the ideas of pan-Arabism discredited and the
Arabs deeply divided. Popular upheavals in the Arab world have not historically pushed toward more liberal political orders.

The popular movements of the 1950s and the late 1980s each
brought huge numbers of people into the streets and into the political
realm. They forced dramatic political change, focused the regional and
international agenda, and shaped political identities and strategies. Now
the question becomes: What do these earlier regional protest waves have
to tell us about the current period? A great deal. Each featured intense
ideological disputes in a fully integrated Arab media space, relatively
weak states, highly mobilized publics, and an uncertain American foreign policy in the midst of a changing international structure.

The fate of the earlier protest waves should be sobering, however.
None of those democratization initiatives offered under popular pressure
led to lasting transitions. The Arab Cold War of the 1950s ended in
the ruthless consolidation of authoritarian rule across the region and
decades of enforced public slumber. The 1980s were no kinder. Algeria's
push for democracy led to a military coup and a bloody civil war.
Sudan's popular uprisings ended in a brutal military dictatorship.
Jordan's and Tunisia's faded under relentless, incremental reassertion
of regime authority. These results offer crucial lessons for postrevolutionary Tunisia and Egypt today, as hopeful publics struggle to redeem
the democratic promises of their revolutions.

Each wave ended with the reassertion of authoritarian state control.
Indeed, much of what we know about Arab politics is actually based on
the repressive, authoritarian state structures that developed in *response* to
the turbulence of the Arab Cold War. The tight control over information,
careful management of public political opinion, and massive "coup-
proof" security services were all designed to blunt the power of transnational radical appeals. The Egyptian-Saudi-American alliance, quietly
linked to Israel, that has dominated Arab politics for decades was the
product of Egyptian president Anwar Sadat's strategic decision to take

his country out of the Arab Cold War and join the conservative, pro-Western camp that Egypt once lambasted. Will this grim history repeat, or are there reasons to believe that the rise of the new Arab public will make things different this time?

The Arab uprising can be seen as the cresting of a powerful third wave of mobilization that began around 2000 in response to the outbreak of the second Palestinian Intifada, the violent uprising that erupted with the failure of peace negotiations. Many of today's activists point to these protests as the moment of their own political awakening and the seed of future mobilization. Ironically, authorities in countries such as Egypt allowed these rallies as a way to let off steam and divert popular anger from domestic concerns. When the protests over Palestine shifted toward resistance to the U.S.-led invasion of Iraq, regimes went along with slightly more hesitation, given their own private cooperation with that campaign. But in both cases, the diversionary principle applied, with the regime permitting and even exploiting mobilization around foreign issues while forbidding domestic protests. The massive protests across the Arab world from 2000 to 2003 revealed enormous pent-up anger, but did not in themselves challenge any of the basic operating principles of the regional order.

The revolutionary change came when the activist groups, particularly in Egypt, turned inward against the regimes that protestors held responsible for allowing systematic foreign and domestic failures. The Kefaya movement challenged the Egyptian regime's efforts to hand power from Hosni Mubarak to his son Gamal. The Lebanese Cedar Revolution brought a million people to Beirut to demand justice for the assassinated Prime Minister Rafik Hariri and the departure of Syrian troops from their country. Bahraini activists demanded human rights and democracy. Those internally focused movements laid the foundations for the Arab uprisings of 2011. But once again, most stalled by the end of the decade, as authoritarian regimes devised new methods of control and repression and old political divides splintered nascent new coalitions.

These earlier historical periods offer at least a suggestive guide to the coming period of highly diverse regimes, ideological polarization, mobilized publics, and transnational media. The structure of international politics may be different, as is the world-historical moment. The 2000s saw new information technologies such as satellite television and the Internet establish themselves as potent challengers to state-dominated media. Arab publics and states alike have different tools at their disposal, different political horizons, and different identities. Islamist movements are far stronger today, and organized Arab nationalist parties far weaker. But for all those differences, it is well worth recalling that this is not the first period of massive regionwide Arab popular mobilization and partial defensive democratization.

THE ARAB COLD WAR

The Arab Cold War pitted powerful states with distinct ideological visions for the region against one another. It played out primarily in the battle-field states of Syria, Lebanon, and Jordan, though it spread into the frontiers of Yemen and into Iraq, the very heart of the conservative Middle Eastern order.

The cold war grew out of the long struggle against Western colonialism and the state system constructed after World War I, and the contested process of forming modern nation-states from the remnants of the Ottoman Empire. For decades, popular mobilization in many Arab states had focused on the demand for independence from direct or indirect colonial rule. In Egypt, the Wafd Party and the Muslim Brotherhood had each challenged British indirect rule within a formally democratic system. In Algeria, a popular and increasingly bloody insurgency challenged French rule.

This unrest began to take on a more urgent character on July 23, 1952, when a coup led by Gamal Abdel Nasser and Egypt's Free Officers finally overthrew the British-backed monarchy in a near-bloodless coup. The Egyptian revolution of 1952 soon helped to spark the wave of popular mobilization that defined the Arab Cold War. This did not take form overnight. For several years, Nasser and his fellow officers had tentatively reshaped Egypt's domestic order, while carefully exploring new international and regional alliances, including a long flirtation with the United States. By 1954, Nasser had consolidated power at home and began the foreign policy reforms that would drive regional politics for the next decade. These had mainly to do with two powers: Israel and the

Soviet Union. A bloody Israeli raid on Gaza, designed in part to humiliate and intimidate the new Egyptian leader, backfired badly. On September 27, 1955, Nasser announced a Czech arms deal with the Soviet bloc, to great public acclaim across the region but with devastating effects on Egypt's relationship with America. With this move, the Arab Cold War began in earnest.

Nasser's challenge won widespread support around the entire Arab world, fueled in part by the Voice of the Arabs radio broadcasts that could reach the farthest corners of the region through newly available, cheap transistor radios. Nasser's pan-Arabism set the agenda for the region, even as the West sought to shore up its alliances against the Soviet Union in an escalating global Cold War. The conflict broke down into two major blocs: a pan-Arabist bloc led by Egypt, enjoying widespread popular and party support across the region but few state allies; and a conservative, pro-Western bloc led by Iraq and Saudi Arabia. Britain and France, the major colonial powers, and the Arab regimes aligned with them bore the immediate brunt of this anti-Western sentiment. The United States, while temporarily made popular by its intervention against Israel, the U.K., and France in the 1956 Suez crisis that forced its allies to withdraw from the territory captured in the initial attack, squandered its popularity by battling Nasser. American efforts to enlist Arab regimes in anti-Communist schemes such as the Baghdad Pact and the Eisenhower Doctrine consistently backfired.

As in the 2011 uprising, the Arab public was intimately involved in power politics. In the 1950s, the public was more an object to be mobilized and deployed by Egypt rather than an independent force of its own (though in 2011, many Arabs would complain that Qatar hoped to use al-Jazeera in the same fashion as Nasser had used Voice of the Arabs). But Arab publics moved in force that relatively young and weak regimes struggled to contain. Between 1954 and 1958, millions of Jordanians, Lebanese, Syrians, and Iraqis routinely came out into the streets protesting in the name of Arab unity. The Jordanian monarchy tottered, forcing the young King Hussein to hand over considerable power to a pan-Arabist prime minister. Syria's government changed hands nearly a dozen times. Lebanon's confessional system, which distributed power among the sectarian groups while preserving the leading position of pro-Western

Christians, required an American military intervention to avoid collapse. And in 1958, the core of the conservative pro-Western bloc in Arab politics collapsed when a revolution toppled the Hashemite king of Iraq. The fall of the Iraqi monarchy in 1958 shifted the balance of power dramatically, if momentarily, in favor of the Arabist camp, and the battle shifted to the political direction of Iraq and then to a civil war in Yemen. The Arabist regimes could not cooperate, however, and Egyptian-Iraqi rivalry quickly returned, despite the new revolutionary orientation in Baghdad.

The Arab Cold War was a battle of ideas more than a battle of arms, with intense ideological polarization between opposites: Should government be a republic or a monarchy, oriented toward the West or the Soviet Union, nationalistic or pan-Arabist? Those ideas were deployed in the service of regional great powers and, as the 1960s ground on, took on overtones of the global struggle between the West and the Soviet bloc. But there could be no question about the importance of Arab public opinion in this era. The sheer level of popular mobilization, which brought down some governments and kept every other potential target on perpetual edge, made the answers to these questions the fundamental currency of political power.

These ideological battles played out in a genuinely transnational media space. Voice of the Arabs brought Arabist ideas to every corner of the Arab world. Most other states and political movements countered by launching their own radio stations, turning the regional airwaves into a dense arena for political battle. The ability of regimes and political movements to credibly align with the norms of pan-Arabism became a fundamental source of power, available to some and withheld from others.[2] None could avoid engaging with the prevailing ideas and arguments, no matter how distant their own behavior or identity might be from the current trend.

In such an environment, the ability to control the domestic front and prevent external involvement became a key element of the balance of power.[3] States that were unable to control the flow of ideas and mobilization within their own borders became the arenas for regional competition. Those with relatively closed political systems gained strength. Egypt enjoyed a relative power advantage over potential rivals such as Iraq and Syria because of its greater ability to destabilize their domestic arenas.

Military coups were the primary mechanism of change, even within a highly mobilized political arena. In addition, most political players sought help abroad when available.[4] The heavy-handed authoritarianism that fell over the region in the 1970s responded directly to this pattern of permeability, as ambitious rulers set out to ensure that they would never again be threatened or weakened by such machinations.

Syria is the prototypical example of the importance of internal strength in making a state an actor or a plaything for others. Under Hafez al-Assad, who seized power in a military coup in 1970 and ruled with an iron fist, Syria was a powerful player in regional affairs. But, like Iraq after the fall of Saddam Hussein in 2003, Syria in the 1950s lay wide open before powerful foreign actors, unable to control its territory or the loyalties of its own people. As long as it remained internally weak, Syria was an arena for regional conflict, not a serious player.

Syrian leaders in this period faced challenges from all sides, and foreign rivals had many instruments by which to meddle in their affairs. The hyper-politicization of the Syrian officer corps turned the military coup into the preferred vehicle for change. Meanwhile, popular mobilization intensified in the early 1950s, channeled through the Ba'ath Party, the Communist Party, trade unions, and the Muslim Brotherhood.[5] Through the early 1950s, social protest focused on rural violence against landowners, but over time, the unrest moved into the cities. In February 1954, parliamentary life was restored, creating openings for political movements that had previously been mobilizing popular support. Over the course of the summer, there was a dramatic uptick in strikes and labor actions, political protests, and electioneering.

The rising popular mobilization destabilized each succeeding government. In June 1954, a national unity government was formed to try to contain popular unrest. In the fall, former Syrian president Adib Shishakli attempted a military coup. Over the next decade and a half, power changed hands seventeen times, almost always through a military coup. Its pan-Arab ideology presented endless opportunities for outsiders to press demands upon its political leadership and to shape its foreign policy. The real pressure was coming from below, however. As the Syrian Chief of Staff Afif Bizri recalled: "Nobody would dare say no, we don't want [unity]. The masses would rise against them. I mean we

followed the masses. The crowds were drunk. . . . Who at that hour could
dare say we do not want unity? The people would tear our heads off."[6]

The decisive turning point in the regional politics of pan-Arabism
came with the ill-considered intervention in Suez by Britain, France, and
Israel—an inflection point that should come as a warning to all those
who today push for interventions in the Arab revolutions. The Western
powers worried about Nasser's nationalization of the Suez Canal and
shared Israel's fear of Egypt's rising regional influence and seeming turn
to the Soviet bloc for support. The cockamamie military scheme that followed, in which the European powers intervened after an Israeli attack,
fell apart when the Eisenhower administration refused to be dragged into
the conflict. Concerned that it would lose the increasingly empowered
Arab public to the Communist world en masse, should the conspiracy be
allowed to stand, the United States forced its own allies to back down.
Nasser emerged a victorious hero despite his military defeat and quickly
moved to parlay his success into a bid for regional hegemony.

What ensued was an exceptional moment in regional and, indeed,
international history: Egypt and Syria joined forces and combined their
states to form the United Arab Republic (UAR). Popular mobilization
does not often lead states to voluntarily merge against the real preferences of most of the political class. In historian Malcolm Kerr's evocative
description,

> The wave of exuberance that swept Syria at the start of the
> union, signified by the triumphant crowds that welcomed Nasser
> to Damascus, and widely shared by Arab opinion in the sur-
> rounding Arab states, reflected a conviction that . . . the initiative
> in the Middle East had passed to the revolutionary pan-Arab
> movement, that before long the people of other Arab states
> would rise up against their tyrannical rulers and join the union.[7]

Anwar Sadat, then one of Nasser's key aides who was sent to handle
the move toward unification, marveled at his reception in Damascus:
"[O]ur Syrian audiences wanted more and more. The crowds couldn't get
enough and seemed to grow increasingly frenzied. All that was said was
hailed, applauded, celebrated. People chanted and screamed and called
for more. For a whole week the crowds besieged the Guesthouse. They

camped outside in the wide square, eating, drinking, and sleeping in the open air."[8] Tahrir Square in Damascus!

The moves toward a union between Egypt and Syria put incredible pressure on Lebanon and the Hashemite Kingdom of Jordan. Lebanon could not avoid its deep organic links to its Syrian neighbor. Its relatively open political system and media and weak central state institutions had made it a prime battlefield for all regional trends. The rise of Nasserist pan-Arabism had triggered a sharp conflict between the Western-oriented, politically dominant Christian community and the Arab-oriented Muslims. By 1958, this conflict exploded into a dangerous crisis. The surreal sight of U.S. Marines landing on the beaches of Beirut to protect the pro-Western government became an iconic image of the Arab Cold War.

In Jordan, under the young King Hussein, the relatively sophisticated political opposition, including Palestinians only recently united with the East Bank following the creation of the state of Israel and Jordan's annexation of the West Bank, posed a serious challenge to the monarchical system and its pro-Western orientation. With only rudimentary national institutions, street protests served as one of the most effective forms of political action.[9] These riots often came in response to regional concerns, with a massive protest in December 1955 against the American-backed Baghdad Pact proposal, an ill-advised effort to bring together the region's pro-Western regimes into a formal alliance, marking the occasion of the first major round of demonstrations.

While they responded to the provocations of Nasser's Voice of the Arabs, the opposition movements also had their own distinct national demands. It is important to recall that even though the Arab Cold War was waged through the idiom of pan-Arabism, there were always local concerns. In Jordan, so deeply shaped by the regional trends, the level of street activism was made possible by rapid urbanization, the influx of Palestinians from all walks of life following their expulsion from their homes in what had become the state of Israel, and the grievances of a repressed population trapped in refugee camps and struggling to find decent jobs.[10]

These protests also drew on the new media technologies of the day. Voice of the Arabs offered a direct, unfiltered channel from Cairo to the streets of Amman. Meanwhile, activists organized themselves in part by circulating pamphlets in the schools, publishing op-eds in the nascent national press, and relentlessly canvassing the urban population.[11] Their efforts produced results. They brought down several governments. On December 19, King Hussein told the U.S. ambassador that Jordan could not join the Baghdad Pact.

The Jordanian prime minister resigned the next morning, and King Hussein dissolved parliament and called for new elections. When the Supreme Court ruled this unconstitutional, renewed riots broke out. This time, John Bagot Glubb, commander of the Arab Legion, brought out the army, putting down riots with a lot of bloodshed. Two months later, Hussein dismissed Glubb—a move that Israeli historian Uriel Dann blamed on "a hate campaign orchestrated from Cairo" but that was met with "an outburst of popular enthusiasm unprecedented in the annals of the Hashemite monarchy."[12]

In the elections that followed, the opposition led by the pan-Arabist Suleiman Nabulsi won a sweeping victory on an agenda of alignment with Nasser's Arabism and a domestic move toward constitutional monarchy. As Dann grudgingly admits, "the support for Nabulsi was wide and deep. . . . It was not easy for a young king with a desire to be loved to adopt a policy predicated on repressing a popular mood."[13] Imagine if he had succeeded in forcing the young king to accommodate the public mood and cede governing power to an elected parliament! The result would have been a constitutional monarchy with a foreign policy based on popular opinion, something that still does not exist in Jordan, or most anywhere in the Arab world, even in 2011.

But it was not to be. Britain and the United States worried deeply about losing their Jordanian outpost, and the king and his men had no intention of surrendering their hold on power. On April 8, 1957, a fateful, failed coup attempt gave King Hussein the excuse he needed to dismiss Nabulsi. Three weeks of crisis followed. On April 24, Hussein declared martial law and never looked back. The experiment with a strong parliamentary system ended, and the monarchy and armed forces established their absolute dominance in political life. There would not be another serious nod toward democracy in Jordan for more than thirty years.

The pan-Arab revolution even reached Iraq, the heartland of the counterrevolution. Hashemite Iraq, with its close connections to the British, conservative ideology, and significant power potential, represented the most potent counterpart to Nasser's pan-Arab revolution. Baghdad dueled with Cairo across all of the arenas of the Arab Cold War, especially in fellow Hashemite kingdom Jordan and the battleground state of Syria. The unification of Egypt and Syria threatened Iraq's regional role, however, particularly since it placed enormous pressure on King Hussein in Jordan. On February 14, 1958, the Iraqi monarchy declared an Arab Federation with Jordan, primarily to protect its smaller neighbor from the new United Arab Republic.

The Arab Federation backfired in the most unexpected of ways, however. On July 12, 1958, rumors of a coup against Hussein prompted the Iraqi monarch to order its Twentieth Brigade into Jordan (much as a later Saudi king would do for tiny Bahrain). But, instead, the Iraqi military marched on Baghdad, not into Jordan, and overthrew the monarchy, at a stroke taking it from the conservative camp into an Arabist one. The bloody military coup in Baghdad ended with the young monarch and his key advisers dragged through the streets and hung from lampposts. The regional balance of power had been overturned in one bloody night, as avowedly pan-Arabist officers took control of the strongest of the conservative powers. Nothing remotely equivalent has yet happened in our times.

The revolutionary change in Baghdad did not have the expected transformative effect on regional power politics, however. Revolutionary Iraq proved every bit as competitive with Egypt as its conservative predecessor. It did not immediately subordinate itself to Egyptian leadership. Indeed, in some ways, Egypt and Iraq became even more competitive because the two states were now competing for leadership of the same pan-Arab camp instead of lobbing verbal bombs across a deep divide. Within a few years, Syria had withdrawn from the UAR, and negotiations to form a new UAR with Egypt, Syria, and Iraq went nowhere in the face of mutual suspicion, partisan self-interest, and power politics. We should remember this as we wonder whether Iraq, which has competed with Iran for hegemony in the Gulf throughout its entire history, will become an Iranian vassal simply because it has an elected Shi'a government. Or, as we contemplate the likely dynamics of a region divided between revolution and counterrevolution, and wonder if a new Egyptian regime will completely change its foreign policy or quietly subordinate itself to Saudi tutelage for the promise of a few billion dollars.

Yemen was the mostly forgotten graveyard of the Arab Cold War. In 1962, a republican insurrection attracted the support of an Egyptian military intervention, as Cairo saw the opportunity to challenge Saudi Arabia on its border. This in turn drew Saudi counterintervention and laid the course for a half-decade of insurgency and civil war. The brutal fighting in the mountains of a faraway land nearly broke the Egyptian military, and certainly diverted attention and political momentum from the heartland of the Arab world. The horrific battles in Yemen's mountains—where Egyptian forces reportedly resorted to chemical weapons—helped break the back of the Arab revolution, as Egypt's energies and armies shifted from Israel and the Levant toward the far reaches of the Arabian peninsula.

LESSONS OF THE ARAB COLD WAR

Popular mobilization had therefore faded even before the 1967 war. As the revolutionary fever broke, Nasser refocused on Egypt and building its socialist economy. While he never abandoned Arabism, his ability to mobilize crowds diminished as politics turned inward. Syrian politics became more focused on competing military coups rather than mass national politics. Jordan's king ruled with an ever more iron grip. Iraq was now in the Arabist camp, but a surly and uncooperative member that soon fell prey to a succession of Ba'athist coups and countercoups.

The era of the Arab Cold War came to a crushing end with the 1967 war with Israel, which was itself very much the result of intense ideological competition between domestically insecure Arab regimes.[14] In 1966, yet another military coup had brought a particularly radical but unpopular regime to power in Damascus. This regime chose to score points at home and in the region through elaborate protestations of fidelity to Arab causes. And above all, it needled Nasser for his weakness and failure to truly confront Israel. The rhetorical battles had goaded the Egyptian president into a series of ill-considered moves, such as demanding the withdrawal of the UN presence in the Sinai. Israel found itself surrounded by ever more hostile rhetoric emanating from every Arab capital and facing a series of provocative moves meant to back up the bold words. Its surprise attack on June 4, 1967, was not a preemptive strike to ward off an expected Arab attack, as is often claimed. It was a preventive war designed to head off a shift in the balance of power, executed under conditions of extreme crisis and psychological pressure. The rapid defeat of all the Arab armies and the Israeli conquest of the Sinai, the West Bank, and the Golan Heights silenced the Arabist outbidding by discrediting Nasser and his rivals alike, and brought the Arab Cold War to a close.

What had begun as a series of revolutions and popular uprisings ended with the Arab defeat in 1967 and Nasser's death three years later. The symbolic end came as the Jordanian military brutally crushed the presence of the Palestine Liberation Organization (PLO) in the East Bank and expelled its remnants to Lebanon, while the Arab League and Nasser stood by silently. The great champion of pan-Arab causes would now do nothing to protect the massacre of Palestinians by another Arab regime—and literally, not symbolically, died in the process. What ensued was the most stifling period of Arab authoritarianism in any era. Leaders who had either survived massive popular unrest or come to power through the streets would now take no chances. The massive upsurge in oil revenues following the 1973 oil embargo by the Organization of Petroleum Exporting Countries (OPEC) gave the conservative regimes the means to finance an unprecedented expansion of security and patronage systems. By the late 1970s, the authoritarian state had the upper hand over once-potent political movements and set out to crush all forms of popular opposition or dissent.

The course of the Arab cold war has many lessons for today's struggles, then. Great powers competed vigorously to appropriate the popular movements challenging leaders seen as illegitimate, inauthentic, or ineffective. Efforts by such protest movements to remain independent, unsullied by association with regimes, rarely lasted long. The more that Arab regimes extolled the virtues of unity, the more they actually competed with one another, and the more brutal the game of competitive interventions and rhetorical combat became. The ability to control one's own territory and population often proved more important to the exercise of regional power than did the ability to project military power abroad. And all those pressures could lead to deeply irrational moves and to unexpected wars—with Nasser's ill-conceived intervention in Yemen in 1962 and foolishly provocative moves against Israel in 1967 standing out.

Finally, this period ended not in democracy or unity but in states imposing the fiercest and most brutal repression the region had ever witnessed. The authoritarian brutality of the 1970s and 1980s was a direct response to the instability of the 1950s and 1960s. But that repression could not prevent popular mobilization from reappearing. New waves of protest and challenge from below would recur—economic protests in the early 1980s, serious pushes toward democracy in the late 1980s and early 1990s, and then a steadily gathering tidal wave of protest that rose over the entire decade of the 2000s.

CHAPTER 3

BUILDING TOWARD REVOLUTION

T HE ARAB WORLD IN THE 1980S was dominated by fierce, brutally repressive states that carefully patrolled the political sphere for any sign of dissent. Regional politics were dominated by Iraq's war with Iran, Israel's invasion of Lebanon, and the fading of any notion of pan-Arabism. But popular protests never disappeared. Episodic challenges over economic stagnation rocked North Africa, the Sudan, Egypt, and other Arab regimes throughout the decade. Those gathered force in the late 1980s with the collapse of the Soviet Union and the turn to democracy across Eastern Europe and in many parts of sub-Saharan Africa.

The Middle East could not help but be affected by those global trends. The first Palestinian Intifada began in late 1987. Bread riots prompted at least temporary defensive democratic openings in Algeria, Yemen, and Jordan. Widespread mobilization over the U.S.-led war with Iraq to liberate Kuwait brought millions of Arabs into the streets, often against policies supported by their governments, for the first time in decades.[1] Over the next few years, however, the democratic gains retreated, either through the slow reassertion of state authority (Jordan, Tunisia) or through sudden, brutal civil war (Algeria, Egypt). Once again, the wave of protest ended with authoritarian regimes ruthlessly reasserting their control.

But that hold on power would never be as secure as it had once been. Many Arab countries experienced the growth of independent civil societies in the 1990s, which could not openly mount political challenges but which helped carve out spaces for independent political action. And all of that laid the groundwork for the seismic transformations that began to take hold in the 2000s.

EPISODIC PROTESTS IN THE 1980S

Pan-Arabism faded as an ideological force after the 1967 defeat of its key leaders by Israel; the rise of the wealthy, conservative oil states; and the consolidation of overbearing state authority across most of the region. Fouad Ajami, an influential conservative Arab academic, famously declared these days to be the "end of pan-Arabism."[2] Egypt's separate peace with Israel transformed the region's strategic equation and removed the longtime center of the pan-Arabist bloc—leading to Cairo's expulsion from the Arab League itself. Saudi Arabia deployed its vast oil wealth to prop up conservative forces and to exercise its control over media and political movements across the region. The 1980s were dominated instead by the brutal war between Iraq and Iran, in which most of the conservative Arab states backed Iraq against the perceived revolutionary threat from Tehran (only Syria, which still declared itself "the beating heart of Arabism," opted to side with Persian Iran over Arab Iraq). As Arab leaders consolidated their domestic control and stamped out popular mobilization, they focused ever more overtly on naked self-interest or national patriotism rather than on grand shared Arab concerns.

The Arab regimes that emerged from the 1970s had perfected the art of pervasive social and political surveillance and control. Few Arab countries enjoyed any kind of press freedom, save for the occasional, limited-distribution, English language broadsheet aimed at the diplomatic and expatriate community. The willingness of these regimes to respond with crushing, brutal force affected the ability of any protest to spread. At the same time, almost every Arab regime developed systematic instruments for internal surveillance and control that barely concealed the brutal violence lurking beneath. All-pervasive intelligence agencies monitored every sphere of public life. Even opposition political parties were generally part of regime survival strategies, allowing managed political competition among generally compliant competing elites, rather than real challenges to political power or legislative alternatives.[3]

Popular unrest did not cease, but fierce, brutal regimes willing to use extreme violence and able to exert near-complete control over the media had the upper hand. The Iran-Iraq war, as well as the horrifying civil war in Lebanon and ongoing tensions with Israel, created a grim, dangerous environment that dictators could use to justify their strict control. In Syria, the brutal suppression of an Islamist uprising in Hama in 1982 ushered in grim decades of iron-fisted control. In Iraq, Saddam Hussein's Baathist regime became increasingly totalitarian in the face of intense internal and external challenges, resorting to the wholesale slaughter of the Kurds in the late 1980s. Jordan became more oppressive as the Hashemite monarchy emulated its hardline neighbors. There were some exceptions. Egypt, for instance, became more democratic after the assassination of Anwar Sadat in 1981, as new President Hosni Mubarak experimented with greater openness and political competition (a move that may have been possible precisely because of Egypt's isolation from the Arab League after being expelled following the conclusion of the Camp David Accords with Israel). But overall, for much of the region, the 1980s were a decade of stifling state domination and creeping totalitarianism.

Nevertheless, turbulence continued, especially in North Africa. Bread riots rocked Egypt in 1977, and Sadat was assassinated by Islamists. In late 1983, cities in Tunisia's south began to violently protest over International Monetary Fund (IMF)–mandated economic reforms.[4] The protests began as angry citizens received news over the state radio station that food price subsidies would be slashed. Furious Tunisians rampaged through the streets, overwhelming local police. Despite the regime's efforts to contain the unrest, the protests quickly spread across the substantial distances separating the towns of the south—without Facebook, Twitter, or even al-Jazeera to spread the word. Protestors tore down statues of former president and revolutionary hero Habib Bourghiba—the ultimate rejection of not only the government but the regime.

On January 1, the protests spread to Kasserine and then to Gafsa, two major industrial centers in the southern region. Massive crowds of protestors swarmed the streets, facing off against police and soon against tanks and armored personnel carriers. As reports of protestor deaths filtered through the country, Tunis itself exploded. Police stations were overrun, cars and buildings attacked, and an antiregime frenzy swept the nation. Street battles spread to almost every part of the country, from Kef along the border to the major hub cities of the southern interior. After about a week, the Tunisian military and police had reasserted control, and significant economic concessions were made to the protestors, but the regime was badly shaken.

The protests did not stop in Tunisia, however. They spread across the border to Morocco in January 1984, and then into Algeria. Violent protests broke out in Marrakesh on January 9. Students and workers across Morocco joined in, though the major cities under heavy security force control remained relatively calm. In Algeria, protests spread rapidly through major cities.[5] In Egypt, Mubarak faced broad economic discontent and dangerous riots by the police in February 1986. Popular protests brought down the Sudanese government in 1985, as major protests broke out over increases in prices for bread, oil, and public transportation, combined with a growing drought.[6] The mobilization culminated in the ouster of Sudan's president Jaafar Nimeiri by a military coup in April 1985 and a surprisingly rapid transition to open multiparty elections in May 1986. In a development with stark warnings for today's transitions, those elections were dominated by the National Islamic Front (NIF) and Umma Party, as the newer parties lacked organization and funds and waged ineffective electoral campaigns. The political polarization that followed led all too quickly to civil wars, military coups, and the rise of a nasty Islamist authoritarian system.

These protests recurred across North Africa for much of the decade, feeding off each other's momentum across borders even as local conditions dominated. Each government responded with its own particular mix of repression, economic reform, and relatively meaningless political shuffling. This economic protest remained episodic and did not at this point come together into a broad regional uprising. Few of the protests of the early to mid-1980s, no matter how intense or violent, had been able to force fundamental changes. They had remained largely contained within a North African arena that was increasingly seen as distinct from the rest of the Arab world. That would begin to change by the end of the decade, when a series of interlocking national uprisings more directly challenged the regional order.

DEFENSIVE DEMOCRATIZATION AFTER THE COLD WAR

The fall of communist regimes across Eastern Europe suddenly offered hope that real change might be possible in the Arab world as well. The fall of the Soviet Union undermined the pillars of the international structure supporting Arab authoritarianism and left numerous regimes suddenly casting about for new sources of international support. The sudden tilt in the global balance of power in favor of the West increased both the ideological appeal and the material benefits of the democratic and capitalist bloc. (Obama's signal that he would not fight for Mubarak played a functionally similar role to Gorbachev's refusal to intervene to save Erich Honecker's regime in East Germany.) This global change helped to spark moves toward democracy not only in the former Soviet space, but also in sub-Saharan Africa where a number of longtime dictatorships moved to contested electoral democracy.

The fall of the communist regimes shaped a world historical moment in which anything seemed possible and where people power seemed greater than the guns and censors of bankrupt dictatorships. The televised images of joyous East Germans or Czechs peacefully overrunning the symbols of their oppression could not fail to resonate with the subdued but discontent populations of the region. Not even the smothering censorship of the Arab autocrats could prevent the circulation of those images. As a cautionary tale, Nicolae Ceaușescu's death in Romania at the hands of the protestors he had attempted to decimate horrified Arab rulers and thrilled their people, increasing the appeal among at least some parts of ruling Arab coalitions of soft adaptation to popular demands.

The protest wave began before the fall of the Berlin Wall, even if that global transformation helped to define and frame its wider meaning. In Tunisia, on November 7, 1987, Bourghiba's thirty-year rule ended with a bloodless coup and his successor Zine el-Abidine Ben Ali offered substantial political reforms and a democratic opening.[7] In December 1987, the Palestinian Intifada erupted. In October 1988, a massive protest wave transformed Algerian politics, driving a proto-democratic transition that would end in blood three years later. In April 1989, riots in Jordan drove

King Hussein to initiate the most profound democratic opening since the 1950s. All preceded the fall of the Berlin Wall.

Of all of the protests, the Palestinian Intifada (1987–1991) had the deepest effect in terms of crafting a broader Arab narrative about resistance and change, probably more than even the fall of the Soviet Union or the North African protests. Where Tunisia had always been on the margins of Arab political culture, the Palestinian issue lay dead in the center, and the sudden outburst of political energy there spoke directly to the deepest political identities of most Arabs. Even in the absence of an open regional media, Arabs followed the course of the Palestinian uprising and acted to support it where they could. This was not a distraction from local problems, as critics often alleged; it was a lesson about the possibility of challenge under even the most hopeless conditions and a rebuke to ineffective leaderships from below.

The Intifada took virtually everyone by surprise, not only Israel, but the leaders of the PLO and of the Islamist group that would soon become Hamas. But like the 2011 uprisings, in retrospect it came to seem inevitable. As the veteran analyst Joost Hilterman observed,

> for many Palestinians in the Occupied Territories . . . the greatest
> surprise, with hindsight, was that the uprising had not occurred
> before December 1987. Smaller uprisings, usually lasting not
> more than one or two months, had repeatedly broken out in the
> preceding decade. . . . From late 1986 on, there was definitely
> "something in the air," with continual demonstrations in various
> locations. . . . Only a decade earlier, however, the assessment was
> that no collective action against the occupation could occur.[8]

The Intifada mobilized all sectors of Palestinian society in the face of great odds, riveting regional and international attention.[9] Its heavy coverage in the international media compensated for the absence of a meaningful Arab public sphere. That international coverage offered new narratives and icons, presenting Palestinians both as active agents of change rejecting obvious injustice and as indomitable underdogs facing an oppressive Israeli occupation. These positive narratives in international media were unfamiliar to supporters of the Arab cause. The Intifada also implicitly challenged the Arab order, as courageous youth with nothing but stones could be seen challenging Israel's occupation in ways that neither Arab regimes nor the PLO had managed for the previous decade and a half.

Protests were still raging throughout the region when the Iraqi invasion of Kuwait inflected the narrative, dramatically affecting the course of the upheaval.[10] As the U.S. assembled a massive military force in the region in the months following Iraq's seizure of Kuwait, massive crowds across the region protested against an American-led war, even as most governments sided with the coalition. That stark gap between rulers and the people was as important to the protest wave as was the widespread rejection of U.S. intervention, even in what many might otherwise have seen as the good cause of liberating Kuwait from invasion by a neighbor.[11] In Jordan and Yemen, the regimes sided with public opinion against their U.S. patron, which weakened their material ability to repress and control their publics and facilitated (limited and temporary) democratization from above. In other countries, such as Egypt, the pro-Iraqi popular sentiment drove a sharp wedge between the people and the regimes, forcing them into heightened repression and media control while mainstreaming popular protests against governments for political rather than purely economic reasons. The Gulf War experience also radicalized many of the opposition movements, whose strength on the streets arguably went to their heads and drove them to take unwise steps.

The Intifada and Gulf War both directly affected Jordan, with its long borders and intimate economic and social relations with both the West Bank and Iraq. The heavy representation of citizens of Palestinian origin in Jordan, and the regular movement between the East and West Banks, ensured that the Palestinian mobilization would be felt across the river. But Jordanians of Palestinian origin initially kept their heads down, calculating that the best way to help their compatriots in the West Bank was to avoid spooking the Jordanian regime. The challenge to the king came from an unexpected direction instead: from the Transjordanian southern tribesmen who had long formed the most reliable base of support for the monarchy.

The riots began in April 1989 in southern cities infuriated by IMF-dictated cuts to subsidies. The royal court was shocked by this unexpected challenge, which came on top of the already tense regional

situation. Rather than crack down this time, King Hussein instead initiated an astonishing round of democratic reforms.[12] His motives appear
to have been entirely defensive, aimed at preventing the escalation of
popular unrest that might unite the people against his regime. In November, Jordan held the freest and most competitive parliamentary elections
seen in the kingdom since the 1950s. The king invited Mudar Badran, a
candidate acceptable to the Muslim Brotherhood that represented the
largest opposition bloc, to form a new government. Hussein's decision to
align with Iraq during the Gulf War was wildly popular at home even as it
badly hurt Jordan's key international alliances with the U.S. and Saudi
Arabia. The monarchy then initiated a novel, large-scale national dialogue
including most political groups, which in 1991 produced a "National
Pact" enshrining the twin principles of the monarchy and democracy at
the center of political order. An independent press flourished, new political parties formed, and a real civic and political life blossomed.[13]

The popularity and political resilience gained through these reforms
and foreign policy stances likely helped the king survive the intense
mobilization around the Palestinian Intifada and the 1990–1991 Gulf
War. It is unlikely that the king would have chosen to side against the
United States, his primary international backer, had he not faced a mobilized public and fragile but popular democratic institutions. His deference to public opinion on a nearly existential question stands to this day
as a key example of the difference that an empowered public makes for
regional politics.

This opening would not survive the king's decision to sign a peace
treaty with Israel. The move toward an unpopular peace treaty led to a
rapid closing of the democratic opening, to prevent effective opposition,
with few international objections.[14] The Jordanian regime cracked down
on opposition parties and on the independent media, while gerryman-
dering elections in order to limit the gains of the Muslim Brotherhood's
Islamic Action Front Party. Jordanians could not block the peace process
directly, but instead mobilized within civil society by forming a broadly
based coalition against normalization with Israel modeled on a similar
Egyptian campaign in the 1980s. The political retreat reopened the old
problems of economic discontent and political alienation, leading to the
outbreak of renewed riots across the south of Jordan in 1996.[15]

Algeria was the site of another key popular uprising in the late 1980s. Like so many other Arab states, the Algerian regime was struggling with a disastrous economy and a stifling, sclerotic political system. In October 1988, a massive wave of cross-societal protest in Algeria challenged the long-ruling Front de Libération Nationale (FLN) that had degenerated into a corrupt, unpopular bureaucratic military regime. The protests had been building for nearly a decade, fueled by economic stagnation and by "the systematic and contemptuous violation of their rights through constant abuse of power and arbitrary rule."[16] Rage at such official contempt would prove as central to the 2011 Arab uprisings as it did in 1988. While there was no immediate trigger for the protests that began on October 5, declining oil revenues and unsustainable social spending undermined the economic foundations of the regime, while the FLN's overbearing and heavy-handed bureaucratic authoritarianism offered few outlets for legitimate dissent.

The democratic opening in response to the protests was controversial within the Algerian regime. The embattled President Chadli Bendjedid defensively sought to introduce democratic reforms, to put off economic demands while also fending off the hardliners in the military.[17] In February 1989, Algerians approved a new constitution by a landslide in a popular referendum. Political parties formed, and a vibrant national press and civil society organizations blossomed. Two very different wings of the Islamist movement, a mainstream and relatively moderate Muslim Brotherhood strand under the leadership of Abassi Madani and a harder-edged Salafi group led by Ali Belhadj, came together to form the Islamic Salvation Front (FIS). In the summer of 1990, the new Islamist party swept local elections and assumed control of a large number of local councils. Far from being overwhelmed and discredited by the hard work of governing, however, the FIS proved tenacious and effective in power, compensating for its limited ability to actually solve massive social and economic problems with ostentatious shows of integrity and personal commitment. Its frequent, massive public rallies kept enthusiasm high, at the cost of terrifying secular opponents.

The rise of the Islamist FIS in Algeria's newly democratic arena cast a shadow over the transition toward democracy—and continues to haunt today's thinking about the risks of moves toward democracy in the region. At a time of great uncertainty over the real power of competing political forces, the ability of the FIS to turn out massive numbers in organized marches and protests signaled real power. A definitive moment early in the process came with the FIS response to a decent-size march organized by women's groups. The response the next week stunned everyone. Hundreds of thousands of Islamists silently marched through the streets of Algiers, in disciplined formation. The show of strength thrilled the rising popular classes, but terrified the Francophone and secular elites. The FIS attempted to "narrowcast" its messaging, sending radical messages to its mobilized base and reassuring messages of moderation to the Algerian mainstream and the international media. But even in 1990, this effort failed, as the confusing mixed messages only intensified doubts about the movement's true intentions. The election results confirmed the impression of the FIS power over the streets.

Then came the fateful parliamentary elections in late 1991. The FIS won by a landslide over the discredited FLN, with the electoral system carefully designed to turn a small FLN victory into an overwhelming ruling majority instead handing that power to the Islamist challengers. The military had seen enough and stepped in to remove Bendjedid from office, cancel the second round of elections ahead of the inevitable results, and assume control. The West, alarmed by the rise of the Islamist movement and its mixed messages about its political intentions, quietly acquiesced in the coup—a message about its lack of real commitment to democracy when Islamists might win that continues to shape Arab views of Western rhetoric on democracy to this day. The leaders of the FIS were quickly arrested, and initially calm seemed to be guaranteed.

But then an Islamist insurgency grew and Algeria descended into a horrific civil war in which by some estimates over a half-million people were killed.[18] That violence unfolded under a near-total information blackout imposed by the military regime.[19] This tight repression included iron control over the national media, the targeting of intellectuals and foreigners, and the expulsion of much of the international press. This created perfect conditions for the spread of conspiracy theories, rumors, and a corrosive skepticism about all government statements.[20]

The fate of Algeria's massive mobilization and democratic opening had the deepest effects on both publics and regimes across the region.[21]

The brutal clampdown had a chilling effect on challengers, while its initial success emboldened the autocrats. The crackdown was not completely unpopular either. The success of the FIS had frightened secular elites in Algeria and elsewhere, and many liberals seem to have quietly accepted the argument for canceling democratic elections to prevent Islamist rule. The unfortunate and still widely accepted idea that Islamists supported "one man, one vote, one time" dates to some of FIS leader Ali Belhadj's more aggressive pronouncements in this era. And the horrific violence that followed, whether the fault of Islamists or of the regime's security services, served the same role as the Iraqi carnage of the mid-2000s in convincing many dissatisfied Arabs that their situation could actually be worse.

Less dramatic but still profoundly important challenges could be seen across the region. Tunisia's democratic window closed even more quickly, as Ben Ali opted for a massive crackdown on the Islamist el-Nahda Party and a turn toward severe authoritarianism. While Tunisia under Ben Ali maintained a formal democracy with regular elections, in fact it quickly devolved into an unusually repressive regime in which the state exercised near-total control over the media, civil society, and all forms of political activity.[22]

In Egypt, Mubarak had liberalized the political realm considerably in the 1980s, allowing relatively fair elections and a more open public sphere in the face of significant economic discontent. In 1990, the Egyptian Supreme Court threw out the 1987 electoral law, requiring new elections, while Mubarak fired his interior minister in response to protests by Islamists and other parts of society. The Gulf War proved a turning point, however, as Mubarak was forced to defend a highly unpopular alliance with the United States against Iraq. Even $60 billion in debt relief won little applause. Most of the opposition boycotted the 1990 election, which the National Democratic Party (NDP) again won with some 80 percent of the vote. Mubarak resorted to tight control over the media and growing repression to maintain control over an agitated population. In 1992, a small but fierce Islamist insurgency broke out, with terrorist attacks in Cairo and upper Egypt. Mubarak responded with blanket repression against all Islamists, including the relatively moderate Muslim Brotherhood, and a broader retreat on human rights, democracy, and public freedoms.

In Yemen, an unexpected move to unification between North and South Yemen in late 1989 created an unprecedented political opening.[23] Political parties proliferated, the independent press flourished, and popular demonstrations broke out across the country. In the midst of this political opening, the Iraqi invasion of Kuwait both mobilized Yemeni publics into massive demonstrations and caused an economic disaster as hundreds of thousands of Yemeni workers who had been in Kuwait were forced to return home. The overwhelming public support for Iraq forced Yemen, like Jordan, to stay out of the U.S.-led coalition to liberate Kuwait—a costly decision, as it lost U.S. and Saudi financial assistance, but hugely popular with the newly empowered public. The worsening economic situation complicated the delicate unification process, as "beginning in late 1991, day-to-day politics was increasingly punctuated by acrimony, popular protests, strikes, riots, bombings and assassinations."[24] Popular demonstrations and protests continued after the formation of the new government, escalating through 1992 until fading after the elections on April 27, 1993.

Even Saudi Arabia faced significant social mobilization, especially over its extremely unpopular decision to host a half-million coalition troops on its supposedly holy soil for Operation Desert Storm.[25] In 1990, a group of influential Islamist activists and Ulema (religious leaders) delivered the first Memorandum of Advice. The Sahwa, an influential network of Muslim Brotherhood–inflected Islamists, advocated from within for political change. The Saudi crackdown on this protest movement pushed some out of politics and radicalized others, including most famously the popular figure from the Afghan jihad, Osama bin Laden. Across the Gulf, muted demands could be heard.[26] Kuwaitis impatiently demanded more democratic forms of government from their restored emir, with patient U.S. pressure pushing to accommodate their demands from below.

The mobilization during the late 1980s and early 1990s therefore had many qualities familiar to today's Middle East. The massive popular movements in the streets crossed sectarian and class lines. They tapped into a clear sense of a common regional narrative, especially as the Intifada and the Iraq War intersected with local demands for political change. But none of those led to a real democratic transition. As Asef

Bayat, a professor of Middle Eastern studies who was one of the keenest observers of these societal changes well before the Arab uprisings, noted, "urban mass protests ebbed noticeably during the 1990s," as "governments imposed tighter controls while delaying or implementing unpopular policies only gradually."[27] Some regimes found ways to divert, repress, or contain popular challengers. Others gave significant ground politically, only to withdraw their concessions when the pressure faded. And others chose to fight bloody civil wars to maintain their hold on power. By the middle of the 1990s, the passion and energy of this protest wave had been blunted, contained in increasingly empty democratic games or diverted into apolitical civil society organizing. It took the launch of al-Jazeera and the second Palestinian Intifada to reenergize popular mobilization, years later.

KEFAYA: BUILDING TOWARD REVOLUTION

The decade of the 2000s was, in effect, one long wave of intense popular mobilization spanning the entire region. The upheaval was fueled by new media and communications technologies, by popular rage at trends in regional and international policy, and by the receding institutional competence of authoritarian regimes. Terrorism and the global war on terror, Israel's wars with the Palestinians and America's war with Iraq, rampaging sectarianism and massive refugee flows, and the increasingly open consolidation of a tacit alliance between Israel and most Arab regimes against Iran profoundly shaped the decade. The regional turmoil fueled domestic discontent, as Arab regimes seemed to systematically take positions at odds with the preferences of their people. Little wonder then that popular upheaval ensued.

The protests of the 2000s were of course not unprecedented, but they were the first to take place within the intensely unified political space shaped by new media technologies. This new social media was neither necessary nor sufficient for the spread of protests. In 1984, Tunisians had had no trouble diffusing riots from Sfax to Gafsa without Facebook, while Saudi Arabia was quite able to contain domestic challengers despite having a deeply wired society, but the new social media profoundly shaped the character and orientation of these protest movements' avant garde.

Al-Jazeera played a decisive role, linking together disparate national struggles into a coherent narrative of popular Arab protests against both foreign intervention and domestic repression. Its talk shows became an open forum for regionwide discussion and debate about shared issues and concerns, while its news coverage crafted a coherent master frame, making sense of the cascade of events across the entire region. As the decade moved on, new social media such as blogs, Facebook, and Twitter evolved into an infrastructure of communication, organization, and mobilization for such debates. I call this period the *Kefaya* wave, after the Egyptian protest movement that formed in 2003 to challenge Mubarak's son Gamal's presumptive inheritance of power. Even though only Egyptians embraced the name Kefaya—and only some Egyptians, at that—the same spirit of frustration and impatience with the smothering role of the authoritarian state permeated the entire region. As the Syrian intellectual Burhan Ghalyoun eloquently argued, this period witnessed "the awakening of the people who have been crushed by despotic regimes." Even where they could not win, they decisively cast aside the taboos and self-restraint that had controlled public life for decades.

Egypt's Kefaya movement itself was only one small part of the broad regional story, of course. Like other protest waves, including the 2011 uprisings, each local movement responded to local windows of political opportunity and domestic particularities, while also being embedded in a regionwide narrative. There were some direct imitators, such as Jordan's short-lived 2005 Qaba'at movement, which Jordanian journalist Samih al-Mayateh described as "Kefaya in a Jordanian dialect."[28] Other movements were completely different in motivation. In Lebanon, the massive mobilization in 2005 reflected the political rage following the assassination of Prime Minister Rafik Hariri and the intense societal and sectarian polarization of the political field. In Bahrain, the online mobilization in forums on human rights issues had to grapple with the sectarian realities of a Shi'a majority dominated by a Sunni monarchy. In Algeria and Tunisia, protest movements provided a new overlay on a nearly continuously contentious and turbulent political environment.

But all of these diverse movements shared a common challenge to the status quo. Kefaya's great success was to force previously repressed issues into the public sphere and to galvanize public debate over these once-taboo subjects. It drew the attention of a much wider segment of Egyptian society to the existence of deep discontent with the status quo and the possibility of organized action demanding change. Along the way, it directly confronted some of the most potent red lines in Egyptian political discourse, including the alleged plans to have Gamal Mubarak succeed his father. Organized around loose coalitions across ideological lines, Kefaya pioneered protest methods, organizational forms, and communications tactics that were adopted by later Egyptian and wider Arab protest movements. And it managed to command the attention of the international media in ways far beyond its numerical strength, pioneering the intricate and intimate interactions between protest movements and the new media that would characterize the coming revolutions.

The spark for the Kefaya protest wave was international, as huge numbers rallied in support of the second Palestinian Intifada, the "Al-Aqsa Intifada" (2000–2002) and against the U.S. invasion of Iraq (2002–2003). Those protests focused attention on a common issue across the entire region, establishing a tempo of protest and of unified political debate shaped by al-Jazeera. Regimes happy to see political energy directed externally might have tolerated or even encouraged those protest movements. But as the political focus turned inward, these movements refused to disband. Activist youth proved creative, determined, and able to stay a step ahead of the authorities through new uses of social media and protest techniques. The deteriorating economic conditions and closing political space kept grievances high and rising, with new protestors entering the fray, from workers in Egypt to tribesmen in southern Jordan.

The second intifada, which erupted in September 2000 following the controversial visit of the polarizing right-wing Israeli leader Ariel Sharon to the Al-Aqsa mosque complex in Jerusalem, had a galvanizing effect across the region. As the first great al-Jazeera regional event, the Al-Aqsa Intifada focused regional attention and galvanized regional debate for several years. This second intifada was very different from the first, however. Instead of a peaceful, unified social mobilization against Israeli occupation, the Al-Aqsa Intifada was intensely violent and divided the Palestinian polity in near-fatal ways.

As violence intensified, the culture of resistance celebrated across the region began to raise troubling questions as suicide bombings arose and open warfare began. And the failure of Arab regimes to do anything concrete to support the Palestinians at their hour of greatest need focused critical attention among a mobilized public on the systemic failings of the Arab order.

The Palestinian struggle, no matter how grim or disorienting, resonated deeply with this emerging new Arab public. For virtually the entire modern history of the Arab world, the issue of Palestine had been the focal point for political activism and political identity. The Palestinian struggle became what Shibley Telhami, a leading American political scientist, memorably termed the "prism of pain" through which Arabs made sense of their political condition. For much of this period, Arab regimes were comfortable with mobilization directed toward Palestine, as this let off steam (in the oft-abused metaphor) and diverted attention from their own domestic abuses. But the Arab regimes' misuse of the Palestinian cause did not make the Arabs' identification and passion any less real.

Al-Jazeera's coverage of the Al-Aqsa Intifada made a real difference in how Arabs related to these events. Its graphic, emotional coverage brought the conflict home to many Arabs in radically new ways. The now-controversial image of Mohammed al-Dura, a young boy allegedly shot by Israeli soldiers while protesting, replayed in an endless loop, a stand-in for the daily horrors Palestinians suffered. The coverage alone was not enough, however. What made the al-Jazeera–mediated Intifada different was the way it was framed within a comprehensive narrative of Arab identity, debated in hotly contested talk shows, and experienced simultaneously by almost all Arab television viewers.

The large protests that broke out in response were themselves covered by al-Jazeera as a part of the story of an Arab nation on the march. Arab citizens saw themselves moving together, sharing a common struggle even if their leaders consistently let them down. These protests had their moments of impact. In April 2002, Vice President Dick Cheney came to the region to drum up support for a move against Iraq, only to find the regional agenda completely consumed by the Israeli reoccupation of the West Bank. But by the fall of 2002, the Arab public was grappling with its own impotence. It had failed to force its will upon Israel,

America, or even Arab leaders. The protests struggled to sustain themselves. Even so, whatever the effect on the wider course of the Intifada, al-Jazeera and the experience of sustained, regionwide collective mobilization laid the foundations for the transference of public energies toward other issues: first the impending invasion of Iraq, and then domestic misrule and abuse.

The protests in support of the Al-Aqsa Intifada morphed seamlessly into demonstrations against the U.S.-led invasion of Iraq. The terrorist attack of September 11, 2001, and the subsequent invasion of Iraq had fundamentally diverted the regional agenda, as well as Western perceptions of the significance and nature of Arab protest movements. By late 2002, the impending invasion had risen to the top of the Arab agenda, covered with the same intensity on al-Jazeera as the still-raging Intifada. Iraq and the Palestinian conflict morphed together with the war on terror to reinforce a seamless narrative of American aggression against Islam, feeding the al-Qaeda narrative, fueling the attractiveness of any form of resistance, and undermining all who would work with the United States even on shared interests.

We will likely never know precisely how important the dream of a long-term transformation of the Middle East was to the decision by the Bush administration to invade Iraq. Public rhetoric before the war focused primarily on the supposedly imminent threat of Iraqi weapons of mass destruction, and postwar rationalizations emphasized the goal of Iraqi democracy. But among neoconservative ideologues, there was always a broader ambition of transforming the region, a vision of democracy promotion that united them with otherwise hostile liberal hawks.

Since the outburst of the new Arab uprisings, some backers of the Iraq War have claimed vindication. They should not. Few Arabs anywhere claim Iraq as an inspiration. Arabs almost unanimously denounced the U.S.-led invasion as an illegitimate act of imperialism. The postinvasion descent of Iraq into a hell of civil war and insurgency, along with the images of a faux democracy carried on the back of American tanks, actually helped to discredit the idea across the region. While some reformists proposed using American power in pursuit of their cause during a rare moment of interest, most saw their prospects dimmed by the "Iraqi earthquake."[29]

Still, the transformation of Iraq did have important regional effects, even if they are not the ones the most ardent war supporters claimed. Arab dictators pointed to Iraq's chaos as a reason to avoid loosening their own hold on power, while Arab publics thrilled to the rise of the Iraqi insurgency. Iranian power rose with the removal of its great enemy, frightening most Arab regimes and perhaps helping to push them closer to the U.S. and Israel in fear. When Iraq did finally begin to stabilize after 2007, many Arabs saw the emerging entity as an Iranian-dominated, war-ravaged cautionary tale. Almost none yearned to mimic its experience.

But it would be too easy to conclude that the invasion and occupation of Iraq do not matter for the emergence of a new regional order. Iraq is simply too central, too powerful, and too key to regional narratives and debates for its occupation to have had no effect at all. For one, it embroiled America in the struggle to pacify Iraq for nearly a decade, draining resources and consuming attention. It empowered Iran by removing its most powerful enemy and opening Iraq to become a new arena for power politics, in ways painfully reminiscent of the struggle for Syria decades earlier. It reinvigorated al-Qaeda at a time when the jihadist organization might have collapsed completely following the destruction of its base in Afghanistan. And it unleashed a vitriolic wave of hostility on the United States across the region that colored the response to any American initiative, no matter how worthy.

The Iraq War also contributed all too directly to the spread of sectarianism across the region. The bloody civil war in Iraq that spiraled out of control from 2004 to 2007 brought horrific images of violence to the entire region. The refugee crisis sent millions of Iraqis into Lebanon, the Gulf, Jordan, Syria, and even Egypt and North Africa. The rise of a Shi'a leadership in Iraq intersected with the long-standing cold war between Iran and the Gulf Cooperation Council (GCC), with King Abdullah of Saudi Arabia convinced that America had handed a powerful Arab state over to Iran. The growth of Sunni-Shi'a hatreds served the agendas of Gulf states such as Saudi Arabia and Bahrain that hoped to muster opposition to the growing power of Iran and Hezbollah, and to browbeat their own Shi'a populations into silence. Anti-Shi'a propaganda flooded the Gulf media, while the horrifying scenes of sectarian carnage in the streets of Iraq spoke for themselves. Such sectarian messages were also spread by the Salafi-jihadists associated with al-Qaeda, who demonized the Shi'a on doctrinal grounds as non-Muslims. Genuinely unprecedented antipathy toward the Shi'a could by the middle of the decade be heard in places such as Egypt and Jordan that had virtually no Shi'a or history of anti-Shi'ism.

For all the American talk of how Iraq's liberation would promote democracy in the region, in fact it clearly strengthened the hand of dictators in the short term. The chaos made democracy seem dangerous to many ordinary Arabs who otherwise would have found it attractive, particularly in Syria, where real fears of sectarian bloodshed would still color the response to the uprising in 2011. The war also weakened the hand of the United States in promoting reforms. The Bush administration was in no position to make real demands of the Arab allies that it desperately needed to help with its Iraqi campaign, particularly as it largely ignored their demands that the U.S. engage seriously in achieving Israeli-Palestinian peace. The intense anti-Americanism of this era put reformists in a bind, making it costly and dangerous to accept U.S. financial or political support. The Bush administration's constant invocation of "democracy" and "freedom" juxtaposed painfully with the images of tortured and abused prisoners from Abu Ghraib prison in Baghdad, discrediting those who had long spoken of the need for democratic change.

The Iraq War did help to fuel protest movements, however, though not in the ways the Bush administration had envisioned. Opposition to the U.S. occupation of Iraq helped to bind together a broad discourse of "resistance" that focused popular hostility against the U.S. and complicit Arab regimes. Al-Jazeera's emotional, intense coverage of the war riveted Arab attention, binding together the regional narrative around this single, shared spectacle. The Iraq War, along with the endless stalemate in Palestine, contributed to the protestors' narrative of the Arab regimes' uselessness and complicity with the hated regional status quo. Marching against the Iraq War played a key part in the evolution of protest networks and repertoires. Indeed, many activists across the region still identify the antiwar protests on March 20, 2003, as the real starting point for the decade's wave of antiregime mobilization.

This unified narrative continued to cohere even after the fury over the invasion of Iraq peaked and protest movements shifted their focus inward. The Arab public was now well primed to view local protest movements as part of a common, unified regional narrative that had evolved in the preceding three years. The Egyptian Kefaya movement, Jordanian bread riots, Bahraini human rights movements—all of these and more came together into a broad-based and increasingly self-conscious Arab protest movement.

If Egypt offered the template for an activist-led reconfiguration of the public sphere, Lebanon presented the first great spectacle of mass mobilization forcing large-scale political change. The Cedar Revolution against Syria's role in Lebanon following the assassination of Hariri brought millions of people into the streets. The media-savvy, telegenic activists of the March 14 movement (named after the first great rally in 2005) expertly cultivated international opinion, coordinating mass mobilization with a sophisticated public relations campaign to maximize their impact. The countermobilization led by the Shi'a resistance movement Hezbollah brought out comparable numbers from different sectors of society. In the end, the Cedar Revolution succeeded in driving Syria from its dominant position in Lebanon.

The revolution did not make any appreciable move toward democratizing Lebanon, however, as it operated within rather than against the entrenched sectarian system. Hezbollah's countermobilization kept the streets alive with competing demonstrations until June 2006 when a provocation likely designed for domestic political consumption triggered a massive Israeli assault. That war badly undermined Lebanon's March 14 government of Fouad Siniora, and empowered Hezbollah both at home and throughout the region after it emerged bloodied but unbowed after thirty-three days of Israeli bombardment and ground invasion.

The Bush administration attempted to take credit for and to promote such democracy and reform movements. Its Middle East Partnership Initiative tried to build regional networks supporting civil society and democracy, and the administration spoke frequently about the need for democratic reform in order to combat both terrorism and anti-Americanism. In a well-received speech at the American University in Cairo in 2005, Secretary of State Condoleezza Rice apologized for past American support for dictatorships and pledged a new support for freedom and democracy. But, in fact, the Arab public in this period was deeply opposed to American policies and wanted nothing to do with U.S. talk of democracy. It is true that Bush's rhetoric on democracy and pressure on some Arab leaders such as Mubarak helped to create at least some space for mobilization, but that was only a marginal part of the story. Arabs wanted democracy for their own reasons, not the least of which was that they hoped to more effectively oppose American foreign policy. Throughout the thriving, rollicking debate about democracy and reform that swept the new Arab public in the mid-2000s, there was near-complete consensus about the indigenous roots of the demands for change and a rejection of any American efforts to commandeer the process.

The moment of ferment could not be sustained. Momentum faded, elites who had been caught off guard regrouped, and the authoritarian states reasserted their iron grip on political life. The year 2006 marked a clear turning point. The Egyptian regime had navigated a constitutional referendum, a presidential election, and—after a crude intervention in the second and third rounds—parliamentary elections, leaving few new openings for political mobilization. The Israeli war with Lebanon and the Arab regimes' tacit alliance with Israel against Iran put most of them on the wrong side of popular opinion, encouraging both tighter crackdowns on popular mobilization and official encouragement of a nasty strain of sectarianism. American ardor to promote democracy faded after Hamas won parliamentary elections in Palestine. Al-Qaeda's rising appeal during this period, fueled in part by the fiasco in Iraq and in part by the Bush administration's intensely unpopular "war on terror" discourse and policies, led the West to put an even greater premium on cooperation in counterterrorism.

The overture for a renewed period of popular challenge actually came from outside the Arab world completely. Iran's Green Movement protests following alleged fraud in the June 2009 presidential elections in some ways offered a preview of what was to come in the Arab world. The Iranian protest movement brought a wide cross-section of society into the streets, but drew heavily on urban youth. Their use of social media, especially Twitter, captivated international attention. Even if such social media played only a marginal role in organizing Iranian protests themselves, they played an outsized role in shaping global narratives. With journalists thin on the ground, the videos and tweets and blog posts out of Iran (especially those in English) became arguably the most important source for information about the unfolding protests and repression. The Green Movement demonstrations raged for weeks, but ultimately state repressive power held. As in most of the Arab cases, the protests revealed unexpected depths of popular resentment and extraordinary competencies to organize and to communicate, but ultimately authoritarian regime seemed to be able to weather the storm.

By the end of the decade, the protest wave appeared to have crested, and the Arab political order restored to the relative stability of the 1990s. The study of authoritarian resilience dominated the academic literature at the end of the first decade of the 2000s. Activists across the region were disheartened and uncertain about their next move. The United States, at both the end of the Bush administration and the beginning of the Obama administration, did not prioritize democratization or reform in its Middle East policy. Nevertheless, this decade is the essential training ground for the mobilization that finally broke through in 2011.

The authoritarian regimes could not fully regain their grip, as the underlying trends in the information environment and in the expectations of political society pushed relentlessly toward challenge and change. The regional agenda fragmented, as media outlets proliferated and regional divisions became more entrenched. On the eve of the uprisings, Arab autocrats felt more confident and activists more despondent than they had in a decade. But they mistook the action for the structural changes beneath—changes that would bring the challengers back even more powerfully at the end of the decade.

WHAT DOES THIS HISTORY tell us about the Arab uprising in 2011? *First,* we should not be overly impressed by the novelty of Arab popular mobilization. There have been several earlier waves of region-wide popular uprisings that have challenged both domestic and regional political order. The idea that some cultural peculiarities rendered Arabs politically passive has always been at odds with reality. We should not therefore assume that there must be some unique new factor, such as social media, to explain a supposedly new phenomenon.

Second, the unified Arab media space has always been something that makes the regional dynamics unique compared to other areas of the world. In each of the earlier episodes of regional mobilization, there were powerful emulation effects as Arabs in each country paid careful attention to events in others. This went beyond simple media attention. Arabs identified with each other across borders and saw their struggles as intimately and directly linked. When the Tunisian uprising began, history tells us that it was almost inevitable that it would spread across the region.

Third, the popular mobilization has always been interwoven with the competition and power politics between Arab states. Domestic challenges have rarely remained insulated from regional trends for long. Powerful states have always sought to exploit openings in their rivals, or to compete with them in the arenas of weaker regional states. This was most obvious during the 1950s, as Nasser and his rivals directly competed to mobilize their supporters across the region. But interventions, direct or indirect, have always been the rule. Nobody should have been surprised when the Saudis, Qataris, and others began to take advantage of the Arab uprisings.

Finally, waves of regional popular mobilization have repeatedly ended not with democratization but with the deeper entrenchment of authoritarian regimes, in perhaps the most sobering and distressing of historical lessons. Revolutionary mobilization ended up in the reconsolidation of state authority, sometimes under new leaders and sometimes under surviving regimes. History warns us that within a few years, the Arab uprisings of 2011 are likely to result in an even more repressive, stifling regional order. Will the transformative role of the new Arab public be able to overcome this tragic fate?

CHAPTER 4

A NEW HOPE

THE WINTER OF 2010 was thus a time when the authoritarian regimes seemed to have regained control after being rattled by the protest wave of the mid-2000s. Many Arab states had faced down significant, creative, and fearless protest movements over the preceding decades, but had emerged unscathed. Activists were scattered and weak, battered by waves of arrests and official pressures, and unable to find points of entry into increasingly repressive regimes. Regimes that had seemed baffled and failing a few years earlier now gave off an air of cockiness, taunting their opposition with stage-managed elections while arresting dissidents with impunity. The American and international agendas were decidedly focused on status quo issues: the interminable Israeli-Palestinian peace process, the Iranian nuclear program, and the Obama administration's efforts to move beyond the war on terror with a high-profile outreach to mainstream Muslims.

But this seeming stability masked the deep structural changes in the public sphere that continued to have an effect. The underlying balance of power was shifting relentlessly away from autocratic regimes toward empowered publics. Momentary tactical defeats for specific protest movements could not blunt the overall changes in the public sphere across the Arab world. The ability of regimes to beat down their challengers did nothing to address the unsustainability of the regional status quo or its rejection by the emerging Arab public.

Despite the façade of stability, the foundations of the regimes were eroding dangerously. State services, already in sorry condition, continued to deteriorate. Families struggled with overcrowded, undersupplied, and poorly administered schools and hospitals. Corrupt and abusive police and indifferent bureaucrats were the primary points of contact between citizens and the state. Rumors of corruption spread relentlessly. (I still remember the first time a taxi driver in Amman began without prompt to rail about Queen Rania's private jet and about who was getting a kickback on a big new construction project in the center of the city. Such public complaint by total strangers, once taboo, had become routine.) Economic woes escalated, the middle class disappeared, the poor scrambled for survival, and youth found all doors closed to them. Sectarian and tribal conflicts broke out unpredictably. Labor strikes intensified and proliferated. A series of deadly disasters in Egypt made this decay all too literal—a rail crash, a capsized ferry, a collapsed apartment building. What could "stability" mean given the palpable decay of the institutional underpinnings of states across much of the region?

This was the context for the uprisings that toppled President Zine el-Abidine Ben Ali of Tunisia and President Hosni Mubarak of Egypt within the span of two months. Those two seemingly successful revolutions marked a discrete phase in the unfolding Arab upheavals. The success of the Tunisian uprising in forcing the flight of Ben Ali galvanized Egypt and inspired protestors across the region, even though it had taken place at the margins of international attention. It incited Egypt's January 25 rebellion, which riveted global and Arab attention for eighteen days and ended with the removal of Mubarak. The fall of these two long-entrenched autocrats to popular uprisings created a palpable sense that anything was feasible. That sense of inevitable change would begin to fade by March, as authoritarian regimes determined to survive struck back hard. But for those first two months of 2011, fundamental change everywhere in the region seemed not only possible, but unstoppable.

The changes in Tunisia and Egypt were important on their own. But their real revolutionary contribution was their rapid and massive diffusion into a regional tidal wave. The coverage on al-Jazeera and the rapid embrace by social media users across the region brought Tunisia from the periphery to the core of the Arab public debate.[1] On an average Friday in February 2011, virtually every city in the Arab world marched to the same beat, chanting the same slogans, watching each other, and feeding off a shared energy within a shared narrative. Al-Jazeera became the primary televised home of the revolution both in Arabic and in English. This role would become more openly problematic in later months, but at this point it seemed natural, given its place in shaping the Arab public sphere, promoting a pan-Arab identity, and advocating for political reform over the preceding decade.[2]

Common themes emerged. Friday became a regionwide day of protest, a focal point that could survive any interference with communications or political crackdown. Protestors imitated tactics, such as the seizing and holding of public squares or the uploading of protest videos to YouTube or other Internet sharing sites. Regimes initially dismissed protestors as dangerous mobs, insignificant minorities, and foreign-backed provocateurs, but over time, they usually found themselves confronting genuine challenges. They then faced a daunting "dictator's dilemma": brutality tended to backfire, sparking more protest than it deterred, while protestors tended to dismiss offers of reform out of hand as insufficient or noncredible. Regimes were transfixed by the novelty of the challenge and had not yet developed or deployed the full range of disruption, co-optation, and repression that would come out in force by the middle of February.

The political field within which these protests unfolded was astonishingly unified. The momentum of events traveled quickly and easily across borders. This wasn't only from Egypt and Tunisia: Protestors in Yemen or Morocco hung on every twist in Bahrain, while Syrians eyed the violence that met the Libyan challenge. Protestors developed a very powerful pan-Arabist outlook even as they focused their energies on domestic change—and saw no contradiction between the two. They adopted identical slogans, as *Irhal* [Leave!] or *Al-Shaab Yureed Isqat al-Nizam* [*The People Want to Overthrow the Regime*] became the lingua franca of Arab society. Terms such as *baltagiya*, an Egyptian term for regime thugs, came into widespread use as far afield as Yemen.

These uprisings may have chanted for democracy, but their energies were not channeled through elections or from established political parties. The authoritarian regimes had largely drained those formal political institutions of meaning through their co-optation of opposition parties, fixing of elections, and pressure on civil society organizations. Protests were driven by networks of networks, loose coalitions of disparate groups and individuals, instead of by organized movements. The key drivers of protest movements tended to be young, urban, middle-class men and women with experience of the outside world and familiarity with information technology. But the movements could only grow into revolutions where they attracted broad-based support from other social sectors.[3]

The Arab upheavals began in the most marginal of marginal locations, Sidi Bouzid, with the December 17, 2010, self-immolation of the young fruit seller and labor activist Mohammed Bouazizi. This tiny, grim town 200 kilometers from Tunis, lacks even a rail link to the capital. Its long history of labor unrest and violent protest against the regime differed little from other, similar towns and cities across the Tunisian periphery. Tunisia itself lay on the edge of the Arab world, both physically and politically. Its tightly controlled political space and media served at best as a cautionary tale about the extent of the smothering control of Arab authoritarianism. Its workers looked north to Europe for work and opportunities more than to the Arab world, while its regional vista rarely extended beyond North Africa.

Nor were the protests that began in Sidi Bouzid themselves especially unusual. Labor protests, bread riots, and large-scale turbulence had been a regular feature of Tunisian politics for decades. The riots that broke out in December 1983, for instance, look eerily familiar from the vantage point of 2011. Those riots erupted in response to economic grievances, perceived corruption, and official indifference. They quickly spread from town to town, and even across the Maghreb into Algeria and Morocco. They were eventually put down through a combination of force and concessions. But had that been all, those riots would have gone down as just another Tunisian protest movement, another bout of turbulence on the Arab periphery.

By the time Tunisia's protests erupted, growing unrest had been episodically appearing across the region for months. The regionwide explosion did not exactly come out of nowhere. In Jordan, riots and a brutal police response in the southern town of Maan in early January had consumed local attention.[4] In Kuwait, a nasty assault on dissident academic Obaid al-Wasmi roiled national politics.[5] A horrifying attack

on a Coptic church in Alexandria inflamed sectarian tensions in Egypt at
the end of December. Algeria had "been in a permanent state of moral
revolt against the regime" for years.[6] Political elites in Jordan and Egypt
were still fuming over the crudely manipulated national elections in
November 2010 that had produced parliaments devoid of any meaningful opposition.

In short, what made January 2011 different was not protest but
rather *success* in driving Ben Ali and then Mubarak from their thrones,
the *backfiring* of traditionally effective regime responses, the *framing* of
multiple local acts of protest into a single coherent regional narrative on
al-Jazeera and social media, and the rapid spread of the protest to almost
every country in the region.

But the upheavals in Tunisia and Egypt also reveal the limits of
change. When I walked through Sidi Bouzid in June 2011, I found it hard
to believe that the revolts that have reshaped the Arab world had begun
in such a remote place . . . and that so little had changed. Sidi Bouzid itself
seemed hardly touched, save for the revolutionary graffiti and shrines
that remain in the main square on the town's one major road. Across the
country, Tunisians continued to complain about the persistence of the
old regime, the uncertainty over the depth of political change, the continuing struggles of the economy, the uselessness of political parties
jockeying for seats of power while neglecting popular concerns, and rising tensions between Islamists and their secular rivals. Tunisians felt forgotten, losing faith in the democratic transition.

By the summer, Egyptians were even more vocal in their disillusion-
ment. The visceral thrill of Mubarak's fall was soon replaced by growing
recognition that existing power structures, particularly the army, had protected the core of their power. A referendum in March on amendments to
the constitution passed with 77 percent of the vote, despite being overwhelmingly opposed by the main spokesmen of the revolution.

Activists fumed over continued police abuses and by high-handed
military rule, while ordinary Egyptians struggled with a collapsing economy and a perception of spiraling crime and instability. The rise of the
Muslim Brotherhood and of more radical Salafi Islamist movements
frightened many activists who saw their secular vision for Egypt under
threat by larger, better organized, and more popular Islamist movements.

Through the spring, supposedly prodemocracy protestors found themselves in the curious position of demanding the postponement of elections, even as this kept the hated Supreme Council of the Armed Forces (SCAF) in power. By July 8, protestors had reassembled in Tahrir Square to protest the behavior of the ruling SCAF and the appointed interim government. Three weeks later, Islamists responded with a massive demonstration, and security forces cleared away the remnants of the Tahrir sit-in.

The limits to change in Egypt and Tunisia were mirrored at the regional level, as authoritarian regimes fought back in what many activists came to call a "counterrevolution." In this chapter, I focus on the two cases of "success," looking at what allowed these protest movements to emerge, grow, sustain, and succeed. The chapter examines the role of both internal and international factors in shaping the calculations of the leaders and protestors, including a behind-the-scenes view of the rapidly evolving thinking of the Obama administration. It explores the importance of al-Jazeera and of social media in the process, both inside Tunisia and Egypt and beyond their borders. It concludes with a discussion of the limitations of change in each case, the ongoing struggle between protestors and interim military regimes over the fate of the revolution. (Chapters 6 and 7 detail the grim battles that followed the protests in Tunisia and Egypt, from Bahrain and Yemen to Libya and Syria to Morocco and Jordan.)

In Egypt, especially, an intense struggle over narratives and legitimacy have defined postrevolutionary politics. The battle has been waged through competing street protests, through the media, and through ongoing debates and discussions across all levels of society. The youth activists who planned the January 25 revolution and fought to occupy Tahrir Square in the early days of the revolution claimed the mantle of revolutionary legitimacy and sought to place themselves above the political fray as its soul and spokesmen. But their narrative was only one of many. The SCAF claimed a decisive role in the revolution by virtue of its decision not to fire on protestors and its move to ease Mubarak from power on February 11. The Muslim Brotherhood claimed a revolutionary role by virtue of its youth activists' early participation and its key role in protecting the square on January 29, as well as its long persecution at the

hands of Mubarak's regime. But others rejected the language of revolutionary legitimacy completely. The revolution, they argued, was made
not by the activists, whose meager numbers could never have threatened
the regime, but by the millions of ordinary Egyptians who joined the
demonstrations and tipped the balance. Legitimacy and power should
henceforth be decided not by who was in the square on January 25 but
through the ballot box or through control of the streets.

Tunisia's protests began for largely unique and idiosyncratic reasons.
The Egyptian revolution almost certainly would not have taken place
without the Tunisian example. Without the Egyptian revolution, the cascade of demonstrations and uprisings that swept the region in February
and March would likely not have ever begun. How did these uprisings
succeed where so many others had failed? Why did they trigger the
broader regional cascade?

TUNISIA

The self-immolation of Bouazizi set the Arab uprising in motion.[7] Its
efficacy will always stand as a great historical mystery. Tunisia, traditionally on the margins of the Arab world, also had a long tradition of popular uprisings challenging the Tunis government, usually originating in
the neglected and marginalized southern cities. Indeed, there had been a
very similar outburst of unrest only two years earlier, in 2008, which the
regime had quickly managed to subdue.[8] But the protests that erupted in
December 2010 dwarfed other recent bouts of unrest.

The regime of President Ben Ali had degenerated into a typical, if
extreme, family kleptocracy. The long-whispered excesses and corruption of Ben Ali's wife and her family had recently been revealed through
U.S. Embassy cables published by WikiLeaks, but few Tunisians had
needed that external confirmation to know of the regime's depravations
(though the pet snow tiger detailed in one of the documents was a nice
touch). This corruption had a particularly sharp salience in a country of
high unemployment, limited opportunities for economic advancement,
and sharp disparities between the relatively wealthy coastal areas and the
struggling interior. Rage at the corruption and flamboyance of the ruling
family, from Jordan's Queen Rania to Egypt's Gamal Mubarak, would be
a common theme across many Arab countries in the coming months.

However, few were hated with the intensity with which Tunisians despised Ben Ali's wife.

Youth in particular felt deeply frustrated with the absence of economic opportunity. They chafed at the heavy-handed restrictions on the Internet and the media. In the height of irony, Ben Ali had declared 2010 to be "the year of Tunisian youth," on January 25.[9]

Ben Ali's regime had maintained one of the most severe levels of control over the media and public discourse in the region, a real achievement in an authoritarian Middle East.[10] Stifling censorship of all local media, along with the regime loyalists' ownership of all private media, prevented virtually any meaningful public debate. Foreign journalists were rarely allowed access, and their reporting was tightly controlled. In the few years prior to the 2010 uprising, the regime's intolerance of public dissent and repression of the media had intensified, even as rumors of corruption spread relentlessly through society. As a result, much real political debate and dissent had migrated into cyberspace. The regime responded with intense censorship of the Internet, including not only political sites but even popular video-sharing services and social networking sites.[11] In return, Internet activists such as Nawaat pioneered methods of online anonymity and personal security, and connected local issues into the diaspora community of migrant workers, particularly in France.[12] Facebook, which was seen as a nonthreatening and popular social outlet rather than a political threat, remained unblocked, even as YouTube, Daily Motion, and Flickr succumbed to censorship. As a result, Tunisia soon had one of the highest Facebook membership rates in the world.

The silence of the official media protected the regime from a great deal of potential opposition, but also created a remarkably brittle structure of control. The transformation of the environment for information and communications, both globally and regionally, made the maintenance of such rigid control increasingly implausible. Dependence on such control left the regime uniquely vulnerable to the introduction of new information or new protest movements. Compared to a country like Egypt or Jordan, where critical information flowed freely through the opposition press and protests were a daily occurrence, Tunisia's tightly controlled public sphere made it distinctively vulnerable to a cascade of dissent once those controls faltered. The very strength of the Tunisian authoritarian state—fierce but brittle—became a weakness once mobilization reached a critical point.[13]

Tunisia was also distinctive in the region for its near-complete decimation of its organized Islamist opposition. Ben Ali had crushed the Muslim Brotherhood offshoot el-Nahda in the early 1990s, driving key figures such as Rached Ghannouchi into exile, imprisoning most of its leaders and many of its cadres. In contrast to most Arab countries, where the Muslim Brotherhood maintained a daunting array of social welfare, religious, and political institutions, Tunisia banished all formal expressions of political Islam. Its Kemalist-style, state-driven secularism and French-style enforcement of the iron line between religion and state set it apart from most other Arab states. The rapid reemergence of el-Nahda following Ben Ali's overthrow suggests that this rigidity, like the censorship of the media, created an unnatural and unstable status quo.[14] It also meant, however, that the mobilization during the revolution itself was uniquely non-Islamist in character and expression.

Bouazizi's act of desperation was not the inarticulate expression of rage that it has been portrayed to be. It was a calculated political act designed to provoke precisely the kind of popular response it achieved. It came in the wake of a series of particularly brazen land grabs in the farmlands surrounding Sidi Bouzid, and attempts by local labor organizations to mount challenges to official abuses. As graphic and horrifying as his self-immolation was, it likely would have had as little impact as previous acts of protest were it not for what would soon become a distinctive combination of factors across the region: a brutal regime response to the protests that broke out, which fueled rather than crushed dissent; the creative use of social media to spread images and reports of the brutality; and an unusually attentive international response once the protests had begun to capture the regional imagination.

Tunisian security forces were quite familiar with outbursts of furious protests in these remote southern towns and cities, and they responded in their traditional fashion. When protestors gathered at Sidi Bouzid's police station, security forces fired into the crowd and sealed off the city by blockading the only roads in and out of the isolated southern cities.

Next, the regime tried hard but unsuccessfully to censor information about the protests.[15] Information Minister Oussama Romdhani imposed a comprehensive ban on any reporting out of the turbulent city. As researcher Rasha Moumneh recalled, "the media blackout is so severe that in the first days of the riots, one Tunisian resident remarked incredulously on Twitter that everyone was lying about the riots, because he had seen nothing of them on TV or in the newspapers."[16]

But neither move proved effective this time. The heavy-handed response, which resulted in several more deaths, infuriated other Tunisians and, instead of dispersing, the crowd grew. The protests quickly spread across Tunisia's southern cities, despite the regime's efforts to isolate Sidi Bouzid. Here, social media, which has often been awarded too much importance in the spread of the Arab uprisings, played a genuinely important role. Tunisia's exceptionally high level of Facebook usage allowed a direct way for activists to spread information about the repression, despite the regime's continuing ability to almost completely control the broadcast media and press. Facebook pages circulated graphic images and information that spread quickly through existing social networks of activists, families, and organized groups.

Al-Jazeera also picked up the story and heavily covered it—perhaps more aggressively than it might have done in another North African country. The relationship between Tunisia and the Qatari TV station had always been difficult, as its fearless coverage clashed with Ben Ali's fierce determination to maintain suffocating control over the flow of information. The al-Jazeera offices in Tunis had routinely been shut down, and in 2006 Tunisia had closed its embassy in Doha, protesting what it called al-Jazeera's "hostile campaign" against it. But over the last two years, al-Jazeera had developed innovative ways to exploit social media and had built strong relationships with many of the online activists who were building an infrastructure of independent communication. When the Tunisian protests broke out, al-Jazeera therefore had both the motive and the means to cover them.

Al-Jazeera framed the Tunisian protest as a pan-Arab event and the fall of Ben Ali as an unmitigated good. The impact was felt not only across the region but also inside the country, as Tunisians could now see themselves protesting on television, feeling their own momentum, and bridging regional and urban or rural divides. The protests dominated the station's political talk shows for the first few weeks of January, with almost all the guests openly sympathizing with the uprisings.[17] In a December 27 episode of the prime-time lead "Behind the News," Tunisian-born host Mohamed Krishan openly enthused about the massive response to the calls for protests and demonstrations across Tunisia. The popular al-Jazeera host Ali al-Dhafiri began a January 10 program on Tunisia by declaring that "the Tunisian people have broken the wall of fear." On January 15, Al-Jazeera's Open Dialogue program hosted el-Nahda leader Rached Ghannouchi, spokesman for the National Council for Freedoms Suham bin Sidris, and others to discuss the "popular explosion in Tunisia." Host Ghassan Ben Jeddo began the program by reciting a poem by the Tunisian Abu Qasim al-Shabi and then launched a torrent of praise for "free Tunisia" and its glorious message to the Arab world, the Islamic world, and the West.

The regime's standard moves of repression and co-optation failed to contain the protests. In the absence of an organized Islamist movement, other social forces stepped forward to lead the Tunisian protests. The Tunisian General Labour Union (UGGT) played a key role, organizing a wide sector of the population. Unions had been organizing protests for years, from the Gafsa miners to underpaid urban teachers. Now they helped move the protests from the periphery to the center of Tunisian politics, organizing solidarity strikes in the major cities and into the capital.

Online political activists also disseminated information, easily sidestepping the military blockades of the roads connecting southern towns. It is easy to mock the cheap activism of changing a Twitter avatar, but it is hard to deny the power of 2 *million* Tunisians changing their Facebook profiles to a revolutionary icon on one day.[18] Human rights organizations, lawyers, academics, and journalists stepped forward to join protests and challenge a regime that had for decades kept them on a tight leash. The personal bravery of these individuals cannot be exaggerated, given Ben Ali's harsh treatment of dissidents over the years.

Popular culture also played its part. The previously unknown rapper El General provided the soundtrack to the revolution with a series of incendiary tracks against Ben Ali. His first rap, "Rais el-Blad," led to his arrest and abuse after he posted it on his Facebook page. Other musicians and artists received less personal acclaim but contributed to the dissemination of revolutionary spirit across society. An overwhelming spirit of youth solidarity pushed across regional and ethnic divides, and soon brought in the older generation, families, and others far beyond the traditional opposition.

Indiscriminate repression also contributed to the spread of a revolutionary spirit through Tunisia. The techniques that had worked in the past against a largely cowed population played out differently when directed against a widely mobilized population. Beatings, arrests, and brutality deployed against ordinary Tunisians touched virtually every family in the country. When these actions were further publicized through the new media that drew from and spoke to all sectors of society, previously passive observers mobilized like never before. Videos and images of police brutalizing unarmed protestors infuriated the previously apolitical and crystallized an entire system of disrespect and shame.

The regional and international environment failed to significantly check the process, as it might have in other circumstances (for example, in Algeria in 1991, Egypt in 2005, or Palestine in 2006). The United States had a working relationship with Ben Ali. It had located the regional office of the Middle East Partnership Initiative (MEPI) in Tunis, ironically locating a democracy-promotion program in one of the region's most repressive countries. But the U.S. did not have a great deal invested in the Tunisian regime and did not play any major role as the upheavals spread. In his January 25, 2011, State of the Union Address, President Obama spoke approvingly of the Tunisian revolution: "And we saw that same desire to be free in Tunisia, where the will of the people proved more powerful than the writ of a dictator. And tonight, let us be clear: The United States of America stands with the people of Tunisia, and supports the democratic aspirations of all people."[19]

Ben Ali's relations with France were closer, and reportedly the French government initially stepped in to offer support to the struggling regime (including a controversial alleged offer to sell riot-police gear). But when these moves were revealed, they were so unpopular that President Nicolas Sarkozy's government backed away. Even the Tunisian regime's regional allies proved unwilling or unable to help. Ben Ali's key regional friends, including Saudi Arabia, might have preferred that he stay in power but did not move quickly or effectively to help. At this time, the outset of the Arab uprising, nobody quite fathomed the nature of the new threat and still saw the Tunisian convulsions as a local issue. Outside forces would not save Ben Ali.

As the protests spiraled, the red lines governing critical discourse in the public sphere that had cowed Tunisians for decades simply evaporated. Tunisians of all ages and orientations began to unload their long-repressed frustration with Ben Ali and his family.

In early January, al-Jazeera host Krishan published the first of a series of scathing essays in the pan-Arab daily al-Quds al-Arabi declaring that for the first time in a thirty-year journalism career, he had to say what he truly felt about Ben Ali.[20] The real message of Tunisia, argued Krishan, was not that people demanded jobs or food, but that they demanded dignity and an end to corruption and repression.[21] This explicit link between political repression and economic despair lay at the heart of the Arab public's articulation of the revolutions. As the Sudanese intellectual Abd el-Wahhab el-Effendi put it in the same newspaper, "the revolution was required so that the people deserved to have bread in the first place."[22]

Ben Ali certainly did not go without a fight. The endgame in Tunisia rested on the decisions of the independent military, which ultimately decided not to use excessive force against protestors and then moved to push Ben Ali out of power.[23] General Rachid Ammar reportedly infuriated Ben Ali by informing him that his professional military would not shoot at Tunisian citizens. His reluctance may have been due to the unique qualities of Tunisia's military, which was smaller, more professional, and less involved in overt political repression than in most other Arab countries. As the Council on Foreign Relations Middle East scholar Steven Cook has noted, Ben Ali kept military spending low and the military's role circumscribed to prevent a coup against his own rule. This had the unintended effect of making it a less effective tool for repression when the challenge came.

Ben Ali offered a series of political reforms as his problems mounted, but had little credibility or bases of support by then. With the streets raging, the military neutral, and his allies melting away, Ben Ali had few options. We don't yet know why he chose January 14 to flee the country and seek refuge in Saudi Arabia. Some point to his poor health, others to his hopes to salvage his personal fortune and avoid being put before revolutionary justice. Many bitter Arab leaders complain that he simply lost his nerve and ruined it for everyone else. But it is difficult to imagine how he could have held on any longer. His decision to flee came as a mercy—and set off a paroxysm of celebration across the country the likes of which Tunisia had rarely seen.

The rest of the Arab world shared their joy. "Thank you to the great Tunisian people for proving to the world that the Arab peoples are not dead," declared the Egyptian dissident journalist Ibrahim Eissa the day after Ben Ali fell.[24] But the liberal Lebanese journalist Hazem Saghieh worried that despite the region's excitement, Tunisia "is now testing the question of change in the Arab world: can a corrupt dictator be overthrown without descending into chaos or a new tyranny?"[25] Tunisians understood better than anyone the daunting challenge of building a democracy in a state that had been under exceptionally heavy authoritarian rule for decades.

TUNISIA'S FALLOUT

Even before Ben Ali's fall, almost everyone in the region was consumed with the question of which dictator would be next. The region focused on the events in Tunisia, with almost all opposition movements and activists openly identifying with the its struggle and almost every Arab regime stressing the uniqueness of its situation. All recognized that the real significance of the Tunisian revolution would be determined less by what happened within its borders than by whether it spread beyond them. Egypt's opposition leader Mohamed el-Baradei called the spread of Tunisia's revolution to his own country "inevitable."[26] Saudi columnist and director of the Saudi-owned TV station al-Arabiya, Abdul Rahman al-Rashed, went even further, half-worrying and half-hoping that breaking the psychological barrier against demonstrating raised the specter of a "domino theory" by which even currently calm Arab states might soon be threatened.[27] The sheer bewilderment of the opinion leaders in Arab societies had never been more palpable.

The prevailing consensus among academics, local commentators, and country specialists was that Tunisia's revolution would remain confined to that small North African country. Other countries had good arguments for why they were not like Tunisia: Egypt was larger, Saudi Arabia wealthier, Jordan protected by a monarch and fears of Palestinian takeover, Syria immune thanks to its regionally popular "resistance" foreign policy. Egyptian Foreign Minister Ahmed Aboul Gheit angrily dismissed claims that Tunisia's revolution might spread to his country as "nonsense." Early on, analysts posited that the Arab monarchies might prove more resilient than the republics, though whether this was due to their greater legitimacy or their greater wealth was unclear.[28]

But these comforting reassurances ignored what was happening on the ground. Across the region, activists and ordinary people were transfixed by events. They were openly asking how they could imitate the Tunisian miracle. And this discussion of the "Tunisia scenario" was everywhere. In Jordan, the Muslim Brotherhood warned that the impending price increases planned by the recently seated new government would lead to an unprecedented explosion like Tunisia's.[29] A Syrian activist tweeted, "Today the world sings [the Tunisian National Anthem] and tomorrow God willing they will sing [the Syrian National Anthem] #Tunisia #Syria."[30]

In the weeks that followed Ben Ali's departure, the rhythm of protest synchronized across the region. Each Friday, when Muslims congregated for prayers, became a "day of rage," while episodic protests throughout the week took turns dominating the regional agenda. Al-Jazeera and other regional media covered all of these protests as a single story. Activists online actively circulated a schedule for national days of protest. One summed up the common itinerary developed online: "Activists are using twitter to line up the dominoes post-Egypt. Yemen Feb 3, Syria Feb 5, Algeria Feb 12—the 'Arab Revolution Timetable.'"[31] And ordinary people, not only these wired activists, could suddenly see an unprecedented hope for change.

The rapid diffusion of the Tunisian experience and the immediate crystallization of a shared narrative across the region are the truly unique contributions of the new media. The new social media were neither necessary nor sufficient for organizing protests. But without them, the amazing images of Tunisian protestors might never have escaped the blanket repression of the Ben Ali regime. Twitter and Facebook weren't enough, however, as there were simply not enough Arab users of social media for that alone to have made the difference. It was the airing of these videos on al-Jazeera, even after its office had been shuttered early in the revolution, that brought those images to the mass Arab public and even to many Tunisians who might otherwise not have realized what was happening in their country. The claim about al-Jazeera's significance should not be seen as an either-or proposition: al-Jazeera and social media were both part of a comprehensively transformed information environment. Al-Jazeera picked up on and carried the framing of the protests developed online, working with rather than against the social media narrative.

Tunisia's immediate neighbors had traditionally been most affected by past turmoil. Algeria quickly felt the shock waves from Tunisia, though the initial calls for demonstrations on Facebook and elsewhere were not successful.[32] To the west, Moroccan protestors were transfixed but initially were lying low; a first attempt in February to organize national demonstrations failed, with widespread protests only emerging on March 20.

Meanwhile, on January 15, 2011, Libya's longtime ruler Moammar Qaddafi blasted the Tunisian people for "destroying" all of Ben Ali's accomplishments, while caustically mocking the Internet:

> This Internet, which any demented person, any drunk can get drunk and write in, do you believe it? The Internet is like a vacuum cleaner, it can suck anything. Any useless person; any liar; any drunkard; anyone under the influence; anyone high on drugs; can talk on the Internet, and you read what he writes and you believe it. This is talk which is for free. Shall we become the victims of "Facebook" and "Kleenex" [a reference to WikiLeaks] and "YouTube"! Shall we become victims to tools they created so that they can laugh at our moods?"[33]

Qaddafi would soon come to regret his nonchalance. Libyans scheduled their day of protest for February 17, but couldn't wait that long; protests actually broke out the evening of the 16th.

In Jordan, the effects were less dramatic, but the regime still found itself confronted with persistent and real social grievances carried by an unusually wired and discontented young population.[34] In 1989, Jordan had been one of the countries most directly affected by Tunisian riots. Now the government attempted to get ahead of the unrest, preemptively cutting food and fuel prices. Even so, on January 14, leftist groups brought a few hundred protestors into the streets in Amman, Kerak, Irbid, and Zarqa. Two days later, professional associations, which typically led political activism in a country with few significant political parties, brought out thousands. The government wavered between repression and concessions, offering more subsidies while also warning of chaos. By the end of the month, weekend protests had become a standard affair, and on February 1, the king sacked Prime Minister Samir al-Rifai in response to the growing dissent.

Tunisia's effects were felt even in the faraway Gulf, where many eagerly watched the events unfold on television and on their social networks. Many equated their own conditions with those of their fellow Arabs, despite the efforts by Gulf regimes to paint the monarchies as inherently, existentially different from their republican counterparts. Yemeni protestors mobilized around the Tunisian example particularly quickly and enthusiastically, despite being the most geographically distant point in the entire Arab world. After Ben Ali's fall, protestors took to the streets daily, demanding political change. They directly challenged President Ali Abdullah Saleh in extraordinary ways and numbers, explicitly invoking the Tunisian example of change: "The revolution is contagious. Thank you Tunisia for your inspiration," wrote one activist on Twitter.[35] Yemen had one of the lowest levels of Internet penetration in the region, but it did have an experienced and enthusiastic activist base that had been challenging Saleh for half a decade.

The spark caught almost as quickly in Bahrain, where the Tunisian example rekindled a massive protest movement that had been challenging the monarchy for nearly a decade. At its peak, some estimated that more than half the country's population was protesting in the streets. The Bahraini protest movement tried to present itself as a nonsectarian movement for human rights, democracy, and constitutional monarchy. It sought to turn the Pearl Roundabout into the Bahraini equivalent of

Tahrir Square. The regime attempted to brand the challengers instead as an Iranian-backed Shi'a movement and to rally the Sunni minority to its side. Bahrain would become a central battleground of the counterrevolution in March 2011. But in these early days, the enormous outpouring of popular demonstrations in Bahrain offered a powerful example of the demonstration effects from Ben Ali's fall.

Kuwait and Oman joined Bahrain in proving that even wealthy Gulf states were not immune. The always tempestuous Kuwaiti political scene grew even hotter, as an emboldened parliament demanded accountability from the prime minister, directly challenging the prerogatives of the royal family in unprecedented ways. A determined youth movement organized regular protests as well. In Oman, usually off the radar even in the Arab world, a small but determined group of protestors repeatedly took to the streets. Even Iraqis, generally alienated from the mainstream of the Arab world and consumed by their own traumas, found inspiration in Tunis as activists occupied their own fortuitously named Tahrir Square on February 25.

IN ISOLATION, Tunisia's revolution had posed little true challenge to Washington or to the region. But its spread touched on the vital interests of virtually every regional and global player. None could remain neutral in the face of challenges to regimes in strategic countries like Egypt, Jordan, Syria, Yemen, or Bahrain. Where Tunisia passed without massive international involvement, outside actors would profoundly shape every other revolution. Especially after the fall of Mubarak, the tensions would become even starker and the competitive interventions even more intense.

EGYPT

For all the regional momentum that spread following events in Tunisia, the mass protests of January 25 in Egypt were the pivotal moment that transformed local domestic political struggles into a single, coherent, regional uprising. It was Egypt that took over the international as well as regional agendas and convinced the world that the protests marked something fundamentally new. Egypt has always been at the center of Arab politics—the largest Arab country with more than 80 million citizens, one involved in all regional political issues, and, despite falling on

hard times over the last decades of Mubarak's rule, still an intellectual
and cultural leader. If Tunisia defined the periphery of Arab politics,
Egypt stood at its core.

By any rational measure, the Egyptian protests should not have succeeded. After Ben Ali fell, the Egyptian regime was fully prepared for
what was coming. Its security forces were on alert and deployed, and the
Internet was disrupted and al-Jazeera was largely silenced (first due to a
still-unexplained decision not to cover the opening hours of the revolution, and then by the Egyptian government's jamming of its signal).
Egyptian protest leaders were well known, the timing of the protest was
openly advertised, and the likely points of convergence were well protected by legions of security forces. And yet, against the odds, hundreds
of thousands of ordinary people poured into the streets, battling the
police in Cairo, Alexandria, Suez, and elsewhere, and put together one of
the largest demonstrations in contemporary Egyptian history.

The differences between Egypt on January 25 and Tunisia on
December 17 are as striking as their similarities. Both countries shared
the affliction of an aged, corrupt, and increasingly out-of-touch president. Both countries suffered from massive unemployment and under-
employment, a frustrated youth population, and a shrinking middle
class. But unlike Tunisians, who had struggled against stifling censorship and political repression, Egyptians had been battling against the
Mubarak regime for over a decade. Over the 2000s the Kefaya movement, the April 6 Youth Movement, labor movements, judges, civil society organizations, and a wide range of new independent newspapers and
critical public figures had arisen to protest against the Mubarak regime's
manifold failings. As they planned the protest of January 25, Egyptians
therefore faced a different challenge from their Tunisian counterparts—
and indeed much of the Arab world.

The real challenge facing the organizers of the January 25 demonstration was not that they would be breaking a taboo against public
protest; the challenge was in persuading potential participants that they
could succeed. They needed to persuade ordinary people that it was
worth the risks and costs to leave their homes and come into the streets
against Mubarak. The example of Tunisia was the single most important
thing that changed those minds. Tunisia's great contribution was to show

Egyptians that they could actually win . . . and how cathartic that victory could be. Indeed, without the Tunisian inspiration, efforts to organize the January 25th protest almost certainly would have failed just as they had for the last few years.

Believing in the possibility of victory was not easy. Over the course of the previous decade, the Mubarak regime had absorbed every challenge and beaten back every assault. The Kefaya movement had disintegrated. The April 6, 2008, movement had failed to replicate its initial success in galvanizing a mass protest in support of workers. The National Association for Change headed by Nobel Laureate Mohamed el-Baradei had focused attention on the failures of the Egyptian regime and galvanized the politically active youth, but had not crystallized into a coherent political challenge. Egypt in December 2010, for all of its deep and intractable problems, looked to be farther away from immediate revolution than at any time in a decade. Most galling for the Egyptian people, the hated Gamal Mubarak was on the path toward taking his father's place as head of state despite nearly a decade of activism against and public criticism of the prospect.

As important as the Tunisian example was for changing Egyptian minds about participation in protests, significant changes in youth activism had been taking place for some time. In some ways, the wave that would become the January 25th protest began as early as June 2010. Khaled Said, a young man dragged from an Internet café in Alexandria and beaten to death by police, might have been Egypt's Mohammed Bouazizi. After the young Alexandrian died from horrific police abuse, a group of then-anonymous administrators created the Facebook page "We Are All Khaled Said" to organize protests in his memory, posting graphic photos and updates on his case. The page was the brainchild of Wael Ghoneim, an Egyptian Google employee usually based in Dubai, who worked with several colleagues, including the former Muslim Brotherhood youth activist Abdul Rahman Mansour and human rights activist Ahmed Saleh, to create and maintain it. The page became a major forum for discussion and debate, expanding the circle of activists and the scope of dissent. The organizers experimented with a wide range of creative protests, including silent protests on the Alexandria Corniche while wearing white T-shirts—identifying them to onlookers as somehow linked, but not a blatant enough political symbol to cause them to be arrested. At least as important as the protests themselves, the Facebook page became a vibrant forum for debate and discussion among a growing sector of the youth. The activists of the April 6 Youth Movement, the remnants of Kefaya, Baradei's National Association for Change, and other groups continued to search for creative ways to organize and protest, building relationships abroad as well as inside the country.

The parliamentary election held from November 28 to December 5, 2010, also contributed to the new environment. In 2005, the Muslim Brotherhood had won eighty-eight seats. The party would have won considerably more seats without some blatant regime interventions in the second and third rounds of voting. Since then, Mubarak's National Democratic Party (NDP) had taken no chances. It had put the Muslim Brotherhood under exceptionally intense pressure between 2008 and 2010, with media campaigns, arrests, and moves against their financing, beyond what had occurred since the 1990s. The NDP sought to modernize its own image, while paving the way for Gamal Mubarak to succeed his father as president. It left nothing to chance, tightly controlling the process. Egyptians responded with mass apathy, producing the lowest voting rate in its modern history and a parliament almost entirely devoid of opposition. That process seemed to close the door on institutional politics as a possible vehicle for change.

However, the fait accompli of Gamal Mubarak's succession continued to galvanize unusual levels of popular outrage. The Kefaya movement had in fact begun as a campaign against hereditary succession and had succeeded in making that once-taboo question a central part of the national debate. Egyptians closely identified Gamal with the small group of crony capitalists who had grown wealthy during a decade of neoliberal reforms, even as most found their standards of living deteriorating and the public infrastructure collapsing. And for all the corruption in the system, Egyptians were still proud of their republican system. They bristled at the prospect of Egypt emulating the backward Gulf countries or, for that matter, Syria.

Even the military had little love for Gamal. He was a civilian who had avoided military service and whose neoliberal reforms might someday threaten their own commercial and industrial empires built through long years of cronyism. Later, one leading member of the Supreme Council of Armed Forces (SCAF) that would eventually succeed Mubarak laughingly told a Washington audience that everyone had known the senior military leadership hated Gamal and had been searching for a way to prevent his rise to power—and that we should "read our WikiLeaks" for proof. But for all that hostility, by December 2010, after the NDP's carefully stage-managed "success" in the election, Gamal seemed to be well on the way to his goal.

The Tunisian protests provided a solution to this problem. At the end of January, ordinary Egyptians watching television suddenly decided to join the activists in a mass push to overthrow the regime. We should rec-ognize that despite retrospective myth making, the protest organizers had no greater expectation of success than the analysts at the time. As they plotted the January 25 demonstrations, Cairo organizers dreamed of perhaps turning out a few thousand people. In Alexandria, organizers debated whether they might muster a better turnout by merging their previously planned demonstration demanding an increase in the mini-mum wage with the new anti-Mubarak protest. The televised Tunisian miracle is what galvanized Egyptians and convinced them that they too could hope for real change.

This is not to deny the creativity or courage of the activists; indeed, their expectation that they would be only a few facing the wrath of a mobilized security state makes their bravery on January 25 even more impressive. The organizers cleverly distributed false information about the time and location of the protests online to fool state security, and then distributed the real information by SMS (text messages) shortly be-fore the event. They craftily used numerous gathering points from which to converge on Tahrir to prevent the police from bottling them up in any one location. They picked up even more supporters as they marched through the streets, dodging roadblocks and police deployments. Their experience from years of clashes with the police served them well in the opening hours. And they adapted creatively as the unexpected crowds suddenly poured into the streets to converge on obvious focal points like Cairo's Tahrir Square and Alexandria's Corniche. Instead of a few hundred experienced protestors challenging thousands of riot police, hundreds of thousands swarmed through Cairo's streets toward Tahrir. In Alexandria, nearly a million people quickly moved to the Corniche before swarming police stations and other government buildings.

For all the meticulous planning and despite all the structural pre-conditions that made revolution in retrospect appear inevitable, nearly everyone was taken by surprise—including the activists. Nobody could have known that so many people would answer the call. Without the Tunisian example, it is extremely unlikely that they would have. How necessary were the activists for making the revolution happen? Would the Tunisian example have been enough for an outraged and frustrated Egyptian population, without the activists to point the way? It is impossible to know.

Mona el-Ghobashy, one of the sharpest academic observers of Egyptian affairs, argues convincingly that the activists had in fact succeeded in reshaping the Egyptian political terrain over the preceding decade. Through seemingly "failed" activism, she argues, a generation of activists had learned how to demonstrate, how to organize, and how to compete with a repressive regime. The political atmosphere was charged, especially after Tunisia, and open discontent could be seen throughout almost all sectors of society. But el-Ghobashy also points out that the key link between the structural problems of the Egyptian regime and the long-delayed revolution was "four continuous days of street fighting, January 25–28, that pitted the people against the police all over the country. That battle transformed a familiar, predictable episode into a revolutionary situation."[36]

This battle was not waged online. On January 26, in one of the most remarkable acts in the short history of the Internet, the Egyptian government almost completely shut off access, nationwide. Vodaphone, the leading SMS and mobile phone service in Egypt, which had close ties to the regime, also shut down its networks. The regime saw the Facebook pages and blogs as an integral part of the protest movement, and clearly expected the shutdown to cripple the communications and organization of their challengers.

The regime was wrong. Once the protest momentum had begun to build, communication and coordination became less essential. Everyone could simply watch al-Jazeera to find out where and when protests were happening. Many youth activists could still upload to Twitter and YouTube via direct satellite uplinks on their mobile smartphones, or else find workarounds to circumvent the Internet cutoff (such as piggyback-ing on the services in luxury hotels, which the regime did not dare cut off for fear of alienating foreign businesspeople or tourists). In addition, the shutdown in Internet access and television coverage likely brought many people out into the streets to see for themselves, rather than following the events from the safety of their apartments.

Al-Jazeera, despite a noticeable silence in the opening moments (it aired a sports documentary even as hundreds of thousands of Egyptians poured into the streets, to the vocal outrage of engaged viewers across the region), became the unquestioned home of the revolution on the air-waves. As in Tunisia, al-Jazeera provided a focal point for audiences everywhere to share in revolutionary protest. Egyptians now watched themselves changing the world, and the messages and images that once reached a few thousand Facebook users now reached tens of millions of ordinary citizens. Al-Jazeera also set the tone outside Egypt, as al-Jazeera English came into its own by capturing large American audiences with its nearly unique coverage. Even President Obama turned to al-Jazeera Eng-lish to watch key events in the Egyptian revolution. But while al-Jazeera owned the revolution, within days, Cairo had become the central focus of the global media, and there was simply no preventing coverage of events.

Al-Jazeera's role was again controversial. Egyptian officials com-plained bitterly about a Qatari vendetta against Mubarak. More subtly, al-Jazeera's coverage contributed to the Tahrir-centric narrative of the rev-olution, as its unblinking focus on the square unintentionally erased the massive mobilization taking place across Cairo and across the country.[37] The millions in Alexandria, the violence in the Suez, and the demonstra-tions in squares across Cairo all disappeared in favor of the central node in downtown Cairo. And there is some reason to believe that al-Jazeera's success in Egypt went to the heads of its management, and that the Qatari royal family began to treat it more as a useful weapon in regional politics than as the prestigious independent symbol it had long valued.

On the ground, in the days to come, the protest marches generated an unstoppable momentum. Ordinary people joined the veteran activists in converging streams of marches. The Egyptian regime did not fail to anticipate the challenge. Security forces were ready. Likely congregation points were heavily guarded, lines of riot police blocked major arteries, and the local media had been placed under tight control. The activists alone could never have hoped to overwhelm the fully deployed security forces. That took the sheer masses of ordinary people in the streets, reinforced by the organized cadres of the labor movement and later the Muslim Brotherhood.

Friday, January 28, was the prototypical Friday "day of rage" that would punctuate politics in the entire region for many months. January 25 had in many ways been only a dress rehearsal for this decisive day. Despite the massive deployment of repressive power and the shutdown of communications, hundreds of thousands responded to the call to protest. The Friday prayer and the centrality of Tahrir Square provided perfect convergence points, reducing the need for coordination. A bout of street fighting enabled the protestors to finally seize and occupy Tahrir Square.

For all the later talk about *silmiyya* (nonviolence), this was a day of violence. Police stations and prisons burned, while protestors savagely attacked police and regime supporters. At the end of that brutal day, the protestors had taken control of Tahrir, and a steady stream of people poured in to reinforce the revolution's newfound home. Later that day, Mubarak made his first televised speech since the revolution had begun, promising a cabinet shuffle and political reforms. Too much had already changed, and his concessions fell flat. Protests continued, and people ignored official curfews.

On January 29, the Muslim Brotherhood officially joined the protests. For the first four days, a large number of individual Brotherhood youth activists had taken part, but the organization itself had held back. Once the Brotherhood threw its weight behind the revolution, however, it provided badly needed manpower, organizational capacity, and experience. Its decision to join was in some ways remarkable, given the deep caution that characterized the Brotherhood's leadership. Most of its politically engaged leaders had been removed from the Guide's Office in controversial 2009 internal elections to the Brotherhood's main leadership body. Its joining the protests openly had many risks, including the potential to frighten the United States, Israel, and other key external actors and to divide the protestors. While from the activists' viewpoint, the Brotherhood was late to the revolution, a major hurdle had now been crossed. Mubarak's prospects for survival dimmed.

For all the power in the streets, the crucial decision that saved the revolution was the army's. On January 29, the military was deployed after the failure of the hated police to control the crowds. No matter the courage of the protestors, the army could have cleared the square with tanks and helicopters, had it been willing to inflict massive loss of life on peaceful protestors. But, whereas the police and regime thugs had used all the violence in their arsenal, the army early on announced publicly that it would not fire on the Egyptian people. It largely stuck to this vow, which proved to be a wise move. Six months later, Interior Minister Habib el-Adly and Mubarak himself were in court charged with ordering the deadly violence against protestors, while the SCAF ruled revolutionary Egypt.

So many other Arab militaries would make a disastrously different choice in coming weeks. Why did the Egyptian army act the way it did? Part of the reason, not fully appreciated by Egyptians themselves, is that the Obama administration had engaged in near-constant dialogues at all levels up and down the ranks of the Egyptian military, pushing it not to fire, with multiple daily phone calls pressing the case. The SCAF itself highlights its patriotism and deeply rooted self-conception as the defender of the Egyptian nation, not of the Mubarak regime. Because it was a professional military, thoroughly depoliticized so as to avoid coups, it could not be deployed for naked regime-survival purposes. Protestors took the military's open hand gratefully for the most part, though gaps appeared almost immediately between the hard-core activists suspicious of the military's shadowy leaders, and the mass public that favored the military without question. Many of the more politically savvy activists speculated that the move was simply self-interest, to jettison the hated Gamal Mubarak and protect its own corporate interests once it saw Mubarak's fall as inevitable.

Whatever the case, the military's refusal to unleash its arsenal to defend the regime marked a key turning point. The seizure of Tahrir had been enough to force a political crisis but not enough to bring down Mubarak's regime. However, once Mubarak lost the military, the real focus shifted to the political bargaining and brinksmanship among the protestors, the military, the Mubarak regime, and international actors (primarily the United States).

Having seized Tahrir, the protestors shifted from dynamic marches to a pitched battle to defend the central square against security forces, the *baltagiya*, and the camels that the thugs rode to break the demonstrators' hold on Tahrir. They set up barricades and a tent city, providing basic services, security, and a joint political leadership to keep the revolution focused. Millions of Egyptians passed through the square during these eighteen days to listen, to observe, and to participate in political arguments. All testified to the extraordinary spirit that pervaded the square despite the tension and fear, as people from all walks of life and all political trends joined in a common project of national liberation. The constant circulation of first-time protestors and new participants prevented the Tahrir occupation from degenerating into a narrow clique dominated by the activists, as arguably happened later in the summer. The protestors held Tahrir until Mubarak fell on February 11. Alexandria, for its part, had largely been "liberated" by early February, with most state institutions and police dissolving in the face of the mass protests, leaving the millions along the Corniche little to do but demonstrate in solidarity with Cairo.

The dynamic then shifted to a tense, multilevel bargaining process among Mubarak, the military, the United States, a variety of political parties and self-appointed spokesmen for the revolution, and the determined protestors who had seized the streets. The bids and counterbids of the next eleven days brought pressures from all sides. The power of the street became a crucial variable, as protestors sought to keep the population mobilized, even as negotiations dragged on and the regime tried to divide its opponents while appealing for a return to calm and order. With the military showing self-restraint and the millions in the street declaring that "the army and the people are one hand," the fear of violent repression receded temporarily. But this opened the space for the regime's delaying tactics, attempts to disperse the protestors with promises that it could later break, and efforts to divide the united front in Tahrir.

By this time, Egypt was no longer simply an Arab concern. The whole world, as the cliché goes, was watching. The key external player this time, unlike in Tunisia, was the United States. The Obama administration was working hard behind the scenes to persuade Mubarak to step down in favor of a transition to democracy. But it encountered great resistance from Mubarak and his advisers, who continued to denigrate the significance of the protestors and to view the Muslim Brotherhood as poised to seize power. This claim did not work with President Obama as it had with President George W. Bush, who had eased his pressure over Egyptian democratization following the success of Islamists in the 2005 elections. Obama had very quickly concluded that the game was up, and that some way must be found to push Egypt toward a real democratic transition, but one that protected core American interests, including the Camp David treaty with Israel, along with the nations' military relationship. A barrage of phone calls to all levels of the Egyptian regime explored possibilities.

Meanwhile, American allies around the region were aghast that Obama seemed to be abandoning America's longtime Egyptian partner. The Saudis were particularly furious at what they saw as Obama's betrayal and urged Mubarak to hang tough. For the first time (though not the last), it became transparently clear that Riyadh and Washington were working at cross-purposes. Other American allies from Amman to Kuwait, Rabat to Sanaa, also watched nervously. If the U.S. would give up on Mubarak so easily, would it stand by them if they faced popular uprisings? Israelis were deeply spooked at the potential loss of their most important friendly regime in the region. Mubarak not only kept their southern border calm but also shared Israeli hostility toward the Muslim Brotherhood and Iran, actively cooperated in the blockade of Gaza, maintained the supply of natural gas from the Sinai, and managed intra-Palestinian politics. Israelis understood the near-universal hostility among the Egyptian public toward them, and saw little good coming from Mubarak's fall.

Iran soon tried to insert itself into the narrative. Supreme Leader Ali Khamenei declared the uprising to be an "Islamic Awakening" directed against American and Israeli hegemony, but found few takers in an Arab public that remembered all too well Tehran's harsh 2009 crackdown on its own protest movement. Egyptians scoffed at Iran's claims. Tehran would not be a player in this game, a harbinger of its declining relevance in the new politics of the region.

Al-Qaeda faced similar problems. Its message that only violent jihad led by a true Muslim vanguard could bring real change rang hollow with millions of ordinary Egyptians alongside Muslim Brothers in the streets demanding their rights. While al-Qaeda's deputy leader Ayman al-Zawahiri no doubt was delighted to see his old nemesis Mubarak on the ropes, and al-Qaeda anticipated a more permissive environment within which to work should his intelligence services crumble, they had no role to play in the unfolding events.

The high-stakes game played out partly in public. On February 1, Mubarak spoke again, offering more substantial concessions than in his first appearance. He offered to step down at the end of his term in September and vowed not to run again. In subsequent interviews, he continued to refuse to step down, but promised to use his remaining time in office to oversee a transition and begin political reforms. He added that Gamal Mubarak would also not stand in elections. With Gamal's succession prospects ended, the main goal of Kefaya had finally been achieved. But now, with the end of Mubarak's regime in sight, the concession was treated as a throwaway and quickly rejected. The people in Tahrir Square heard only vague promises and rambling condescension. Nor did Washington hear the key words it had been seeking. With Obama's prestige now on the line, the only acceptable outcome for the United States would be Mubarak's ouster.

On that same day, President Obama therefore quickly came before the television cameras to warn bluntly that "an orderly transition must be meaningful, it must be peaceful, and it must begin now." While it has become folk wisdom in Egypt and much of the Arab world that America acted slowly and overcautiously during the Egyptian revolution, in fact, the speed with which it acted is truly remarkable. Only *six days* after Egypt's protests began, the United States had unequivocally and publicly called for the president of its closest Arab ally to step down. Privately, it delivered the same messages through multiple channels. But the immediate impact was muted. Mubarak refused to listen, and his inner circle grew more obstinate at the public rebuke. Activists were unaware of the private communications, mistrusted American intentions, and found the words empty when they did not immediately succeed—and in Twitter time, results must be truly immediate.

The next day, February 2, in the infamous "Battle of the Camels," pro-regime thugs launched violent attacks on Tahrir Square with swords and sticks, many of them riding camels from the nearby market. The violence failed to empty Tahrir or to break the spirit of the protestors. Instead, in a dynamic that would characterize the entire region for the coming months, the violence galvanized even more Egyptians to rally to the protestors' side, withdrawing legitimacy from any regime that would inflict such horrors on its own people. And it strengthened the arguments of those outside Egypt who saw a transition as inevitable and Mubarak as a liability rather than an asset.

By now, efforts to find a political solution were escalating from all sides, both international and domestic. On February 3, a self-appointed group of twenty-four "wise men" from the Egyptian political elite presented a plan for political reform—an offer that the regime received coolly and that many of the protestors mistrusted as a potential sellout by an unrepresentative, self-appointed elite. The Obama administration repeated and clarified its message that Mubarak must step down. Privately and publicly, it warned the military that it must avoid using violence against civilians if it hoped to maintain a positive relationship with the United States after Mubarak fell. But nothing seemed to work. America's message was muddied when one-time envoy Frank Wisner told a European television interviewer he believed "that President Mubarak's continued leadership is critical." Even though this was a light year away from current administration thinking, Egyptians still continue to cite his position as evidence of American duplicity.

On February 6, intelligence chief Omar Suleiman, who Mubarak had appointed vice president as part of his belated attempt to meet some of the demands of the protestors, began talks with representatives of the opposition, ostensibly to find a road map toward a political transition. The protestors, who worried that a self-appointed group of representatives would negotiate away the gains of the revolution, found these talks extremely controversial. The factors that contributed to the success of the seizure of Tahrir and mass-mobilization of Egyptian society were less well adapted to navigating this political snake pit. Who could speak for this leaderless assembly, these networks of networks? Who was authorized to make specific demands? Who could credibly commit to sending the crowds home if demands were met?

In the end, the very incompetence of the Tahrir leadership likely saved it. The leaderless crowd was unable to agree on anything more than the simple, clear demand that Mubarak must go. It was therefore impossible for anyone to negotiate away the momentum of the revolution. No leadership could effectively respond to the various offers the regime made as it scrambled to survive. The clever gambits to divide and conquer, or to clear the square as a precondition to political negotiations, fell flat in the face of a revolution without a leader. By the time Suleiman offered some serious concessions to a handpicked group of opposition representatives in a carefully staged meeting, nobody in Tahrir was listening. The inconclusive negotiations finally exhausted the patience of the SCAF, and Mubarak dug himself too deeply into a hole by refusing to meet the one core demand of the protestors.

The spirits in Tahrir were low on February 7. The negotiations with Suleiman had cast a pall over the assembled protestors, who could see a long stalemate stretching before them and feared a loss of revolutionary enthusiasm. They were revitalized when the previously anonymous administrator of the "We Are All Khaled Said" Facebook page, Wael Ghoneim, emerged from prison where he had been kept since the revolution broke out. In an interview on Dream TV, he declared, "I am not a hero. I only used the keyboard, the real heroes are the ones on the ground." His appearance galvanized the Egyptian protestors, restoring hope, and—almost as important—gave the protest movement an attractive face for the international media. Months later, Obama reflected, "What I want is for the kids on the street to win and for the Google guy to become president. What I think is that this is going to be long and hard."[38]

On February 10, momentum had built up to the expectation that Mubarak would step down, including, evidently, his own government and the Obama administration. Instead, he refused once again. He offered to delegate some powers to the vice president, but otherwise remained defiant and patronizing toward the protestors.

The collective astonishment, bafflement, and downright rage that gripped not only the Tahrir demonstrators but the entire Arab public at this moment are hard to exaggerate. The protests escalated across the country and refused to calm throughout the entire next day. Could Mubarak really plan to continue? Could the protests sustain themselves for another week without a collapse into violent anarchy? The SCAF finally stepped in and quietly removed Mubarak from office. He never appeared before his people to deliver this news and never publicly acknowledged his loss of power. Within months, he would be on trial in a closed court, lying in a sickbed in a cage hearing testimony to his perfidy.

THE NARRATIVE I HAVE PRESENTED of the Egyptian revolution is messy by design. There are many key moments, many important actors, and many stories still to be told. The battle to claim revolutionary legitimacy out of this confusing and tumultuous process became a key political battlefield. Should the organizers of January 25 own the subsequent revolution? What about those who took and held Tahrir Square on the 28th and then defended it during the Battle of the Camels? What about the SCAF itself, which made the crucial decisions to refrain from violence and then to remove Mubarak? These questions have far more than academic or historical importance. They were a key terrain of political battle and source of power in the months that followed. Activists constantly invoke their revolutionary legitimacy when they press political demands. So do their adversaries. In late September 2011, I was struck by the sudden appearance of billboards in Cairo calling on Egyptians to "work with the SCAF against the demonstrations which threaten the revolution"—a remarkable claim given that most activists had long since turned against the SCAF as a force for counterrevolution.

Surveys in Egypt and Tunisia after the fall of their dictators revealed an uncertain public trying to make sense of their new environment. Few political parties enjoyed widespread support. While the Muslim Brotherhood in Egypt and el-Nahda in Tunisia were quickly revealed to be the most popular parties, they rarely commanded more than 20 percent support. Over 50 percent of people in each country described themselves as undecided. Surveys also showed remarkable optimism about the future and support for the revolutions. Surveys in April 2011 by both YouGov and Information Resources found that 9 percent of Egyptians believed their country was heading in the wrong direction. In April, a Pew survey found that 65 percent of Egyptians were satisfied with conditions in their country, up from 28 percent the year before, and 77 percent were pleased that Mubarak had stepped down.[39] A Gallup Abu Dhabi survey of Egypt released in June, for instance, found 83 percent supporting the revolution. And even as economic conditions deteriorated, Egyptians expressed high hopes for the future; the "wider gap between their assessments of today and their hopes for tomorrow reflect an optimism Egyptians have lacked for several years."[40]

The fall of Mubarak on the heels of Ben Ali's flight from Tunisia created an unprecedented tidal wave of protest and change across the region. The uprising became a truly Arab one, happening simultaneously across virtually the entire region. Young protestors took to the streets wielding the same slogans and the same protest methods used in Egypt. They had real hope that they might actually succeed, and in those delirious moments, their victory indeed seemed almost unstoppable. But within a week of the fall of Mubarak, the Arab uprising was about to take a very different turn in the tiny island kingdom of Bahrain, where the al-Khalifa family had no intention of following the Egyptian president off the throne.

CHAPTER 5

THE TIDAL WAVE

IN THE WEEK FOLLOWING MUBARAK'S FALL, protestors and governments across the region marveled at what had just happened. In Tunisia, an extreme secularist regime that had imposed exceptionally stifling repressive control over its people for decades had vanished. In Egypt, a decade of protest and challenge had suddenly and shockingly broken the power of a cocky regime that had believed it had regained near-total control over its turbulent population. At that moment, anything seemed possible.

The impact of their example on the region could not have been more direct or clear. A veritable tsunami of protest swept the region as discontented publics took to the streets almost everywhere. All the explanations for why each country was different were quickly washed away by the reality of massive protests explicitly modeled after Tahrir Square in almost every Arab country. The enormity and the simultaneity of the wave of protest that followed Tunisia and Egypt transformed very different local challenges into a unified Arab uprising. The feeling of unity in this shared historical moment demanded action, not applause. The sudden collective empowerment and recognition of possibility that followed the fall of Ben Ali and Mubarak drove frustrated and discontented citizens who had never believed in the possibility of change to now seize the opening.

The role of momentum and shared identity cannot be overstated. The Arab protest movements watched, supported, and emulated each other in real time. They identified with each other within a common narrative, one that identified all protestors as the "good guys" and every

regime as the "bad guys." They lived and died together. When one country surged forward, others shared their momentum, and when one
suffered a calamitous reversal, the others rallied to their defense. In just
one of a million examples, in mid-February, a Yemeni tweeted, "Right
now in Freedom Square, Taiz, #Yemen, all the protesters are praying in
one voice for saving their brothers n sisters in #Libya."[1]

Political entrepreneurs in many Arab countries sought to emulate
Egypt's protest methods, language, and, of course, success. Many chose
to adapt Egypt's hashtag, #jan25, to their own countries, by branding
their protests with its own identifying label. Each hashtagged date
marked a symbolic starting point, although most nations had been
experiencing protests of some kind earlier. These Twitter hashtags did
not *cause* the revolutions, of course. They played a role in framing each
local protest as a chapter in a wider Arab story. The hashtag labels con-
ferred significant power within the dynamics of the new Arab public,
raising local conflicts to the attention of the region at large and granting
new moral authority to movements that in the past had been one of any
number of competing political forces.

The proliferation of hashtagged protests marked a new stage in the
Arab uprising. The first two weeks of February were the last time that
the Obama administration, or anyone else, could focus on a single
clearly defined struggle. During the Egyptian revolution, the regional
and international agenda had an exceptionally tight focus on Tahrir
Square. After the fall of Mubarak, the lens widened to a disparate set of
struggles that, though similar in form, took on dramatically different
characters. This phase unfolded in a much less coherent, less unified
way than the first phase, with its tight, sequential focus on Tunisia and
then Egypt.

The sheer proliferation of crises and protests in this period taxed
the ability of the United States—or anyone—to maintain focus. In the
White House, national security staff had been in full crisis mode since
late January. The new environment did not offer the sort of clear, focused
target of attention that the Egyptian revolution had presented. The
rapidly escalating war in Libya consumed what oxygen remained. Important arenas such as Yemen or Bahrain simply dropped off the radar of
global media or international politics. It became perhaps too easy for

Washington to leave Yemen to the GCC and the counterterrorism bureaus, while quietly acceding to Saudi demands in Bahrain.

The narrative of the hashtagged Arab uprisings could at times be misleading, in potentially dangerous ways. The comparison to Egypt and Tunisia exaggerated the real prospects for victory, which could lead hopeful but naive protestors to their deaths, provoke panicked regimes to crack down harder than necessary, or cause onlookers to misread the true nature of opposition movements. Consider, for instance, how we may have been misled by the presentation of a Syrian protest movement that was in fact very small, isolated, and largely directed from abroad as a chapter within the unfolding Arab narrative. Did their placement within the Arab uprising narrative lead external observers to make unwarranted assumptions about its prospects for success, its ideology, or its political aspirations? Did it cause Bashar al-Assad and his regime to exaggerate the threat it posed and thus employ unnecessarily brutal repressive force that turned the Syrian uprising into a self-fulfilling prophecy?

This chapter traces the progress of the second phase of the Arab uprising through the succession of Fridays, the days of rage, as the regional agenda fragmented, the course of the struggles diverged, and confusion reigned. The upsurge from below had common characteristics, but the outcomes diverged widely from country to country. Some protests quickly faded; others consumed media attention and caught fire. Some regimes sought to deflect challengers with preemptive reforms, while others took a hard line and struck back with violence. Each regime made different calculations as to whether the long-term costs of repression outweighed the immediate benefits of breaking the momentum of public challenges.

The wave of ferment may have seemed unstoppable, but seasoned observers of Arab politics knew from the start that the authoritarian status quo would not go easily. Leaders learned from the failures of their counterparts and resolved not to repeat one another's mistakes. The great powers of the region quickly sought to exploit the new opportunities, defending their own interests while seeking to expand their influence where possible. The GCC countries came together to act in an unusually coordinated fashion, after long years of being divided and contentious, to crush dissent in Bahrain and prevent its emergence elsewhere on their home turf. They took the offensive outside their usual sphere of influence, particularly in Syria and in Libya (where Saudi Arabia's King Abdullah had a long-standing grudge against Qaddafi over a reported Libyan-sponsored assassination attempt, and Qatar's emir still resented Qaddafi's grandstanding that had wrecked a Doha Arab Summit meeting). The tentative rapprochement between the two long-feuding Gulf powers, Saudi Arabia and Qatar, would not likely last, but it did hold for long crucial months during the Arab uprising.

The second phase of the Arab uprising therefore passed from the heady rush of regional momentum in February to a more fragmented, contentious crawl. The GCC's intervention in Bahrain and the NATO intervention in Libya, both in mid-March, marked the pivot from the second to the third discrete phase of the Arab uprising. Chapter 6 tells the story of this counterrevolution. But before turning to that shift, it is worth going into some depth about the early moments of enthusiasm and collective movement that defined the first months of 2011—when very similar and deeply interconnected popular uprisings appeared at the same time, but met very different fates.

HASHTAG PROTESTS

The assigning of protest hashtag dates started as something of a joke on Twitter, on a par with the "Arab Dictators Survival Manual."[2] I do not mean to assign too much power to the hashtags, or indeed to Twitter, the importance of which to the organization and influence of protests is often grossly exaggerated. My intent here is more limited: to demonstrate the importance of the process by which distinct national protests merged into a single, coherent, and almost universally shared narrative of region-wide uprising.

This unified political narrative demands far more explanation than is usually offered. It is not intuitively obvious that Tunisia's revolutions should matter to Yemenis: The two countries have virtually no economic, social, or political interaction, have different political institutions and histories, face very different political challenges, and even speak very different colloquial forms of Arabic. Nor is it obvious that Bahrain's protests should have been accepted as equivalent to other Arab protest movements, given the Sunni-Shi'a sectarian hostility that had shaped so much of the preceding decade.

The answer lies in the renewed pan-Arab identity and unified political agenda shaped over the preceding decade by the new public sphere. The hashtags that began as a casual coordination device quickly became a symbol of the unification of diverse national struggles into a single campaign. The hashtags very explicitly defined each uprising as one chapter in a single unfolding story. Not every country revolted on schedule, but the hashtags told a story that bound together the chaotic regional events into a comprehensible narrative with identifiable heroes and villains and encoded with certain expectations. And that shared narrative made sense to Arabs immersed in the new Arab public sphere—even if it confounded outsiders who failed to appreciate its importance and predicted limited diffusion or demonstration effects.

#FEB3: YEMEN

That the Yemenis were the first to follow this script should be no surprise. Protests in Yemen began even before the fall of Mubarak. Indeed, despite being literally on the opposite end of the Arab world, the Yemenis were among the first to be motivated by the protests in Tunisia. Even with relatively low Internet penetration—roughly 2 percent of the population compared to Egypt's 21 percent and Tunisia's 34 percent—Yemenis were deeply invested in the new Arab public sphere and had an impressive tradition of political protest.[3] They had been challenging President Ali Abdullah Saleh through a variety of political actions for years, especially since he broke his promise not to stand for reelection in 2006. The protests that began in late January explicitly invoked the Tunisian inspiration.

Activists set February 3 as their first big day of rage. To almost everyone's amazement, thousands turned out in a surprising show of popular support for the campaign against Saleh's thirty-year rule. *The Guardian's* Brian Whitaker quickly saw the importance of the moves in Yemen and turned his attention from Cairo to follow the unfolding protest. Al-Jazeera noted the Yemeni developments as well, but it was difficult to keep attention on Yemen as the dramatic events unfolded in Tahrir Square.[4] Mubarak's fall gave a renewed momentum to the protests

in Yemen, both by inspiring protestors to believe in their chances of success and by attracting the attention of regional and international media
now keen to identify the next domino to fall. The demonstrations on
February 11 were the largest yet.

Early on, the protest movement drew heavily on youth activists and
diffuse social networks, rather than on traditional opposition parties. As
political science professor and Yemen expert Sheila Carapico described it,
"bypassing the formal opposition coalition of the so-called Joint Meeting
Parties, mostly youthful demonstrators thronged to public squares. They
chanted the North African slogans, 'Irhal' and 'Isqat al-Nizam,' calling for the
immediate removal of the president and his whole regime."[5] One observer
remarked, "In Taiz, a highlands city of half a million, people painted Irhal
on huge banners; in Sanaa they baked it into bread; and everywhere they
chanted it. Go. That single Arabic word has united Yemen's fractured
political opposition, turning old enemies into temporary allies and pushing President Ali Abdullah Saleh's regime to the brink of collapse."[6] As it
rolled forward, the protest movement fitfully began to draw in almost all
of the usually divided and mutually mistrustful opposition: southern
secessionists, the northern Huthi movement that had been fighting government forces for years, powerful tribes, the Islamist movement.

Saleh's regime responded with both concessions and force in the
face of the rising challenge. He had mastered the art of dividing his enemies and surviving through deception, repression, and corruption. On
January 23, even before the large protests began, the worried Saleh
regime arrested the dynamic young protest leader Tawakul Karman and
other protest organizers in a failed attempt to stem the rising protests.[7]
Ahead of the February 3 protest, Saleh had promised not to seek reelection in 2013 in order to mollify his critics, but after breaking a similar
promise in 2006, he found no takers. Protests continued to expand. On
February 21, Saleh offered to begin a dialogue with the opposition, but
refused to make any fundamental concessions or to promise to step
down from power. His opponents rejected Saleh's various offers as lacking credibility, given his past performance. One told The Guardian, "What
the president offered yesterday was just theatre, I don't trust him."[8] As in
Egypt, the diverse and decentralized protest movement could unite only
around a single, clear demand that Saleh must go.

Despite the clarity of this single consensus demand from the protest camps, in fact Yemenis were deeply divided over the challenge to Saleh. Many had very real fears about the dangers of anarchy or civil war, should the state collapse. Saleh enjoyed both tribal support and the backing of many who had thrived under his rule. Others enjoyed profitable ties to the current regime and worried about their future under any new political order. Western governments valued Saleh's counter-terrorism cooperation, and Saudi Arabia (Yemen's most important neighbor) was deeply invested in Saleh's survival. The pro-regime demonstrations that began to appear to challenge the anti-regime protes-tors represented a real constituency. Not all of their anger and numbers could be dismissed as just the protests of hired thugs. On February 23, pro-regime demonstrators—not just thugs—clashed with protestors in several locations, with police stepping in to separate the rival demonstra-tions. On February 25, a harsh military crackdown in Aden introduced a new level of violence to the Yemeni environment. Protestors responded with a "day of wrath" denouncing the violence.

A familiar cycle emerged. The larger the protests became, the more violence they encountered at the hands of the regime's security force. That violence in turn hardened the protestors' demands, galvanized new constituencies' anger at the regime, and brought more tribes and families into the protest movement. Unlike most other Arab countries, the Yemeni military divided, as key officers defected from the regime with their supporters. On March 19, snipers opened fire on protestors at Sanaa University, bringing Yemen to a new level of violence, tension, fear, and rage. What began as a hopeful emulation of the strategies used in Egypt and Tunisia soon diverged and became something else entirely—a descent into a frustrating stalemate where rival militaries clashed and not even the wounding of the president in a failed assassi-nation attempt could produce a political settlement.

#FEB12: ALGERIA

Closer to Tunisia and Egypt, Algerians had been protesting regularly since early January, partly in imitation of the Tunisian revolution but also because such protest activity had become highly common across the country in recent years. All the usual grievances existed, including high unemployment, a struggling middle class, an out-of-touch elite, and pervasive corruption. "What all these forms of riotous assembly over the years have had in common," noted Hugh Roberts, a specialist on North Africa, "is the visceral refusal of *la hogra*—the arrogance and contempt with which the authorities at all levels routinely treat ordinary Algerians."[9] The term was unique to Algeria, but it captured a concept common to the entire region.

On January 1, in the midst of the Tunisian revolution, the government had perhaps unwisely raised prices for key goods. Riots and protests that began in poor urban areas on January 5 at first followed a familiar rhythm. Angry youths protested the cost of living, attacked police stations, and rampaged through the streets. But, here we see an intriguing example of how Tunisia's tight, rigid enforcement of public quiescence rendered it brittle compared to its more traditionally turbulent neighbors. The security forces and regime in Algeria had had the benefit of long experience with protests. This was not a country like Tunisia or Syria or Libya where all forms of public dissent were crushed and even small protests introduced a qualitatively new factor into the political equation. Algeria's searing experience in the 1990s when more than 100,000 people had died in a brutal insurgency probably also placed a ceiling on the willingness of many ordinary people to join in mass protests. Their fears of instability and civil war ran deep and needed little reminder from the regime.

Despite all of this, however, the Tunisian revolution and the regional surge gave even these familiar protests a new significance, and activists hastened to articulate a political message and to align their struggle with the broader regional trend. Algerian activists called for February 12 (#feb12) to become a breakthrough day like Egypt's #jan25.[10] In one joke that made the rounds, the Algerians, whose soccer fans had recently experienced a shockingly violent and unpleasant fight with Egyptians during a match that had turned into a diplomatic crisis, could not allow themselves to lose in the dictator-toppling competition.

The police deployed to stop the protests, but more cautiously than in other cases. Though the police beat and arrested the protestors, their techniques did not include the use of deadly force. They thereby avoided triggering the cycle of violence seen in so many other countries.

The protests did not grow week to week as they did in other Arab countries. Only about 5,000 turned out on February 19. The security forces
were always a step ahead of the protestors, deploying in massive force
and overwhelming efforts to establish a real street movement. As one
blogger noted, perhaps with some exaggeration, the police outnumbered
the protestors 40,000 to 2,000 at one march for change.[11] Established
political parties avoided the demonstrations, while some of the more
prominent faces in the protests, including Islamists associated with the
past violence, frightened or alienated potential partners.[12]

The government remained unpopular, but its response of lower
prices for basic goods and ferocious police retaliation, and the general
weakness of the opposition movement kept the uprising in check. The
regime made some political concessions, including lifting the unpopular
emergency laws that had been in place since 1992. Overall, despite pervasive discontent and a worrisome stagnation at the heart of the regime,
the Algerian system seemed able to handle the challenge of persistent
strikes and occasional riots without major adjustments.

#FEB14: BAHRAIN

The same could not be said of Bahrain. Like Yemen, Bahrain's uprising
emerged from the context of a long-running political challenge. The
Sunni al-Khalifa monarchy had since the state's creation ruled a Bahrain
that had a large Shi'a majority. It had been fighting for years to defend its
royal prerogatives against popular challenges that had both a sectarian
and a democratizing potential. For nearly a decade, the monarchy
had faced persistent political movements such as the moderate Shi'a
al-Wefaq, more radical Shi'a movements such as al-Haq, and an amor-
phous group of nongovernmental human rights organizations, bloggers,
and online activists who strove to focus on democracy rather than sectarian grievances.

The Bahraini movement could draw on a long history of activism
online and off, with contention on issues of human rights and democracy.[13] Since the late 1990s, forums such as Ali Abdulemam's Bahrain
Online had become fully engaged public spheres where Bahrainis openly
discussed human rights and broader politics. The forum had landed
Abdulemam in prison in 2005. Bahrain Online had been used to

organize protests for the 2002 parliamentary elections and for a wide range of concerns. The activists understood the sensitivity of the sectarian and identity issues in the kingdom, and worked hard to overcome the perception that their complaints were Shi'a rather than universal. This decade of engagement is one reason why the Bahraini uprisings were initially embraced by other Arab activists as one of their own, and why the efforts to paint them as sectarian, Iranian-inspired Shi'a fifth columnists did not initially succeed.

These Bahrainis had been highly energized and engaged during the Tunisian and Egyptian protests unfolding on al-Jazeera. Youth activists moved to emulate Tahrir by setting up a camp in the Pearl Roundabout under the #feb14 hashtag.[14] Two days after the activists settled in, regime security forces moved to forcefully clear the square. Their crackdown backfired, however, and protests swiftly escalated beyond the activist core in response to the pressure.

Organized political parties and movements got involved, while the Bahraini regime divided over how to best respond. Unrestrained violence provoked wider protests, in a familiar dynamic, as funeral marches became protest marches and repression infuriated ordinary people offended by such treatment at the hands of the state. At its peak, an estimated half of the country's population joined the street protests—a truly astonishing moment in the history of Arab popular mobilization. The now-familiar images of peaceful protestors facing off against grim security forces, of carnivalesque popular efforts to hold a shared public space, and of online activists employing the common language of Arab uprisings all reinforced the regional sense that Bahrain should be understood as part of the unfolding Arab story of people demanding democratic change and not, as the monarchy suggested, an Iranian-backed challenge to a Sunni king. The Arab public saw the Bahraini protestors as part of its shared struggle, and the regime as equivalent to its own hated regimes.

Serious negotiations soon began, in public and private and with significant American and Saudi input, toward some kind of agreement on reform between regime soft-liners and moderate protest leaders. Opposition leaders tried hard to maintain unity and to focus demands on reforms rather than on regime overthrow, even as more radical groups and individuals pushed more extreme demands. Meanwhile, parts of the regime—including, reportedly, the crown prince—seemed open to moves toward a constitutional monarchy. But just as a deal seemed to be in reach, everything went wrong.

On March 14—the day, coincidentally, that I was scheduled to fly to Manama, the capital of Bahrain, to meet both the foreign minister and the protest leaders—the regime moved to forcefully crush the opposition with the help of Saudi-GCC military that crossed the causeway connecting Saudi Arabia and Bahrain. The forces demolished the Pearl Roundabout, scattered the protestors, and began a massive crackdown on not only protestors but almost all suspected sympathizers. The hospitals were flooded with the wounded and dead. Universities and professional associations were purged. Activists, journalists, students, and many others disappeared into the prisons. Thousands lost their jobs or university appointments. The crackdown, later exhaustively documented by the Bahrain Independent Commission of Inquiry, quickly became one of the most comprehensive, brutal, and oppressive of any in the region, while largely avoiding international condemnation.

Where other Arab countries maintained a united popular front against a hated regime, Bahrain would soon sharply divide along sectarian lines. The Sunni minority rallied furiously behind the monarchy, buying in to the sectarian narrative and defending its privileges against the perceived threat. A ferocious online battle broke out across Twitter and other social media between activists and regime supporters, making it almost impossible to discuss the country in any forum without unloosing a flood of invective and propaganda. While most of the core Arab activist communities across the region originally embraced the Bahraini protests as their own, doubts began to grow. The steady barrage of sectarian accusations took its toll, with demonization of Shi'a activists as Iranian cat's-paws falling on fertile ground prepared by a decade of such sectarian propaganda. The Bahraini regime and its allies pushed relentlessly to separate their own challengers from the wider Arab uprising narrative. By the autumn, Egyptian activists would refuse to even meet with the Bahraini opposition, and previously supportive political figures had distanced themselves. This movement would become one of the first great reversals of the Arab uprisings, perhaps the only case where a repression strategy succeeded. Or, at least, it succeeded in the short term, but likely at the cost of a generation of alienation and sectarian division.

#FEB17: LIBYA

Libya might have seemed the least likely place for a hashtagged revolution. Moammar Qaddafi's regime was famously brutal toward dissidents, and Libya had limited Internet access and virtually no organized civil society or political opposition. Nevertheless, the demonstration effects of Tunisia and Egypt proved potent. Protests in Libya began in earnest the night before the previously scheduled February 17 "day of revolt," in the hopes of catching the regime security forces off guard. Libyan protestors organized a major demonstration in Benghazi and other cities. They initially looked very familiar in the unfolding Arab narrative, with youth activists and a wide swath of the population coming out to demand change. But Qaddafi's regime had a far lower threshold for the kind of public activism it was willing to tolerate.

In response to the protests, the Libyan military showed what could have happened had professional militaries not exercised restraint in Egypt and Tunisia. Qaddafi's troops almost immediately opened fire with live ammunition rather than waiting for the situation to escalate. The brutal response made even Bahrain's early moves look tame. Within a week rampaging security forces had killed at least 1,000 unarmed protestors, but did not prevent Benghazi from falling to the opposition. Like Egypt, Libya quickly cut off all Internet access in hopes of blocking the social media coordination of protests and the transmission of information to the outside world.[15] Al-Jazeera's coverage put a spotlight on the Libyan brutality (even as it ignored the crackdown happening next door in Bahrain). The indiscriminate violence infuriated previously neutral Libyans, and the Benghazi-based rebellion quickly gained support from new tribes, regions, and sectors of society. And as videos and images of the state-led assault circulated on al-Jazeera and across the Internet, the pressure to intervene grew stronger and stronger. The massive show of force had backfired. A horrified international community condemned the bloodshed. This had little effect initially, but laid the groundwork for the formation of an unprecedented international and Arab coalition. Chapter 6 describes that intervention.

#FEB18: OMAN

An Omani protest movement seemed unlikely. A tiny, wealthy sultanate that was determinedly isolated from the political currents in the region, Oman had few of the elements usually associated with the Arab upheavals. Nevertheless, what became known as the Green March began in the shadow of an impending transition to the unknown, with public debate about an aging sultan who had no sons absolutely forbidden. Unlike other countries' protests, the Omani uprising did not call for overthrowing the sultan. Its demands were limited to ending corruption, fighting inflation, and increasing social spending, especially on struggling youth. Still, by Omani standards, such public protest was revolutionary.

Oman's first protests began only three days after Ben Ali fled Tunisia and began in earnest on February 18, the Friday after Mubarak's removal from power. Those protests continued with little interference for over a week before they sparked a massive wave of protests in the industrializing city of Sohar. The security forces finally began to clamp down on February 27. In response to the clashes, a Facebook group called for a March 2 demonstration, but few protestors showed up, partly because of the regime's concessions, including a government text message sent to Omani mobile phones promising increased welfare payments and other measures.[16]

But that moment of calm was misleading. On March 4, small protests crystallized into the largest demonstration in the modern history of the isolated emirate. The protests continued episodically for the next few months. At the end of March, the army broke up a small, month-old sit-in at the Globe Roundabout. It was increasingly aggressive with the protestors, shocking its own people with what seemed an un-Omani show of force and raising questions of whether the sultanate was losing its grip.

In response, the regime made a range of political concessions and lavished money on disaffected constituencies, rather than relying only on the iron fist. The sultan himself remained above the fray, declining to comment. Early on, the regime shuffled the government to bring in fresh blood and remove some of the more disliked ministers. It raised civil service salaries and hired 50,000 new government employees, raised salaries for military and security agencies, and increased the subsidy for university students. The GCC offered financial support. It also announced on March 13 that the previously consultative parliament would for the first time be given legislative and regulatory powers. On October 15, Oman held those unprecedented parliamentary elections. None of these reforms touched the sultan's absolute power or opened the system to serious discussions about the system's future—but the resilience of the protest movement and the frantic regime response in a wealthy Gulf state as far as any Arab state could be from Tunisia demonstrates the power of its example.

#FEB20: MOROCCO

Moroccans chose February 20 as their symbolic starting point, launching a series of protests explicitly modeled on the Tunisian and Egyptian examples.[17] They had to proceed cautiously in a system where the monarchy personified the state and enjoyed considerable popular support despite the usual catalog of political and economic grievances afflicting the country. They carefully balanced protestations of loyalty to the king with their complaints about corruption, the cost of living, and the absence of opportunity.

The movement organized on Facebook drew the kinds of young, Internet-savvy activists familiar in other Arab countries, while the protests grew in strength after receiving the support of the popular Islamist movement al-Adl wa al-Ihsan.[18] The government allowed the protests to proceed peacefully, in line with its usual policy, and was careful to avoid violence that might trigger escalation.

The February 20 protest turned out a surprisingly large number of people across the country. The movement then sustained weekly protests that grew in size and representation as a wide range of political trends joined in. The protests remained peaceful, and the security forces refrained from the worst sorts of violence used in other countries. Protestors focused tightly on calls for democracy, accountability, and the rule of law, and carefully avoided direct challenges to the king.

The extent to which this uprising focused on bringing oppressed voices into the public arena was captured beautifully by a "multicolored banner that quoted the famed lines of the Algerian poet Tahar Djaout:

'If you speak, you die. If you stay silent, you die. So speak, and die.'"[19] The king responded with preemptive moves toward political reform, including a package of constitutional changes put successfully to a referendum in May. As later chapters will discuss, the question was whether this was enough. When parliamentary elections approached in November, most members of the February 20 movement opted to boycott.

#FEB25: IRAQ

Even Iraqis joined the regional trend on February 25 with a series of protests against their deadlocked and endlessly bickering political class, the continuing failure to provide basic services, and the continuing U.S. military presence. It is remarkable that the inspiration of the Arab uprisings carried even to an Iraq scarred by long years of war and insurgency, divided along ethnic and sectarian lines, and largely alienated from an Arab public sphere that many saw as indifferent to their suffering, but it did. On February 25, a day of regionwide mobilization, six people were killed in clashes across the country.

Protests became a weekly ritual, with activists defying a vehicle ban and tight security to occupy Baghdad's Tahrir Square on March 4. But the protest movement struggled to gain broader relevance in the face of steadily increasing violence and the still shaky political equilibrium. Protests could gain real numbers when they involved unifying concerns such as rejecting the extension of the American military presence beyond 2011, or when backed by a political party. But the deep sectarian divides and the legacy of all-too-recent horrific violence put sharp limits on how far the Iraqi population was willing to go in challenging the authorities. While the protests continued in various places, they never cohered into any systematic challenge to the political status quo.

#MAR11: SAUDI ARABIA

The biggest prize for a real Arab revolution would have been Saudi Arabia, which, like Iraq in 1958, was the center of the regional conservative axis. Had there been true uprisings in Saudi Arabia, all bets would have been off—oil prices would have gone into orbit, the American alliance system shaken, and the other conservative regimes cast adrift. Many Arab revolutionaries viewed Saudi Arabia as the hidden hand lurking behind the scenes, crushing their hopes and scheming against their dreams.

Nor was a Saudi uprising inconceivable. The veteran Saudi dissident Madawi al-Rasheed wrote in late February that "Saudi Arabia is ripe for change."[20] The conditions certainly appeared conducive to a Saudi uprising. A large, underemployed youth population had more than enough economic grievances and resented the privileged ruling al-Saud family. The rigid media control and enforcement of public morality looked increasingly at odds with a society saturated with satellite television and the Internet. The infirmities of both King Abdullah and Crown Prince Sultan (who passed away in October 2011) highlighted the uncertain and contentious potential succession and deep-seated intrafamily rivalries. And the kingdom had a long history of political demands and petitions from a variety of Islamist and "liberal" (in the Saudi context) movements.

On March 11, all eyes turned to Saudi Arabia's planned protest. Would the Arab uprisings come to the very heart of the counterrevolution? No. This was not Baghdad in 1958, even after the Saudis risked repeating the Iraqi monarch's mistake of dispatching troops to help a threatened neighbor. The Saudis took no chances. Very few protestors risked joining the demonstration announced on Facebook. Indeed, there were probably more journalists on hand than actual protestors. A week later, King Abdullah went on national television to announce a breathtaking package of financial inducements to his population, including increased subsidies and targeted aid to key sectors such as the religious establishment.[21] Those promises might have compromised Saudi Arabia's long-term fiscal prospects, but in the short term, they effectively met the most urgent demands of many potential protestors.

This dramatic fizzle took Saudi Arabia out of play, and enthusiasm for change has not yet returned to the country. On March 14, the Saudis would move into Bahrain in force and help break up one of the largest and most dynamic of all the protest movements in the region. It would extend its largesse to other GCC states, offering a "Marshall Plan" of economic assistance to less wealthy Gulf monarchies and inviting distant Jordan and Morocco to join the king's club. The kingdom smoothly navigated the death of the crown prince in October despite frequent predictions that the succession would trigger domestic unrest. Its cosmetic reforms, including granting women the right to vote for largely power-less advisory councils, created the appearance of movement without conceding any real powers.

#MAR15: PALESTINE AND SYRIA

Both the Palestinians and the Syrians chose March 15 for their move—a coordination failure that could hardly have been more symbolic of the long years of ineffectual Arab (and Syrian) support for the Palestinian cause.

Palestinians were at the heart of the imagined community of the Arab uprisings, but struggled to take part in the collective movement. There were as many wired, ambitious, and frustrated youth in the Palestinian areas as anywhere else in the Arab world, and as much contempt for the dinosaurs who ruled them. Physically divided by the network of Israeli roads, settlements, zones of control, and checkpoints and with almost all political movements discredited and divided, most Palestinians felt they had nowhere to turn.

While some, like the lonely independent Mustafa Barghouti, called for a new nonviolent Intifada directed against both Israel and the Palestinian Authority, few seemed inclined to take up the call, even as the rest of the Arab world rose around them. Exhausted by years of struggle against occupation and deeply traumatized by the lingering effects of the bloody years following the Al-Aqsa Intifada (2000–2002), Palestinians showed few signs of eagerness to take to the streets. Even if they did, where would they go? Marches on the checkpoints or the security wall dividing the West Bank from Israel, which happened with increasing frequency, invited military responses. Gatherings in Ramallah's central square put little pressure on anyone. Gaza at least offered a central gathering point, but the Islamist movement Hamas that had controlled Gaza since 2007 left little opportunity for uncontrolled mobilization.

There were certainly Palestinian youth eager to emulate the Arab uprisings around them. But they struggled to find a specific target for their anger. Israeli occupation? The Palestinian Authority? Fatah? Hamas? The zero-sum nature of Palestinian politics meant that either Fatah or Hamas would seize upon almost any kind of mobilization, producing dynamics closer to Lebanon's 2005 polarization than Egypt's unified national uprising against Mubarak. In the end, the marches in Gaza, which may have reached 100,000 people, focused on a demand for reunification with the West Bank and the transcending of entrenched political differences.[22] In the West Bank, the Palestinian protest movement fumbled toward a nonviolent movement that had a tenuous and uneasy relationship with the Palestinian Authority (PA).

Few Palestinians could truly get excited about the PA's plan to demand recognition as a state at the United Nations in September, given their deep disenchantment with their political class and lack of faith that anything would change on the ground. President Mahmoud Abbas attempted to deploy protests in support of his diplomatic initiative, but strategic uses of the street were not really what the Arab uprisings were about. The PA sponsored a rally held in Ramallah in mid-September, designed to demonstrate popular support for the statehood bid; it came off as a painful caricature of other genuinely spontaneous and authentic protest movements across the region. Still, the PA's bid at the UN did at least refocus attention on the Palestinian cause and spark some tentative moves toward political reunification between the competing factions.

Similarly, little was expected from the March 15 demonstration called for in Syria. Many who believed that the uprisings were directed against the Western-backed regimes thought that Damascus would be immune to the wave of protest. The Syrian repressive apparatus seemed impregnable. No networks of activists or civil society or opposition movements existed to take up the call to action. But here, the dynamics of regime violence spurred a powerful wave of protest into action. When troops opened fire on peaceful protestors in the grim southern town of Deraa, the bloodshed was captured on video and widely distributed through a growing infrastructure of opposition new media. The Syrian regime created its own catastrophe by unleashing unnecessary violence and bungling offers of reform, and soon found itself caught in a vicious cycle of self-perpetuating escalation. The horrifying and systematic brutality forced Syria's increasingly desperate opposition to rethink its commitment to peaceful protest and rejection of foreign intervention. As chapter 7 details, the turn to violence and open warfare in the streets in Syria would ultimately color the entire course of the Arab uprisings—and not for the better.

#MAR24: JORDAN

The Hashemite Kingdom resembled Egypt more than Tunisia or Syria in terms of its history of political contention. Jordanians had been episodically protesting for decades and had enjoyed moments of real democratic participation, most notably from 1989 to 1992, now regarded as something of a golden age of Jordanian politics. A robust civil society, including both a wide array of nongovernmental organizations and a strong Islamist movement, regularly took to the streets during the 1990s and 2000s to challenge government policies. Relatively independent newspapers regularly published critical opinions.

This was not Jordan's first bout of protest and democratic demands. Jordan had experienced a democratic opening following riots in 1989 (see chapter 3), but since the peace treaty with Israel signed in 1994, political democratization had been steadily closed down. With public opinion remaining sharply hostile to Israel, the palace had little choice but to crack down on the political opposition in order to maintain the new treaty. Each election after 1993 generated more complaints, with the Islamist opposition opting to boycott in 1997 over a controversial election law. King Abdullah, who succeeded King Hussein in 1999 after his father's death following a long battle with cancer, dismissed parliament in 2001 and ruled by decree for two years. Elections in 2003, 2007, and 2010 all retained the widely criticized electoral laws and produced legislatures dominated by pro-regime and tribal figures and devoid of significant political opposition. The 2010 parliamentary election was widely viewed as a farce, with virtually no opposition representation despite the easily visible popular discontent. Throughout this period, the regime cracked down ever more forcefully on the Islamist Muslim Brotherhood opposition movement and exercised ever tighter control over the domestic media.

At the same time, the Jordanian economy had grown progressively worse, with the middle class coming under intense pressure in the last years of the decade. Unemployment and poverty soared, as did the cost of living. A pervasive sense of the corruption among the political elite drove popular resentment, as economic struggles escalated. The failures and trials of the Palestinian-Israeli relationship brought despair as well as impatient frustration to the Jordanian front, with some political groups—notably a Hamas-oriented wing of the Jordanian Muslim Brotherhood—pushing for a renewed focus on Palestine rather than on domestic political issues.

Jordan's combination of economic and political discontent alongside a closing political system therefore put it very much at risk of popular mobilization. Yet Jordan's regional environment buffered it in important ways. Financial and political support from Saudi Arabia, including the offer of GCC membership, along with the unwavering support of the United States, ensured that no serious external pressure could supplement its inevitable internal rumblings. And, as always, its intimate connections to the Palestinian arena represented both a point of vulnerability and a source of strength. Warnings of Israeli intentions to solve the Palestinian issue at Jordan's expense through the "Alternative Homeland" option of declaring Jordan to be the Palestinian state remained a trump card in Jordanian politics, silencing Palestinian political aspirations and mobilizing Transjordanian support for the king.

The long history of Jordanian political turbulence also counterintuitively gave it some resilience in the face of mobilization. In contrast to a Tunisia, a Syria, or a Libya, where any political activism delivered a major shock to the system, the Jordanian regime had long experience in dealing with its opponents. It had spent years perfecting models of riot control, built an urban architecture of roads and bypasses that made it difficult to assemble and march, and maintained pervasive surveillance and monitoring of all groups. The state lavished patronage, military, and civil service jobs on the Transjordanian communities, overrepresented them in parliament, and maintained extensive relationships with the tribes that made up its traditional political support base. The only serious opposition movement, the Muslim Brotherhood, had been seriously hurt by years of repression, while Palestinian movements understood the need to maintain a low profile if they wished to remain active in the kingdom.

But Jordanians were unusually deeply embedded in the new Arab public. The strong Palestinian representation in Jordanian society ensured that they were highly attuned to the trends and ideas across the wider region. For that reason alone, no country is more deeply affected by the ups and downs of the Israeli-Palestinian conflict. During the Arab Cold War, Jordan had been one of the most turbulent of battlefields due to the intensely pan-Arabist sentiments in the population. In 1990, Jordanian sympathy with Iraq had been powerful enough to force King Hussein to side against his primary international patrons in Washington. There was no way that the Arab uprising could pass them by.

The Jordanian protest movement began earlier than the others, except for Yemen's, albeit relatively timidly.[23] The first major "day of rage" came on January 14, before the Egyptian revolution.[24] When protests first broke out in response to Tunisia's revolution, the chants pointedly focused not on the monarchy but on the unpopular Prime Minister Samir al-Rifai. They tended to be dominated at this point by the traditional opposition parties, including the Islamic Action Front and the well-established reform coalition. Weekly protests beginning in mid-January picked up steam as traditional opposition parties and new youth activists joined forces and began to attract greater numbers.

In late January and early February, as protests grew and the regime stonewalled, a palpable change in the public sphere could be felt, as previously taboo subjects became the object of open contestation.[25] As early as January 17, the editor of one Jordanian daily newspaper had warned that Jordan was ripe to follow in Tunisia's footsteps.[26] The Hashtag Debates, organized by a group of young Internet activists, generated surprisingly direct and blunt discourse on core issues of politics. Facebook groups, online newspapers, political websites, and many other new sites of public debate emerged. In this context, even local incidents that might previously have been covered up were brought to public attention, including an incident in Tafileh back in June 2011 during which the king was pelted with vegetables during a ceremonial visit. Several sensational corruption stories exploded that implicated top regime figures and kept the government on the defensive.

In early 2011, the nascent protest movement had scored a real gain by forcing the dismissal of unpopular Prime Minister Samir al-Rifai and the appointment of a fifty-two-member National Dialogue Committee. In the early spring, the Jordanian protests seemed to be on the brink of breaking through to force serious constitutional changes. Their success in driving Rifai from office on February 1 gave them a new confidence and sense of their own power. Whispered complaints about corruption, from a series of controversial land deals to rumors of a new royal jet for the glamorous Queen Rania, fell on fertile terrain in tough economic times and a closing political system marred by exceptionally fraudulent parliamentary elections and increasing regime efforts to control the media. But it was not to be, at least not immediately.

The protests failed to catch on more widely for a number of reasons. As in Bahrain, the regime exploited persistent societal cleavages to prevent the emergence of a coherent movement.[27] Transjordanians were deeply dissatisfied with the stagnant economy, but remained even more hostile to expressions of political strength deemed "Palestinian." Angry young toughs attacked and denounced protestors of Transjordanian origin as "Palestinians." The military remained completely loyal to the king, as did international support. Saudi Arabia and the GCC stepped in to shore up the Hashemite regime, with financial assistance and an offer of GCC membership. And the king was able to play the traditional political game of repeatedly sacrificing a disposable prime minister and bringing in new faces (as he did once again in November), and even offering some constitutional revisions, without making fundamental political changes.

But youth activists were not appeased. This unusually wired and creative group of activists may have been only a small, elite circle. But they had introduced real innovations, such as the 3iber.com citizen journalism website and the Hashtag Debates promoting serious, civil debate about the most sensitive political issues. They saw little change with yet another meaningless government shuffle, empty promises of future reform, or another iteration of fruitless national dialogue. They therefore chose March 24 as their symbolic date to launch a new protest movement by staging a sit-in around the interior ministry.[28] They carefully couched all of their demands in the language of the king himself, and did all that they could to paint themselves as a patriotic, fully Jordanian movement, rather than as representatives of the Palestinian population. But it did not go well.

As the sit-in progressed, a crowd of southern Transjordanian tribesmen assembled around the protest; whether hired thugs for the regime or genuinely aggrieved regime loyalists, their assault on the sit-in scared the protestors. Their movement could not escape well-entrenched discourses about their identity and political lines of division. Regime loyalists tagged them as "Palestinians" and as "elitists," both moves designed to contain and limit their representational claims. But this "Palestinianization" of the domestic arena was risky. The fate of the peace process always hung over such a Jordanian game, with the risk that collapse of the Palestinian Authority or chaos in the West Bank could all too easily spill over into the East Bank in Jordan to ignite a very different kind of crisis.

#LEBANON

One of the few countries to experience virtually no mobilization during this period, oddly enough, was Lebanon. There were good reasons to expect more: the country had a recent history of mass mobilization, a deep dissatisfaction with its political class, and extremely high levels of Internet and media penetration. But when I traveled through Beirut in March, I found virtually no political activism.[29] The Lebanese who were involved in the regional political upsurge tended to focus externally, particularly on the Syrian arena. The Hariri-led March 14 movement schemed about mobilizing mass protests against Hezbollah's weapons, but as a partisan rather than national issue, it went nowhere.

Lebanon proved largely immune from the Arab uprisings for a few reasons. The sectarian system meant that there was no obvious central focus for youth opposition, with no unifying figure such as Mubarak or Assad all could agree to oppose. "The people want to overthrow the sectarian system" did not have the same clarity as did chants directed against a single leader. The March 8 coalition, which included Hezbollah and the Christian Free Patriotic Movement led by Michel Aoun, was at the time ascendant politically after bringing down the government of Saad Hariri, and had little interest in an upheaval at the moment. Soon, Hezbollah and the March 8 coalition would be consumed with the fallout from the unfolding Syrian catastrophe, trapped between its continuing support for the Assad regime and the outrage of most Arab public opinion. Indeed, Hezbollah may have been the single political force in the region whose reputation most suffered during the Arab uprisings, as it went from one of the most popular political movements in the region to widely despised for refusing to break with the Syrian regime.

Youth movements did organize protests, drawing on all the tools of their Arab counterparts—sit-ins, Flickr picture collections, Twitter hashtags, Facebook groups, videos uploaded to YouTube. But their protests remained small and relatively marginal. The Lebanese political system offered no clear point of entry for demands for change: "sectarianism" was too abstract and too deeply embedded to make a clear target. By the autumn, these protests had faded away.

Finally, a certain Lebanese self-absorption kept them from identifying closely with the Arab uprisings. Lebanese tended to pay more attention to their own television stations than to al-Jazeera, and to be immersed in the details of their political maneuverings. Many of the pro–March 14 Lebanese saw themselves as already in a democracy, more Western than Arab, and distant from Arab concerns. And they believed that they had already had their moment of mass mobilization in the Cedar Revolution of 2005. Indeed, I even heard some complain bitterly that they, and not the Tunisians and Egyptians, should be given the credit for sparking the Arab upheavals. Few outside of Lebanon bought this argument, however.

THE NEW ARAB PUBLIC AFTER EGYPT

The wave of protest described in this chapter feels so natural and obvious to us now that it is easy to forget how extraordinary such diffusion really is. Most political scientists had dismissed the prospects for such demonstration effects or diffusion of protests. Drawing on the experience of other regions and their assumptions, they found little reason to expect that Tunisia would affect Egypt, or that either would spread protests to the rest of the region. They expected each state to follow its own course, with marginal regional demonstration effects at best. As this chapter has shown, these expectations proved to be deeply wrong.

Why? What political scientists and experts from other regions missed was the real significance of the new Arab public sphere in unifying political space. Al-Jazeera, satellite television, Facebook, and Twitter bound together these national struggles into a single, coherent narrative of an Arab Intifada. And every local protest movement could now appeal to the power of this public by labeling a protest with a hashtag and declaring it the next stage in the Arab uprising. This created a far more unified regional space than most analysts would have expected, with far more diffusion and far more resonance. The common language, shared identity, tight focus, and dense communication across countries created a genuinely unique regional configuration. Political scientists were not wrong to be skeptical of such diffusion effects. It's just that the Arab world was the one region of the world where the conditions existed to bind together the disparate protests within a shared identity and a common narrative.

The intensely unified political space meant that there was an extraordinary flow of influence, momentum, and despair across very different arenas. The fate of Benghazi affected the region because protestors and regimes everywhere were watching it carefully for signals about their own future. The ruthless crushing of Bahrain's protests mattered not only in the Gulf but throughout the entire region, partly because it showed that full-spectrum repression could succeed and partly because it seemed to expose the hypocrisy of American policy. The various movements would each be of interest to their own countries on their own terms. But they took on broader geopolitical significance because they were seen to add up to more than the sum of their parts.

There is strong evidence for the power of momentum and regional diffusion in the heady initial days of 2011. The simultaneous outbreak of protests in multiple countries, regardless of antecedent conditions, simply makes no sense otherwise. The explicit adoption of Tunisian and Egyptian slogans in Yemen, Jordan, or Kuwait argues against any mechanical, unconscious theory of diffusion. And activists and the media talked about the protests as a regional process and hung on every twist and turn in the regional narrative. Meanwhile, international moves to intervene militarily, to invoke the International Criminal Court, or to impose targeted sanctions against those accused of brutality against peaceful protestors—or, of course, the failure to do so—held the attention of potential repressors elsewhere in the region.

As the power of the new Arab media grew, so did questions about its intentions, impact, and role. Al-Jazeera became increasingly controversial during this period. After serving as the de facto home of the Tunisian and Egyptian revolutions, where a single story unified the public sphere, al-Jazeera now found itself in a position to make or break uprisings. It made several controversial decisions that tarnished its image as the home of the Arab uprising, and that marked it in the eyes of many as an instrument of Qatari foreign policy rather than as an independent voice of the new Arab public. First, it largely ignored Bahrain, to the fury of an Arab public that saw the uprising as an integral and organic part of its own struggle. Second, it focused heavily on Libya and later on Syria to the exclusion of other peaceful struggles. More broadly, its coverage seemed ever more blatantly to follow Qatari foreign policy, which undermined its efforts to portray itself as an independent voice of the Arab street.

Finally, al-Jazeera decided to move to a 24/7 news format and close down all of the live political talk shows that had been the heart and soul of its claim to be an Arab public sphere. It had done the same for six weeks during the 2003 Iraq war, but had resumed the open political debates almost immediately after the fall of Saddam Hussein. This time, the closure became the new status quo, extending indefinitely in an environment not likely to calm down any time soon. A number of its top on-air personalities quit in protest over the new direction, including Ghassan Ben Jeddo (head of its Beirut office and star of its 2006 coverage of the Israeli-Lebanese war) and a half-dozen top female presenters (including Joumana Nammour, the presenter who had hosted the live call-in programs in the weeks following the Iraq War). In September, the station's visionary managing director, Wadah Khanfar, resigned for reasons that remain unclear.

As for the social media, as actors on each side came to appreciate its power, it became a contentious battlefield. Bahrain became a scorched-earth topic on Twitter, akin to the famously difficult Israeli-Palestinian issue, where rational discussion became virtually impossible as abusive pro-regime voices flooded social media. The role of online activists became ever more controversial, particularly in Syria where few news organizations had a presence on the ground. Who could authenticate claims of regime brutality or videos seeming to show murdered peaceful protestors? Did it matter that activists with a clear political agenda circulated the videos?

The overwhelming identification with this narrative could also interfere with rational analysis by silencing those who might question the prevailing consensus. Any protest movement became part of a shared identity, which could not be interrogated or challenged without risk of excommunication from this passionate new group. Analysts who asked whether, for instance, Syrians might fear an uprising that might unleash Iraq-style sectarian conflict were savagely attacked as regime apologists. Those who questioned the tactics of Egypt's leading protest movements were tarred as counterrevolutionaries. Compromise with regimes was viewed as treason, with only complete revolution deemed an acceptable goal. The moral imperative ran in one direction only.

This contest to speak for the Arab street is as old as the Arab regional order itself. Competing claims of revolutionary or pan-Arab legitimacy have defined the battles between political forces from the anticolonial struggles of the 1930s and the Arab Cold War of the 1950s to the internecine struggles to control the legacy of Tahrir Square. Those competing claims were fought out not only rhetorically but also on the streets. Nasser's ability to bring thousands of people into the streets of Amman gave power to his pan-Arab rhetoric, just as the relevance of the Egyptian activist groups ultimately depended on their ability to consistently mobilize large numbers.

The core protestors at Tahrir Square presented themselves as a model of the future Arab public. While they were often called "youth," they were not children; these youth were often highly accomplished men and women in their twenties and thirties, many of them veterans of a decade of street struggles. They included representatives from most political parties and factions, labor and trade unions, professionals, lawyers, and university professors. Islamists stood side by side with liberals in pursuit of a common cause. They formulated common demands and refined protest strategies in intense public debates. I often heard from participants in the protests in Tahrir Square that "those eighteen days created a bond" of shared sacrifice and struggle that washed away differences of class, ideology, and generation. But this bond could not survive the return to normal politics. And it did not. Instead, revolutionary legitimacy became part of the currency of power politics.

In the new regional environment, the ability to speak for the revolution became a form of power in its own right. Similarly, the claim to speak for the Arab nation had defined political power during the Cold War of the 1950s, which generated as much conflict as cooperation between would-be Arab nationalists.[30] Activists who succeeded, particularly in Egypt, claimed a unique moral authority over the course of subsequent events. But such authority is not as easily granted as it is claimed. For activists who stood in Tahrir Square, January 25 mattered enormously. For others, this claim was of only historical interest, as real political battles played out in terms of the ability to mobilize people in the streets, to win votes, or to drive media narratives.

Revolutionary legitimacy carries particular weight and moral authority in this new public sphere, just as pan-Arab legitimacy was the currency of the realm in the 1950s. But this can pose real problems. The prominence of revolutionary activists on Twitter and in the blogosphere does not guarantee that they speak for the mainstream of their own societies. Indeed, they often systematically overrepresent secular, cosmopolitan, well-off urban youth whose views are a distinct minority in the broader society. Revolutionary legitimacy would inevitably clash with democratic legitimacy when their claims were put to the test of the ballot box. The influential Egyptian columnist Fahmy Howeydi put his finger on a real concern when he wrote in early July that the problem was not the proliferation of parties and movements but rather "when one of them tries to impose its opinion on all the others as the sole legitimate representative of the street or the revolution."[31] That way lies not democracy, but the old Arab politics of revolutionary despotism.

Yet, at the same time, it would be too easy to dismiss these activists. Their ability to bring vast numbers of people into the streets is only one measure of their importance. They also occupy an essential place in the emerging public sphere and shape broad narratives about those revolutions. They have the makings of a true counterelite, one that makes its views of greater import than its demographic weight could bear. Public opinion is not simply the aggregation of individual attitudes. Public opinion is rooted in the ideas, narratives, and discourses that circulate in the public sphere. The disproportionate influence of these activists through their ability to set narratives cannot be lightly set aside.

In other cases, the questions were even more intense. Who spoke in truth for the Syrian people in the absence of any clear, legitimate opposition leadership? Could we take the word of a murky, semi-anonymous group of Internet activists about what was happening inside Syria? Who were the anonymous Libyan activists pushing the cause of the Libyan revolution, and for whom did they speak? Did the Bahraini protestors who initially dominated social media represent their country more than those who later poured onto Twitter to argue the cause of the Sunni minority and the monarchy? Who represented the Yemeni people in the blizzard of tribes, movements, NGOs, parties, regional aspirants, and local warlords?

Then there were questions about how much weight to give different contributions to the revolution. What mattered more for explaining the Arab upheavals? The efforts of a specific group of human beings whose actions changed the course of history? Or the structural conditions that made their success possible? Could Egypt have had a revolution without the determined, dangerous, desperate efforts of a few thousand people to hold Tahrir Square at all costs against regime thugs? Or were the conditions of an Egypt of decaying institutions and increasingly empowered and frustrated youth sufficient to ensure that at some point change would come, with the efforts of individuals significant only for the exact timing and nature of the outburst?

This tension has become a crucial part of the emerging Arab politics. In the successful cases of change—Tunisia and Egypt—the appeal to revolutionary legitimacy cuts against both continued military rule and the transitions toward democratic politics. Youth activists have been relentless critics of the transitional governments, particularly Egypt's SCAF. But at the same time, they have resisted rapid timetables for elections for various reasons, including the need to first write and ratify a constitution and the need for more time for secular and liberal parties to organize. The upshot was that these avowedly democratic activists found themselves urging the SCAF to remain in power and to postpone elections. In Tunisia, the young, impoverished revolutionaries from the south feel once again left out of the political system that has emerged from their struggles.[32]

This may seem odd, but in fact it makes sense, given the nature of their social, political, and representational power. The power of the activist class lies in its ability to go to the streets and disrupt normal economic and political life. Some, at least, understand that they are unlikely to do well even in the most fair and free electoral process. Many seem unwilling or unable to embark on the kind of political party building, outreach, and organization that is required in democratic competition. Some activists are deeply skeptical of liberal democracy on its merits and prefer anarchist or leftist models of political order. They find it better, then, to remain in an institutional limbo and exert power through the streets.

The questions of representation play out differently but just as urgently in every other arena, whether violent or relatively peaceful. In some cases, there are real constituencies for the status quo. In others, protest is channeled through entrenched patterns of sectarian, ethnic, or political divisions. Regimes generally claim to speak for the silent majority, and the uncomfortable truth is that there is often more to those claims than activists care to admit. Revolutions only happen when that claim falters, when regime brutality or corruption turns the mainstream away.

The absence of real democracy intensified these representational struggles. With no elections to determine the real balance of power, movements resorted to indirect means to demonstrate their strength. Rhetorical battles played a prominent role here. Student union or professional association elections could become important proxy competitions. But getting people out into the streets in numbers became the currency of the realm, particularly in periods of contentious mobilization. The priority placed on the Arab street therefore reflected not only the fears of unrest or the authentic voice of the people, but also a barometer of the relative strength of competing trends. Democracy in this sense poses a real challenge to those groups whose strength rested on the ability to mobilize thousands into the streets, not on the ability to deliver millions of votes.

Beginning in March, threatened regimes chose to drag conflicts down into the mud of protracted political—and, in some cases, literal—warfare. Bahrainis, Yemenis, Libyans, and Syrians presented very different faces to the Arab world than did the delirious Egyptians and Tunisians. The fragmentation of the arena and the more difficult terrain clearly slowed the regional momentum of this first phase and brought on the next, in which, with momentum broken, it felt as if each country's national particularity reasserted itself and regional groups lost their dominance. In March, the empire struck back.

CHAPTER 6

THE EMPIRE STRIKES BACK:
THE COUNTERREVOLUTION

T HE WEEK OF MARCH 14, 2011, was a pivotal turning point, as hope turned to violence. More than forty protestors were killed by Yemeni regime security forces in Sanaa on March 18. Syrian protests in the town of Deraa were consumed by bloodshed. The Bahraini protests that had brought a majority of the country's population into the streets came to a brutal end with the deployment of the GCC Peninsula Shield military intervention forces and a systematic campaign of arrests. And Qaddafi's troops closed in on Benghazi, driving a furious debate across the region about international intervention.

Saudi Arabia's actions in Bahrain and the GCC's endorsement of the NATO airstrikes in Libya were the most overt intervention. But it acted across a much broader spectrum to consolidate the regional status quo. The GCC invited Morocco and Jordan to join the council, building what looked increasingly like a monarchical, conservative bloc straight out of the classic Arab Cold War. It made huge financial promises to cement relations with a variety of Arab governments, from a $1 billion gift to Jordan to a $4 billion grant to revolutionary Egypt. It also drew upon long-established media and religious networks to advance more conservative forces in the newly open environments. Even the GCC's eventual backing of the Libya intervention might be seen as part of the counterrevolution, since it helped to direct Western energies away from the GCC's own allies and to remove one of its long-standing irritants from the game board.

This should not have come as a surprise. For all the power of the hashtagged revolutions, the remaining Arab dictators were never going to give up as easily as Ben Ali and Mubarak. Its ferocity did surprise many observers, who had perhaps too quickly believed that history had only one right side. This was the flip side of the regional demonstration effect. If the protest movements had come together into an unorganized but intensely felt common cause, Arab regimes also came together in pursuit of what they held most dear—their own political survival. Arab leaders quickly learned the lessons of those fallen peers, and the lesson was not that they also should depart. The GCC took the lead in this initiative and soon supplanted the Arab League as the primary driver of inter-Arab politics. Across the region, regimes quickly developed survival strategies designed to either crush emerging protest movements or adapt to them in ways that preserved the core of their power and interests.

These efforts soon became known as the "counterrevolution" in Arab political discourse. There is significant disagreement about the extent to which this counterrevolution was a coordinated, effective, centralized Saudi campaign or, for that matter, what its ultimate objectives might have been. There is a fine line between a coordinated counterrevolution and an opportunistic effort to protect national or partisan interests. Nevertheless, the new energy and regional focus in Saudi diplomacy and its unusual cooperation with other key Gulf states were impossible to mistake. In addition to political and media support, the GCC states offered a $10 billion bailout to Oman and Bahrain. Saudi Arabia promised $4 billion to Egypt and $1.4 billion to Jordan, while the UAE followed with a $3 billion promise to Egypt, and Qatar added $500 million (though such promises were rarely quickly or completely fulfilled).[1] The GCC directly intervened in Bahrain, provided key political cover to the NATO intervention in Libya, and eventually campaigned against Bashar al-Assad's regime in Syria. It was almost universally believed (though difficult to prove) that the GCC countries were also covertly funneling money and support to their allies within other countries—Qatar supposedly supporting Muslim Brotherhood parties, Saudi Arabia promoting Salafis, and so forth.

Regional politics increasingly took on the character of a new cold war, but one that lacked the clear dividing lines that characterized the struggles of the previous decade. The Saudis, for instance, would have far preferred that the region's politics return to the previous decade's focus on Iranian perfidy rather than demands for democratic change. But other important players had very different priorities. And where to place Qatar, a key GCC member that cooperated with Saudi Arabia in some arenas but actively pushed pro-revolutionary narratives through al-Jazeera? The regional powers commenced direct meddling in the domestic affairs of states experiencing turmoil, while escalating their propaganda and media campaigns through all media available to them. These new struggles threatened to overtake the original popular movements from below and to break that powerful sense of popular unity that had bound together the many disparate struggles.

"Counterrevolution" itself became a common term of abuse, with an ever less obvious specific meaning. The scope and unity of the counterrevolution varied, with the ruling military regimes, Islamists, Saudi Arabia and the Gulf, America, and the remnants of the old regimes all at times identified as culprits in spite of their many obvious political disagreements.[2] The unity and coherence of this alleged counterrevolution was often exaggerated, but the efforts by various actors to shape the uprisings in their own interests were clear. Particularly in the Gulf and Syria, this new cold war was layered on top of a decade of a regional order defined by an alliance of "moderate" autocracies aligned with the United States and Israel against a "resistance" axis. This placed some of America's closest traditional allies at odds with the Obama administration in key theaters, disrupted long-standing relationships, and brought high-level political wrangling into the unfolding Arab uprisings.

Were the interventions and offers of aid to remnants of the old regimes and promotion of sectarian clashes and monarchical reforms all part of an intentional plan to "abort the democratic revolution"?[3] Feverish accounts of a coordinated counterrevolution that became popular on the Arab Left and among many Arab activists over the summer may impose far more coherence and agency than actually existed. "Counterrevolution" became a convenient, easy label for not only Saudi-backed foreign policy but also all competing political interests pursuing their own agendas. Where should the line be drawn between the Egyptian Muslim Brotherhood angling to maximize its electoral performance and a Saudi agenda to abort the revolution? But like the "Arab Cold War" or the "moderates versus resistance" frameworks, the fracture of forces into revolutionary and counterrevolutionary blocs helped make sense of the political changes for many throughout the region. It helped to fix political actors within a particular narrative, to draw lines of friendship and enmity, and to consolidate some stable alignments within a turbulent region.

At the same time, the trope that sees counterrevolution everywhere gives too much credit to the Saudis. They were certainly trying to shape regional politics to their liking, but the results have not been particularly impressive. For example, the Saudi effort to broker a transition plan in Yemen went nowhere. The near-collapse of the Yemeni state left politics gridlocked, and not even the mysterious near-fatal attack on President Ali Abdullah Saleh and his subsequent flight to a Saudi hospital could break the stalemate. His shocking return to Yemen in September, when almost everyone had expected him to never leave his hospital bed in Saudi Arabia, made Saudi policy look ineffectual and incoherent. Elsewhere, results have been similarly ineffectual. The regime long seemed baffled by the unrest in Syria, unable to decide how to respond to the turbulence, and when it did come out against the Assad regime, it struggled to produce any practical steps to bring about change. More broadly, such meddling often provoked a backlash, as when leading Libyan politicians began to publicly denounce Qatar for interfering in their affairs following Qaddafi's fall.

Nevertheless, the revolutionary momentum did slow, and it became common to hear frustrated complaints about "hijacked revolutions" from Tunisia and Egypt to the still unresolved struggles. The secular activists who claimed authorship of the Egyptian revolution, frustrated at the limits of change, threw themselves back into the streets repeatedly seeking to revive the revolution, but with diminishing returns. At the same time, conservative forces played an old, reliable card by pointing to a hidden foreign hand behind the unrest. Journalist Bilal al-Hassan argued that "all Arabs can now see the Western position standing firmly with Israel against us all."[4] In Egypt, the SCAF accused the April 6 Youth Movement of taking American funding. Backers of Bashar al-Assad accused an American-Israeli (and, at times, Muslim Brotherhood) conspiracy of manufacturing an inauthentic Syrian opposition.

Saudi Arabia's alliance with the United States has been sorely tested by the Arab uprisings. Where the Obama administration sought to place itself on the side of history, supporting popular aspirations against autocracy, its most important Arab ally chose instead to double-down on autocracy. The U.S. recognized the damage done to its policies by the crackdown in Bahrain, but declined to openly challenge the Saudi initiative. Washington and Riyadh still agree on the challenge posed by Iran, but increasingly diverge not only on the traditional Arab-Israeli front but also on the response to the Arab uprisings.

The United States remained at arm's length from this counterrevolution led by its purportedly closest allies. The Obama administration continued to identify with the aspirations of the "revolution," even when the Arab public took stances distinctly hostile to America's regional posture. The U.S. pushed for reform and change in the same arenas where the Saudis sought to slam on the brakes, even as it sought Saudi financial assistance for Egypt and Tunisia. It actively sought Saudi support for intervention in Libya, pressure on Syria, and a resolution to the festering Yemeni stalemate. It recognized the damage done to its agenda by the Saudi intervention in Bahrain and struggled to find a political path out of the devastation there. This delicate negotiation within the alliance caused considerable tension and deep confusion, and cut to the heart of regional order. In the emerging new Middle East, was the United States still on the same side as its closest regional allies?

DIRECT INTERVENTION: *BAHRAIN*

Bahrain was the first great battlefield of the counterrevolution. Launched on February 14, the tenth anniversary of Bahraini King Hamad's declaration of reformist National Action Charter, for the most part the protest movement demanded reform rather than revolution. In doing so, it built on more than a decade of campaigns for human rights and democratic change, and drew on robust activist networks that had evolved through the years. Bahrain had long had one of the most active online communities in the Arab world, and the most active and visible democracy and human rights movements in the Gulf. Its intermittent protests and vibrant civil society had created a generation of experienced, savvy activists.

The Bahraini monarchy might have been willing to entertain political concessions, given its past reform initiatives. But by the fall of 2010, the regime had become increasingly intolerant, arresting bloggers and

journalists and various activists on trumped-up and widely disbelieved
charges of conspiring with Iran. Nevertheless, the al-Wefaq society entered
October elections to the relatively powerless parliament and won eighteen
of forty seats. Despite the advance warning on Facebook, the king declined
to attempt any preemptive reforms, and the security forces seemed caught
off guard by the size and energy of the actual demonstrations.

The #feb14 movement included a wide range of political groupings
as well as many of the newly energized activist youth so familiar from
the rest of the region. Their initial protests began joyfully, but were then
met with shockingly harsh force. The regime's initial responses against
protests began the violence-mobilization spiral so typical of most Arab
cases. Bahraini forces cleared the Pearl Roundabout on February 14, but
this only enraged the activists and galvanized much of the population.
The troops withdrew after the first day, but then found that Bahraini citizens, shocked by the seemingly indiscriminate use of force, began to join
the protests. This repeated a key moment in Egypt, when the activist core
was joined by ordinary citizens to transform a typical protest episode
into a potentially revolutionary moment. By March, according to some
estimates, more than half the population had come into the streets.

The Bahraini regime wavered between confrontation and accom-
modation. At one point, the monarchy tried to buy off protests with
financial subsidies and gifts. As the protests escalated, moderate groups
within the regime headed by the crown prince pushed to strike a deal
with the opposition on serious political reforms—a path firmly resisted
by the conservative, long-serving prime minister and his backers in
Riyadh. The crown prince met secretly with al-Wefaq and a half-dozen
other legal opposition groups, and seemed ready to organize some sort
of national dialogue and move Bahrain past the crisis. The sketches of a
pact allowing transition toward constitutional monarchy, which political
scientists had long identified as the best way to move from authoritarian
rule to democracy, began to emerge. Both sides had credibility problems:
the crown prince bargained beneath the shadow of decades of broken
promises, while al-Wefaq and its partners could not guarantee that the
wider protest movement would be satisfied by what they negotiated.
As the momentum grew, their political demands begin to escalate. The
United States quietly worked to shepherd the deal to fruition, with

Assistant Secretary of State Jeffrey Feltman traveling to Manama in mid-March expecting to seal the deal by backing it against conservative opponents within the regime and guaranteeing its implementation to cautious opposition leaders.

But then it all fell apart. Hardliners in the regime, centered around Prime Minister Khalifa and backed by the Saudis, rejected outright the terms of the emerging bargain. The crown prince found himself increasingly isolated within the regime's inner circles. Meanwhile, radical voices in the decentralized opposition movement, including the al-Haq movement that had long fought with al-Wefaq for leadership in the Shi'a dissident community, gave the hardliners the excuse they needed by escalating demands beyond what any compromise could bear.

The radicals on each side fed on each other to prevent the achievement of an eminently possible agreement on serious political reforms. Angry shouts demanding that not only the hated prime minister but the king must go only fueled the determination in the palace to shut down all the demonstrations. As sectarian rhetoric increased, many disenchanted Sunni participants in the uprising as well as more moderate Shi'a quietly left the streets. Al-Haq and other more radical protestors pushed the limits, planning a march on the royal palace itself and calling for the overthrow of the monarchy. Even if they did not speak for the broad mainstream of the protest movement, their actions fueled the monarchy's suspicions, while also offering it useful fodder for its propaganda campaign designed to tarnish the entire protest movement.

No one can know what the Bahraini regime and opposition might have achieved on their own. But it was soon clear to all that Saudi Arabia had decided to draw a line against the spread of upheaval into the Gulf. It torpedoed the attempted political bargain between moderates in the al-Khalifa regime and the organized opposition in favor of a draconian, scorched-field assault on all independent political life. On March 14, Saudi tanks rolled in to enforce the hard-line policy at the invitation of the Bahraini regime, invoking the GCC mutual defense pact for the first time in thirty years. The Saudi forces backed up the Bahraini police and military as they destroyed the Pearl Roundabout, cleared the streets, and established martial law over the entire island.

After clearing the streets, the Bahraini regime began a comprehensive campaign of repression and intimidation that collectively punished almost the entire Shi'a majority.[5] The extent of this repressive campaign was truly shocking, even by Arab standards. Protest leaders were hunted down and arrested, and many were killed. A nasty sectarianism swamped the island. The independent organization Human Rights Watch dubbed it "an unrelenting official campaign of punitive retribution against Bahrainis who participated in or otherwise supported the protests."[6] Thousands were fired from government jobs. Many more were arrested, tortured, and harassed. The campaign touched almost every sector: the universities, the civil service, labor organizations, professional associations, and schools. Security forces targeted hospitals, set up checkpoints across the island, and fiercely punished anyone even tangentially involved with the protest movements. Newspapers, blogs, and any form of independent media suffered intense pressure. Dozens of opposition activists were killed and many more wounded or harassed.

The sectarian crackdown shocked even hardened observers of Bahraini and Gulf politics. To see doctors convicted and imprisoned for treating wounded protestors, students and faculty dismissed from universities for the vaguest of associations with the protest movement, or indiscriminate arrests of suspected activists was to despair of the country's future. Even if the crackdown preserved the throne in the short term, how would such depravations be forgotten any time soon? Most likely, the short-term stability had been purchased at the cost of international opprobrium and decades of domestic instability. But for a regime that perceived an existential threat, such a price seemed worth paying.

The crackdown was not done by force alone. Instead, Bahrain pioneered the full-spectrum ideological and media counteroffensives that would come to characterize other arenas in the coming months. With the ample assistance of the Saudi-backed Arab media, as well as American public relations firms, the hardliners raised the specter of Iranian intervention to justify their brutal crackdown and muddied the waters with an endless flow of dubious information. They accused the democracy protestors of being Iranian agents, offering a catalog of alleged abuses and connections to turn the struggle for power sharing into a sinister campaign of subversion. They swarmed social media sites such

as Twitter and Facebook with pro-regime arguments and helped to pub-
lish pro-regime op-eds in newspapers around the world.

The accusations outraged the engaged Arab public, which viewed
Bahrain's protests through the lens of their master-narrative of peoples
and regimes and not through a sectarian lens. But the accusations
worked in other arenas, including in the Bahraini Sunni population and
key sectors of the Gulf and farther afield. It was too easy for outsiders to
miss the extent to which Bahraini Sunnis really did believe the worst of
their Shi'a counterparts and really did fear Iranian designs on the kingdom. The sharply sectarian turn, as the Sunni dynasty painted a Shi'a
and Iranian face on its domestic opponents, marked the first point in the
Arab uprisings when the cold war of the 2000s fully imposed itself upon
its successor. The alleged Iranian role became the justification for a massive crackdown on the entire Shi'a population and a vehicle for rallying
the Sunni population's support, while intimidating moderate Shi'a who
had no love for Iran but hoped for more democracy and respect for
human rights. It also helped to revive an angry sectarianism that spread
to Lebanon and Iraq and beyond, and gave Iran a temporary and largely
undeserved cameo appearance in a season of Arab protests that had
largely left it behind.

Bahrain experienced the sharpest division between the online and
the televised Arab public spheres. No major Arab television station covered the Bahrain crackdown closely. Al-Jazeera, to the shock and outrage
of the activist public, followed the Qatari government and the rest of
the GCC in siding with the al-Khalifa monarchy. It declined to cover the
spiraling catastrophe in any detail. When I pushed its journalists on
the coverage in March, they grew rather red-faced, arguing that Yemen
and Libya had greater importance at the moment than a small Gulf country. Al-Jazeera English did slightly better, managing to air a controversial
documentary on the protestors in August, but it was aimed more at
international audiences than at the Arab public. Al-Arabiya and the rest
of the Saudi media of course followed suit, highlighting the alleged Iranian threat to the Bahraini monarchy, while barely mentioning the
massive crackdown. And Bahrain transformed its own media, including
the previously independent *al-Wasat* newspaper, into full-throated propaganda outlets advancing its version of events.

When the protests were at their peak, Bahrain became a top priority of the online Arab activist community. On Twitter and Facebook, people clearly viewed Bahrain as part of the broader Arab uprising and its suppression comparable to that of any other despised regime. Regional activists castigated al-Jazeera and the United States for failing to deal seriously with Bahrain.

But now social media itself became the battleground. Supporters of the Bahraini monarchy fought back against the activist narrative in cyberspace, with a regime-sponsored campaign swarming Twitter, Facebook, and Internet comment threads. This campaign changed few minds, but did serve to pollute the formerly pure stream of solidarity. Posting about Bahrain, or retweeting leading activists, would invite dozens or even hundreds of hostile, abusive responses. Over time, more and more people began to simply ignore Bahrain in order to avoid the stream of invective that would invariably follow.

The United States kept its head down during the repression as well, a decision that badly crippled its credibility across the entire region. The U.S. Fifth Fleet, stationed in Bahrain, loomed large over an administration that saw the containment of Iranian power and influence as a core strategic priority. The Saudis made extremely clear to the Obama administration that it considered Bahrain to be within its sphere of influence. The administration clearly calculated that it had little choice but to defer to the Saudis and accept the fait accompli. It understood the costs, but deemed them worth paying for the broader panoply of regional interests. Still, when Obama gave his May 19 speech on the regional transformations, his advisers pushed hard for a pointed mention of Bahrain, knowing that failing to do so would compromise everything else he might say. But the mild reproach he mustered failed to appease an angry Arab public that saw Bahrain as the graveyard of American credibility in the Arab uprisings.

The scorched-earth campaign in Bahrain produced one of the only clear-cut victories for repression in the course of the Arab uprisings. It came at a steep price. Efforts to heal the wounds went nowhere. A National Dialogue arranged in June quickly collapsed; it was difficult to have a meaningful political dialogue with most of the opposition in prison. An investigation headed by the respected jurist Dr. Cherif Bassiouni released an unexpectedly thorough and damning report documenting the regime's abuses in November, but this could not force the regime to make the necessary political changes. Al-Wefaq and other opposition parties decided quickly to boycott promised parliamentary elections. The survival of Bahrain's monarchy came at the expense of long-term societal divisions and memories that may take generations to fade.

MONARCHICAL REFORM: MOROCCO AND JORDAN

Saudi Arabia also extended its defensive interventions beyond the Gulf to include the other pro-American, conservative monarchies. Jordan and Morocco offered limited reforms in an attempt to placate the moderate wings of their opposition movements. King Mohammed VI of Morocco went further, putting significant constitutional changes to a snap referendum that disrupted the opposition and bought both domestic and international breathing space. Jordan's King Abdullah had less to offer his restive population, but for many months continued to navigate the turbulent space using traditional levers of control.

MOROCCO

Morocco's #feb20 movement had gained considerable traction after initially struggling to attract support. The initially sparse crowds had grown and moved beyond the capital city. On March 9, in a televised speech, King Mohammed VI responded by appointing a committee to explore constitutional reforms and promising to give up some power and respond to legitimate complaints.

Despite this well-received speech, the protest movement continued to grow. The turnout on March 20 was possibly the largest and again passed peacefully. A terrorist attack on April 28 that killed over a dozen people at the tourist center of Marrakesh derailed the protest momentum, however, as all sectors of society joined in shock and outrage at the atrocity. The attack itself remains mysterious in its origins and motivations, but seemed to have little to do with the protest movement. But its effects were dramatic as frightened citizens rallied around the throne, and the regime's security forces took advantage of the shock to call for a return to public order in the name of security.

In the aftermath, security forces began to take a much harder line toward protestors, with increasing reports of police abuse. That tougher approach in turn began to radicalize some of the activists' demands. As one activist wrote, "the more the government uses violence to suppress demonstrations, the more the people will take to the streets to voice their dissatisfaction. We are not far from the day when young demonstrators will stop running, and instead clench their fists on the throats of those uniformed brutes and their walkie-talkie toting commanders. The odds for a peaceful transition are slim. I fear the worst is yet to come."[7]

At this point, Morocco might well have tipped in the direction of massive mobilization. But before the familiar violence-mobilization cycle could kick in, the king moved quickly with a preemptive reform initiative. At the end of May, he called for a snap referendum on a sweeping set of constitutional reforms, which maintained the core powers of the monarchy but did offer some real concessions to more representative and participatory government. The amendments passed overwhelmingly, with a disoriented opposition unable to mount any sustained campaign to vote against it. They protested in vain that the reforms left all of the important powers in the unchallenged hands of the monarchy. Most of the February 20 movement chose to boycott the parliamentary elections in November, in protest over what they saw as sham reforms. But it was soon clear that the king had deftly regained the initiative from the streets, deflected the appeals for more fundamental change, and had reframed the terms of political debate.

The Gulf media raved about the constitutional initiative, praising it as a model alternative to regime overthrow or violent insurgency. A Mauritanian columnist called the new constitution the most important event in Moroccan history after its revolution and independence.[8] The Egyptian analyst Wahid Abdel Meguid said it showed that "change is possible through gradual reform and that popular uprisings and revolutions are not the only path to democracy in the Arab world."[9] This verdict reflected the regime's narrative and the preferences of the counterrevolution, and resonated abroad with audiences conditioned to appreciate the "moderate" monarchy.

The constitutional changes fell short in fundamental ways. They were far from adequate to ensure a transition to anything resembling democracy. It was not clear that they offered a model for anyone else, though a few months later, Jordan would try.

JORDAN

Jordan's politics have long been shaped by Arab identity, and its political arena thoroughly penetrated by regional actors and political movements from Baathists and the Muslim Brotherhood to a variety of Palestinian groups. Furthermore, the high percentage of citizens of Palestinian origin has always given an outward orientation to Jordanian politics, along with a long history of transnational linkages. Finally, its young, restless population has one of the highest levels of Internet activism and entrepreneurship in the Arab world. These cosmopolitan young Jordanians, frustrated with the limits of their political system and desperate for change, offer a textbook example of the potential of the new Arab public. As described in chapter 5 they had moved early to seize that opportunity but had struggled in the face of deeply entrenched political obstacles.

For months, the Hashemite monarchy had attempted to meet societal mobilization with its usual formula of selective repression, shuffling governments, and the formation of meaningless national dialogues and reform committees. The king responded in traditional fashion by announcing a new package of subsidies and salary increases for state employees (January 20), dismissing Rifai (February 1), and appointing a number of committees to once again study ideas for reform (March 13).[10] The new government led by Prime Minister Marouf al-Bakhit demonstrated little interest in deeper reform, however, and discontent rapidly grew.

The regime responded defensively, with unusually blunt attacks on the press and on protestors. Most Jordanians believed that the regime's intelligence services were behind the frightening attacks by thugs on the March 24 protest at the interior ministry, which proved to be a turning point in blunting the momentum of this protest movement.[11] On that hashtagged day, a group of young activists tried to set up a camp outside the interior ministry along the Tahrir model of seizing symbolic public space. They were attacked by a group of thugs. One protestor was killed. The ugliness of that day shocked both sides. It galvanized public attitudes, forcing all sides to take seriously the magnitude of the challenge

that protests could pose to Jordanian stability. It also chagrined the protestors, whose carefully formulated strategies to avoid repression and
ethnic division failed to protect them.

In June, the veteran journalist Randa Habib's office was ransacked
and she was harassed. Later in the month, a group of journalists wearing
government-provided orange vests were singled out by regime thugs and
beaten while covering a demonstration.

But these attacks did little to chill the rambunctious Jordanian public
sphere. Jordan's new generation has proven to be unafraid, rejecting
the red lines that constrained their elders and willing to discuss everything publicly. Marwan Muasher, a leading liberal who had suffered a
painful political defeat over his own attempt to push reform through the
2005 National Agenda project, told me of his amazement during his
first appearance in a Hashtag Debate in July 2011. He was peppered
with questions about constitutional monarchy and mukhabarat (secret
police) abuses that even a year before would have been unthinkable in a
public Jordanian setting. He could only urge the youth not to give up on
their dreams.

As in Bahrain, the monarchy was able to turn to deeply entrenched
ethnic suspicions to divide and isolate the protest movement. The protestors went to great lengths to portray themselves as nationalists,
singing patriotic songs, waving Jordanian flags, and repeatedly quoting
the king's own words. But the young toughs who attacked them saw
them as Palestinian elitists bent on overthrowing the monarchy, bringing
together class, ethnic, and political resentments into one toxic brew. This
ethnic divide gave the regime the opportunity to shift the narrative away
from popular opposition toward intrasocietal conflicts—a risky strategy,
which many Jordanians believed helped to perpetuate and even acceler-
ate societal disintegration, but one that did work in the short term.

The protest movement subsequently spread outside Amman into the
southern towns and cities where it took on very different characteristics.
The emergence of local committees in almost every town in the south
brought a distinctly Transjordanian face to the protest movement that
the regime could not as easily dismiss. It also brought in issues of class
and distributive justice with which the middle- and upper-class Amman-
based protestors had struggled.

As protests continued, and the regional environment grew more treacherous, the Jordanian regime switched to the Moroccan model of preemptive, limited constitutional reforms. Impressed by the success of Morocco's King Mohammed VI, on June 12, King Abdullah gave a televised speech promising sweeping reforms, including—crucially— a parliamentary form of government in which the prime minister would be chosen by the elected legislature rather than appointed by the king. The reform package the king presented in mid-August offered more sweeping constitutional changes than ever before, but without touching the core of monarchical power or the scope of the security services. It proposed explicit guarantees of political and media freedoms, limited the king's ability to dissolve parliament or to rule through temporary laws, and outlawed torture. But the regime offered no referendum, as in Morocco, and no path whatsoever toward constitutional monarchy.

Reactions were tepid: "too little, too late"; "more of the same empty promises"; "ignoring the real issues such as corruption." Some activists acknowledged that the proposal might be sufficient to split the opposition and blunt protest momentum. But few saw the reforms as even coming close to their hopes. The constitutional reforms eventually passed through parliament, to little public notice and without a referendum, leaving most of the big questions unaddressed. In October, the king again replaced his prime minister, this time turning to well-respected jurist Awn al-Khasawnah and giving him a mandate to carry through the promised reforms. But yet again, the palace avoided more fundamental reforms to state institutions, the electoral law, or the economy. Protests continued to simmer, not only in cosmopolitan West Amman but increasingly throughout the tribal south and across all sectors of society.

The cynicism in the Jordanian public about such promises ran very deep by this point. Perhaps the most incisive response came from the leading Jordanian political columnist Mohammed Abu Rumman. The palace, he observed, still saw a country in which only a few hundred political elites mattered, and the rest of the population was only a problem to manage, an uneducated and emotional mob to either beat back or buy off. How, he asked, could a regime that viewed the people with such contempt and approached them with a security mentality ever seriously rebuild the broken bonds of trust? Those fundamental questions remained unaddressed by the constitutional reform package and the government reshuffle.

STALLED REVOLUTIONS

"Have the Arab movements for change failed?" asked Bilal Hassan in the Saudi pan-Arab daily *al-Sharq al-Awsat* in mid-July.[12] He argued that the movements had across the board failed to achieve their goals, even where leaders had fallen, while internal conflicts in each country grew and international interventions became a more open secret. The counter-revolutionary commentators could be forgiven their self-satisfaction. As arenas became confused and divided, the revolutionary momentum of a unified Arab public shattered. The monarchical center of the conservative axis appeared to have weathered the storm.

The stalled momentum was evident not only in the monarchies. The same sense of frustration permeated Tunisia and Egypt, the two great early success stories of the Arab uprising. Revolutionary actors in Egypt and Tunisia were reduced to fighting among themselves about whether to abandon street politics in favor of elections or to continue public mobilization.

TUNISIA

After Ben Ali fled the country, the Tunisian military took power, presiding over an unsteady process toward a democratic transition. Its first interim government, headed by the elderly Mohammed Ghannouchi (no relationship to Rached), proved unpopular. The military simultaneously had to decide how to deal with the vast membership of the old regime party, the Constitutional Democratic Rally. Protestors demanded its immediate dissolution, while others worried about the perils of inadvertently decapitating an entire state bureaucracy and political class, as had occurred in Iraq when the Ba'ath party was dissolved and its members barred from public life.

The challenge of creating a new Tunisia was steep. All Tunisian institutions, whether state or civil society, were irreparably shaped by decades of authoritarian rule. The existing political parties were either deeply compromised by their relationships with the former regime or else weakened by years of exile and repression. Civil society and the media were thoroughly compromised by the requirements of survival in Ben Ali's Tunisia. Protestors were leaderless and empowered, determined to push for radical change at a pace that alarmed the conservative military as well as the old elites. The absence of well-developed parties could have become an advantage in a democratic transition, if all groups were willing to show patience and tolerance in the process.[13] This collective agreement to seek consensus worked for some months, as a broad political front cooperated to "preserve the revolution." Over time, after the delay of the promised elections, the agreement predictably began to fray around the edges.

The most powerful and popular movement quickly turned out to be the long-banned el-Nahda Party. The rise of el-Nahda in Tunisia following Ben Ali's fall surprised even veteran observers of Islamist movements. Unlike the Egyptian Muslim Brotherhood, el-Nahda had been thoroughly crushed and its public presence erased for decades. It had no social sector to provide services, no dominant position in the religious establishment, no political offices, and no media empire. It had a small role in the revolution. And yet when the political space opened, it thrived. The long repression meant that el-Nahda had to start from scratch to reconstitute itself and did not have deep existing relationships with Tunisian youth. But that also meant the party was absolutely uncompromised by any relationship with the old hated regime and could claim an attractive mantle of principled resistance and clean hands.

El-Nahda set out to quickly rebuild itself. Its leaders had been increasingly active in Tunisian opposition circles since the mid-2000s, including convening a forum where representatives of most major political trends came together for sustained dialogues about democracy. A movement that had been largely shaped by its leaders in exile for decades began to find its feet again on the ground, even though continuing regime harassment of members, even after their prison terms ended, had prevented any rebuilding of the organization.

On March 1, el-Nahda was legalized by the new interim government. The ruling military council granted an amnesty to el-Nahda leaders, which allowed its long-exiled leader, Rached Ghannouchi, to make a dramatic return to Tunis from London after more than twenty years. When I asked him about this return, Ghannouchi admitted that he had no idea what kind of reception he would have in Tunis and said that el-Nahda had asked its followers to stay away for fear of provoking a violent incident. Nevertheless, he received a rapturous reception, sparking the astonishing rebirth of the movement across the country as well as the first fears in the international community that Islamists might win the Arab revolutions.[14] This triggered a potent national debate about the role of Islam in politics and the identity of the state.[15]

El-Nahda's core leadership immediately reached out to the tens of thousands of former activists now out of prison, many of whom were locally respected business or civic leaders. They established offices in every Tunisian province, quickly setting up sections for youth, women, social services, and politics and holding internal elections to select a new leadership. Many Tunisian critics of el-Nahda have asked about the source of its money, often pointing to foreign support; I was told that the financing came primarily from the successful former members now rejoining the cause. Whatever the case, money alone is clearly not the whole story. El-Nahda threw itself into tireless organizing and mobilization, with Ghannouchi himself visiting twenty-two of the twenty-four provinces. If el-Nahda is currently better organized with more presence at the local level than its rivals, this is due less to some natural "Islamist" appeal than to a tireless organizational campaign.

Still, by the summer of 2011, polarization between Islamists and secularists rose, with bitter complaints that el-Nahda represented part of the regional counterrevolution. Familiar warnings of Islamists hijacking a secular revolution spread widely. The poor cities and towns of the south such as Sidi Bouzid, which had sparked the revolution, continued to struggle economically and to complain of being ignored by the political elites in Tunis. With former regime figures still occupying commanding positions across the political and economic order, Tunisians were posing biting questions about whether the revolution had succeeded at all.

But Tunisia rallied. On October 1, the campaign for parliamentary elections officially kicked off, with hundreds of parties and candidates enthusiastically leaping into the electoral game. The election went almost unbelievably well. Turnout was high, with nearly 90 percent of registered voters (though still less than 50 percent of the total eligible population) casting a ballot. There were few complaints of fraud and near-universal praise for the performance of the Independent Election Commission. The Progressive Democratic Party, which had been projected to do well while running a fiercely anti-Islamist campaign, immediately accepted its defeat rather than contesting the legitimacy of the results. El-Nahda won 41 percent of the seats in the new Constituent Assembly, enough to make its victory decisive but not sufficient to rule alone. It quickly formed a coalition with two secular parties and vowed to pursue national consensus policies in the constitutional formation period. Ghannouchi issued a series of statements designed to reassure anxious Tunisians and the West, assuring them that el-Nahda would not seek to impose religious law. While much remained unresolved, including the actual writing of the constitution, Tunisia's election seemed to have brought it back from the brink and set it on the path of real change.

EGYPT

The struggle to maintain revolutionary momentum, along with complaints about the military rulers and fears of Islamist gains, was more intense in Egypt. There may have an Egyptian revolution, but the revolutionaries never took the reins of power. Instead, the SCAF acted as a caretaker, leaving the core of the old regime firmly in control without any elected parliament or president to check its power. The SCAF initially appointed a caretaker government stocked with former National Democratic Party officials and headed by Ahmed Shafik. As the SCAF dragged its heels over more serious reforms, protestors planned a massive rally for March 3 to revive the revolution—the first of many such efforts in the months to come.

This first call to remobilize shook the SCAF, which could not be certain of its ability to withstand the return of millions to the streets so soon after Mubarak's fall. Faced with a return to turmoil, the SCAF accepted Shafik's resignation and replaced him with Essam Sharaf, a figure still popular with the protestors due to his positive role during the revolution. This sequence sent a message to the activist groups that the threat of street protests still carried power and might be the only way to get the SCAF's attention. This set in motion a dynamic that would drive Egyptian politics for months, of protests both threatened and actual, matched by SCAF concessions and crackdowns.

Two weeks later, however, the activists had an unpleasant shock. The SCAF had appointed a committee headed by the widely respected jurist Tariq al-Bishri to suggest a package of constitutional amendments. It scheduled a referendum for March 17, the first opportunity for the Egyptian people to vote. It coupled those changes with an ambitious timetable for political transition that included parliamentary elections in September, presidential elections in December, and the formation of a body to draft a new constitution.

Activists divided over how to respond. Some saw real progress in the changes, which removed many of the most hated provisions in the constitution. But others wanted to hold out for a comprehensive rewriting of the constitution rather than tinker with what they saw as a fatally flawed document. Many of the liberal activists shied away from the aggressive election time line. They worried that this schedule would not give adequate time to prepare or to form new political parties, and would thus unfairly privilege existing movements such as the Muslim Brotherhood or well-known local figures or wealthy individuals. The major activist groups came together to campaign against the amendments, urging a no vote. But 77 percent of Egyptians voted yes—a sobering rejoinder to their claims of popular leadership and a vote of confidence in the increasingly vilified SCAF. While many activists complained that Egyptians hadn't really understood what they were voting for, a new narrative of a silent majority supporting the SCAF had been established that would shape the course of the subsequent political jockeying.

The activists regrouped and responded with a series of large-scale demonstrations in Tahrir and across the country. On April 1, they organized a demonstration to "save the revolution" and followed that a week later with a "Friday of Cleaning." The turnout at these protests was significant, but nothing on the order of the protests that unseated Mubarak. They succeeded in making their presence felt, however, and the SCAF responded to several of their key demands. The activists and the SCAF continued to duel over the following months. Twice, the activists managed to organize truly massive demonstrations in support of political reform and social change: the "Second Day of Anger" on May 27, and the "Friday of Determination" on July 8. These were successful because they expressed a wide popular consensus, brought in the participation of all major political forces, and won large popular support. But in general there was a clear trend of diminishing returns on popular protests, with ever smaller numbers turning up and less consensus on the demands to be pressed. The SCAF encouraged that trend with a nasty media campaign designed to tarnish the nationalist credentials of key protest groups, to emphasize an alleged popular desire for a return to normalcy, and to fan class resentments against the protest movement.

Following a relatively successful demonstration on July 8, the activist groups blundered by organizing a sit-in in Tahrir to press their demands on the SCAF. This gave the military rulers the opportunity they had been seeking. Public opinion rapidly turned against the protestors, as they disrupted traffic and their tent city inhibited local businesses. Regime-backed Egyptian media fanned the flames of frustration with the protestors. Thwarted by their failure to gain traction, a group of activists decided to force the issue by marching on the ministry of the defense to directly confront the SCAF. It turned into a fiasco as local residents in Abbassia attacked the protestors with bricks and clubs while the army stood by passively. On July 30, a massive Islamist rally had taken over Tahrir for one Friday, but with Ramadan rapidly approaching, the activists decided to leave the square. After most had left, the army swept in to forcibly expel those left behind and to clear away the remaining tents, to the cheers of local residents. Clearly, the protestors were losing the support of the masses whose participation had made the revolution a success and were floundering in their attempts to find any new, workable strategy to recover that support. In the following weeks, the activists called for "millions" to come out to protest almost every Friday, but rarely produced more than 10,000.

Meanwhile, as in Tunisia, polarization between secularist and Islamist groups rapidly rose. The Muslim Brotherhood, long the most organized and powerful opposition group, built on its advantages in the new environment. It formed a legal political party, the Freedom and Justice Party, and aggressively planned a political strategy for elections. Salafi movements that had long stayed out of politics rapidly organized into several political parties. Even the former jihadists of the Gama'a al-Islamiyya joined the democratic game. Several personalities began to campaign for president, from the estranged Muslim Brotherhood figure

Abd el-Maneim Abou el-Fotouh to the Salafi firebrand Hazem Abu Ismail. With liberal parties weak and poorly organized, fears of Islamist political power increasingly defined the Egyptian political system as much as resentment of the SCAF, which in turn led inexorably to accusations of a counterrevolutionary conspiracy between the Islamists and the SCAF. Some political parties, such as the Free Egyptians Party funded by Coptic millionaire Naguib Sawiris, openly campaigned on an anti-Islamist platform.

In spite of the widespread narrative that secular groups drove the Egyptian revolution, Islamists were well represented in the uprisings. Muslim Brotherhood youth had played a key role in holding Tahrir and keeping the protests alive during those eighteen days. Indeed, Brotherhood youth I met after the revolution were eager to explain their role in the revolution. Brotherhood leaders insisted that their decision to send thousands of tough young cadres to Tahrir is what saved the square on January 29 and February 1. Either way, they had mastered the rhetoric of democracy. Why should majorities not make laws, they asked? Why should their participation as part of Egyptian society be less legitimate than that of small secular, liberal movements? But while they contested the realm of revolutionary legitimacy, they ultimately put their bargaining chips in the ballot box. While activist groups focused on repeated protests in Tahrir, and liberal parties complained about an unfair playing field, the Brotherhood and the Salafis focused on building their outreach and preparing for elections from the first day.

The reality is that the Muslim Brotherhood faced a complex Islamist field after the revolution and could no longer simply present itself as the only clean alternative to Mubarak or as the "Islamic" choice. The Salafi group, which had defined itself in opposition to the Brotherhood's political participation, almost immediately abandoned its ideological convictions and jumped into the political realm. The Salafis had been building their own parallel society for years. They had two popular television stations, well-known personalities, and a dense network of charitable institutions. Mainstream Egyptians tended to find the Salafis more frightening than the Brotherhood. The Salafis had never bothered to perfect the art of blending into society and changing it from within. Their mode of dress, untrimmed beards for men and the *niqab* (veil covering the face) for women, marked them as alien within urban Egyptian society. The Salafis did not participate in the January 25 revolution, but quickly moved to join the new political process. Their retrograde views on gender and on liberal values raised serious concerns, even among those who had reconciled themselves to the Brotherhood's place in Egyptian democracy.

By the late summer, the counterrevolutionary conspiracy between the SCAF and its foreign supporters including the United States had become an article of faith in many Egyptian activist circles—a charge that baffled senior American officials, who saw themselves as clearly on the side of the Egyptian people. The limits of change became painfully clear. With the military ruling and no functioning civil political institutions, it was hard to point to concrete political change. But at the same time, activists terrified of Islamist power pushed against any rapid transition to democracy for fear that they would badly lose early elections. When they lost the referendum on constitutional amendments, they moved to draft a set of "supra-constitutional principles" to limit the freedom of an elected legislature, an antidemocratic move that placed the liberals in an odd place indeed.

Amid all this maneuvering, the United States found itself damned by all sides: The SCAF accused America of interfering in its domestic affairs with its democratic transition assistance, the Islamists viewed the U.S. as profoundly hostile to their legitimate political participation, and the activists with whom President Obama had sought alignment were convinced that the U.S. had sided with the counterrevolution. The protests that began after the Israeli killing of six Egyptian soldiers in the Sinai and then expanded on September 9 to the sacking of the Israeli Embassy tied the United States to its Israeli ally in the most vivid possible way, washing away months of efforts to focus instead on the shared goal of building Egyptian democracy.

But Egypt pushed ahead toward elections, nonetheless. The elections proved deeply controversial, with many liberals and secularists complaining that they would only advantage Islamists and former regime members. The absurdly complicated election law, clear institutional deficiencies, and the short time for parties to prepare all generated great uncertainty.

A week before the scheduled start to Egypt's Parliamentary elections, all hell broke loose. After a massive, disciplined demonstration in Tahrir led primarily by the Muslim Brotherhood broke up on November 18, a small group of protestors attempted a sit-in. Regime security forces moved in to forcibly expel them but found themselves locked in an epic battle. Activists rushed back to Tahrir, and over the next few days more than forty civilians were killed and thousands wounded. On November 25, just days before the elections, massive numbers of citizens poured back into Tahrir to protest the violence.

A political whirlwind followed. Many in Tahrir, along with the United States and France, pushed the SCAF to quickly cede power to an interim civilian government with real executive power. Amidst the chaos in Tahrir and running battles in the streets of Alexandria, many called for the elections to be postponed. The SCAF dismissed the government of Prime Minister Essam Sharaf, and after entertaining a variety of possible replacements settled on the 78-year-old Kamal el-Ganzoury. The SCAF also agreed to move the date of the presidential elections and the transfer to civilian rule up to June 2012, after previously suggesting that the transition would extend well into 2013.

But the SCAF refused to make broader concessions. It insisted that the elections go forward on schedule, and on November 28 the six-week process began on time, to high turnout and great popular enthusiasm. The calls for boycott in Tahrir did not resonate with a public eager to vote. Only days after a second revolution seemed inevitable, the gap between the protestors in Tahrir and the broader Egyptian public suddenly seemed wider than ever.

But the deeper issues all remained unresolved. Islamists appeared poised to sweep the elections, posing difficult choices for both themselves and others about what would follow. The constitution remained unwritten, with no clear demarcation of the powers of the new parliament. And the violence and political chaos of the preceding ten days demonstrated all too clearly the dangers of the failure to resolve these core political issues.

Still, as bad as things got at times, Egypt was a relative success story compared to other Arab countries.

THE FORGOTTEN REVOLUTION: *YEMEN*

Amid all the counterrevolution and stalled revolutions, Yemen went along its own path. Protests continued to escalate through February and March, with massive crowds moving against fierce repression. The Saleh regime slalomed between offers of political concessions and harsh crackdowns. After long decades of deftly maneuvering Yemen's political terrain, Saleh seemed unable to find the right response to this challenge from below. What had begun as a youth movement, organized by a new generation of activists, was rapidly consolidating into a nationwide political coalition bringing together almost every sector of Yemeni political society. Southern secessionists agreed to drop their demand for independence and join the movement. The Huthi movement, a northern armed insurrection that had grown in recent years over the regime's heavy-handed treatment, threw its support behind the protests. Major tribes, civil society organizations, political parties, and key Islamist groups all moved toward the opposition.

Saleh's offers of political reforms failed to derail this momentum. In part, he simply faced overwhelming problems of credibility. Yemenis could not forget similar gambits over the years, including his broken promise not to seek reelection in 2006. Protestors knew well that his proposed reforms would be easily dropped or diluted once they went home. One opinion survey in late February 2011 found a 15 percent drop in confidence in the government since September of the previous year, and over 70 percent described the government as corrupt.[16] More broadly, as in many other Arab cases, the decentralized nature of the movement made it very difficult for the protestors to agree on any specific demands or strategy besides the single unifying "Saleh must go."

On March 18, Yemen's regime made a key miscalculation by resorting to excessive violence against peaceful protestors. Snipers opened fire on protestors outside Sanaa University, killing at least fifty, in the single bloodiest day of the two-month-long movement. As would happen in Libya and Syria, this violence backfired and galvanized support for the protestors rather than deterring or intimidating them. The furious response brought over 150,000 into the streets in the largest demonstration yet.

The escalation came at a pivotal time in the Arab uprising, only days after the Bahraini counterrevolution and at the same time the bombing began in Libya. Al-Jazeera broke away from its wall-to-wall coverage of Libya to air gory footage of the brutalized protestors, focusing regional and international attention on Yemen.

The regime's collapse seemed imminent. In response to the violence and escalating protests, Major General Ali Muhsin defected, declaring his support "for the peaceful revolution of the young people and their demands." His move was followed by a cascade of resignations and defections by government officials, party members, and even military officers. The momentum seemed irreversible, and Saleh seemed to be on the brink of joining Mubarak and Ben Ali. The Arab public sphere focused on the unfolding events in Yemen, eagerly anticipating a new jolt of momentum for the Arab uprising.

Saleh responded by blaming "armed elements" for the bloodshed and declared a national state of emergency and curfew. The United States issued a rare condemnation of its ally, calling on Saleh "to adhere to his public pledge to allow demonstrations to take place peacefully." On March 22, Saleh warned of civil war if the protests continued, a threat that he risked turning into a self-fulfilling prophecy. Violence escalated across the country, and as the body count grew, protestors and outside observers alike feared that Yemen was going down Libya's path of total civil war. On April 3, the New York Times reported that the Obama administration had quietly shifted its stance on Saleh and now hoped to ease him from power.[17] On April 22, millions came out to join "Last Chance Friday" in an attempt to force Saleh over the brink.

But Yemen instead devolved into a seemingly perpetual stalemate, in which Saleh could no longer rule but nobody could take his place. Saleh and his family clung to power in the face of a near-total loss of both domestic and international support. As a grinding, sometimes bloody status quo took hold, Saudi Arabia and the GCC put forward a plan for a political transition that would have given Saleh immunity and set in motion a transition to a new elected government. The initiative bogged down in arguments about the details and skepticism among the revolutionary public.

Then on June 3, rumors spread like wildfire through the Arab public of an assassination attempt on Saleh. He had in fact been badly wounded by a bomb and had left the country for urgent treatment in Saudi Arabia. The assassination attempt shocked the country and seemed to suddenly open up a horizon for change. There has yet been no claim of responsibility or explanation of how the bomber penetrated Saleh's personal security forces.

But even with the possibility that Saleh was out of the country permanently, no progress could be made. The remnants of the regime held fast. Protestors vainly attempted to put pressure through peaceful demonstrations. The Joint Meeting Parties (JMP) began to fracture, with internal contradictions becoming weightier. When momentum stalled, the protest movement began to flounder. An uneasy tension emerged between the earlier youth movement and the later "opportunistic opposition."[18] As one activist wistfully tweeted, "I wish JMP, Islah, Alahmar's & AliMuhsin would all go away so #Yemen's youth would be free from their influence to revolt & rebuild Yemen."[19]

By late spring, Yemen had largely been forgotten. No major Arab country dropped so completely off the international and regional radar as did Yemen. With no resolution in sight, the situation seemed too hopeless, too marginal, and too distant from the core of the region's concerns to capture much attention. The humanitarian situation deteriorated along with the economy, politics remained hopelessly paralyzed, and authority devolved from the capital to local governments and nonstate networks.

The U.S. was largely paralyzed in the face of Yemen's political turmoil. Its primary interest remained al-Qaeda in the Arabian Peninsula, and it seemed to care most about continued counterterrorism cooperation and permission to carry on with drone strikes. While the U.S. periodically called for a political transition, including a strong statement at the United Nations by Ambassador Susan Rice on August 3, Washington generally deferred to Saudi Arabia and the GCC on the plan for political transition. The failure to push for a meaningful political transition in Yemen would likely be seen as a major mistake.

That mistake came home to roost at the end of September, when Saleh suddenly returned to Yemen from Saudi Arabia amid intensified fighting. Months of stagnation and stalemate had undermined the cohesion of the opposition and inexorably shifted the struggle from peaceful protests against the regime to dueling armed camps. In November, Saleh finally signed the GCC transition plan and promised to step down, but even this only set the stage for ongoing machinations. What could have been a great success story driven by an almost unbelievable resilient protest movement risked turning into a dreary failure, with or without Saleh.

THE FRAGMENTED ARAB PUBLIC
AND THE STALLED REVOLUTIONS

If the delirious spread of protests in February demonstrated the power of diffusion effects in the new Arab public sphere, the counterrevolution's successes and the bloody protests in Yemen, Bahrain, Libya, and Syria spread a darker mood through the Arab public. By April, the delirious spirit of inevitable triumph had long faded. Watching battles and fire-fights rage in Libya on al-Jazeera had a very different effect than watching the surging, exuberant crowds of Egypt and Tunisia. Arab citizens who had identified with those seemingly unstoppable movements now found themselves identifying with people being repressed, massacred, or left in limbo. To their immense credit, few lost hope. But even fewer seemed to know how to break these hurting stalemates.

As the momentum slowed and the agendas fragmented, concerns closer to home began to drive out the former sense of a unified struggle. Egyptian activists, for instance, had difficulty rallying for the Syrian revolution at a time when their own struggles with the SCAF, Islamists, and each other consumed them.[20] The relentless Bahraini pro-regime propaganda made online discussion of that kingdom difficult and did spread a sectarian reading of the events, sapping the unity of purpose that had characterized the earlier phase. Yemen dropped off the map much of the time, lost in a confusing stalemate. Events in Libya ground on for months, the initial enthusiasm of the international intervention sapped.

Old political divisions also reemerged, breaking the façade of revolutionary unity. Transjordanians viewed protestors of Palestinian origin suspiciously. A qualitatively new Sunni-Shi'a sectarianism infected Kuwaiti politics.[21] Leftists suspicious of the Muslim Brotherhood shied from the Syrian and Libyan revolutions when they perceived a leading Islamist presence in their leaderships.[22] Regimes fueled xenophobic suspicions by alleging foreign funding for protests or by mobilizing sectarian suspicions.

A darker period had begun. The challenged Arab regimes proved that they would not easily surrender their power even in the face of this newly empowered Arab public. Real change would come with an ever bloodier price tag. And now the question of international intervention, beginning in Libya and soon spreading to the Syrian struggle, distracted attention from the internal struggles for democracy. Could the international community play a positive role in breaking these stalemates, or would its interventions turn out to make the problems worse?

CHAPTER 7

INTERVENTION AND CIVIL WAR

B Y LATE SPRING, the fervent hopes for a rapid, peaceful, and irresistible wave of regionwide change inspired by the Egypt's and Tunisia's uprisings had thus long since faded. As most regimes recovered their footing and revolutionaries faltered, the old balance of power seemed to reassert itself. But the unprecedented NATO intervention in Libya to protect its rebels and ultimately to assist in the overthrow of Colonel Moammar Qaddafi introduced something dramatically new into the equation of regional politics.

Libya and Syria shifted the lens away from peaceful protests to violent civil war and international intervention. In these two battlefields, peaceful protest quickly gave way to brutal force, and the question of international intervention imposed itself on the dynamics of domestic challenge. Here, the Arab uprisings most thoroughly crashed into regional and international power politics. The new ideas of peaceful protest and democratic change gave way to the familiar world of great power politics, covert interventions and naked violence.

The countries most in play, such as Syria, Libya, and Yemen, were locked in the grip of stalemate and civil war, with the stakes high and the body count higher. An odd stasis spread through the region, even as battles raged furiously on the ground. Libya degenerated into a frustrating battle for territory between two evenly matched forces, while the Benghazi-based National Transitional Council struggled to maintain political cohesion as it gained more and more international recognition. Bahrain's once-ebullient protestors suffered outrageous abuses with little international protest. Yemen's struggle began to resemble a zombie

movie, as protestors and the old regime battled on after the badly injured
Ali Abdullah Saleh fled to Saudi Arabia for urgent medical treatment.
Syria's cautious protests rapidly turned into a bloodbath. For the Arab
public, this was a dispiriting time.

The argument for nonviolence lost traction during this period,
though many still saw its moral and strategic logic. Some opposition
forces concluded that such deeply entrenched security states, willing to
use any level of brutal force against their own people, simply could not
be overturned through peaceful protest.[1] Who could reason with leaders
like Saleh, Assad, or Qaddafi, who clung to power and refused all exit
options?[2] Faced with such odds, more Arabs were willing to publicly
argue that Western military intervention and external pressure could tip
the balance. This was a rather shocking proposition, given prevailing
suspicions of and hostility toward American foreign policy across the
new Arab public sphere. As Qaddafi's troops closed in on Benghazi in
March, the abstract questions of a Western role in the unfolding uprisings became painfully real. Would Arab publics prefer to be ideologically
pure at the cost of defeat, or would they align themselves with Western
power to be freed of brutal rulers bent on revenge? What should Arab
protest movements realistically expect from the West, and what price
might their external saviors extract in exchange for their intervention?

The answers were not obvious, and they triggered an important
public debate that spanned the Arab public sphere. Less than a decade
had passed since the trauma of the Arab public's impotence before the
American invasion of Iraq. The ghost of the Iraqi opposition in exile,
particularly Ahmed Chalabi and his Iraqi National Congress (INC),
loomed large over any efforts to organize opposition from abroad. Arab
publics tended to view with deep suspicion any opposition leaders in
exile willing to deal with the West. They remembered all too well the
suave but deeply dishonest posturing of the exiled Iraqi opposition, and
many held them accountable for the horrors of civil war and insurgency
inflicted on Iraq in the years following the invasion. And, of course,
resentments of Western support for Israel, alleged double standards and
pursuit of Arab oil, decades of support for the worst Arab dictators,
and the rampant abuses of the global war on terror ran deep. The shift
from George W. Bush to Barack Obama may have pulled some of the

poison from the wounds, making appeals for Western help more acceptable, but those deep historical forces had in no way faded.

Anyone who remembered the intensity and passion of those public debates about America's invasion of Iraq, which had dominated Arab (and international) discourse for half a decade, therefore had to be baffled by the sudden reversal in the spring of 2011. But, in fact, both the Arab regimes and much of the new Arab public forcefully called for an international intervention to save the Libyan uprising. In this new emerging narrative, protestors were the good guys and regimes the bad guys, with the U.S. and NATO potentially useful allies rather than the central protagonists in some grand clash of civilizations. The NATO intervention, when it finally came, was expressly invited by the Arab League, with UN Security Council authorization. And while there was certainly a vocal group that continued to oppose any military intervention and a great deal of muttering about NATO imperialism, a remarkable Arab consensus emerged in favor of action by the West.

The support for Western intervention spanned both the official Arab order and the new Arab public, another rarity in the polarized era of the Arab uprisings, where regimes and the people were almost always adversaries rather than allies. When Gaddafi's forces began massacring protestors in Libya, a consensus formed quickly across almost every part of the usually divided Arab political spectrum. Certainly there were prominent Arab voices, echoing those on the Western Left, who warned against Western military adventures, imperialism, and Israeli conspiracies. But at least initially, the majority of the Arab public sphere welcomed and demanded the action. In Syria, tentative calls for Western action only came as Assad's brutality became unbearable, and even then most Syrian opposition leaders firmly rejected any military action. Nevertheless, rarely in modern Arab history had there been such a unified demand from both the regimes and public opinion, from al-Jazeera and the Saudi media, for the West to use its military power inside the region.

This consensus is worth contemplating. For the first time in the history of the modern Middle East, Arab regimes and peoples alike had rejected the claim that state sovereignty should shield Arab leaders who commit atrocities against their own people. The appeal for international intervention in Libya, the GCC's initiative in Yemen, and even the Arab

League's belated appeal for a cease-fire in Syria all appealed to a radically new norm that regimes would lose their legitimacy when they crossed a threshold of domestic violence. This was obviously partial—Bahrain, for instance, was not included in the new concern. And it was only unevenly enforced—condemnation did little to protect Syrian or Yemeni victims of state violence.

Nonetheless, the significance of this new regional acceptance of the global "Responsibility to Protect" norms represented an almost unbelievable change. In 1970, the Arab states did nothing to protect Jordan's slaughter of Palestinian fighters. In 1982, Arabs did nothing as Syria slaughtered its domestic challengers in Hama. In 1987–1989, Arabs did nothing as Iraq slaughtered its Kurdish citizens. In 2002–2003, Arabs almost universally rejected the humanitarian argument for invading Iraq to overthrow Saddam Hussein as a nakedly transparent excuse for self-interested military action.

But in 2011, the debate was entirely different. The Arab publics who demanded a stop to the killing and called for international interventions appealed to global norms and rejected all appeals to Arab exceptionalism or mutterings of foreign conspiracy. The Arab leaders who signed on to the Libya intervention and tentatively challenged Syrian and Yemeni brutality knew perfectly well that it could just as easily be them under this new microscope. They may not have meant the Libya intervention to create a precedent, but it did all the same. The idea that their legitimacy rested upon respecting such global norms was now enshrined not only in public debates but in official Arab League declarations.

From that point forward, the possibility of UN sanctions or International Criminal Court referrals or even foreign military interventions has entered into every discussion as a legitimate and plausible possibility. Some American officials involved, such as journalist turned White House official Samantha Power and America's UN Ambassador Susan Rice, had been deeply affected by the international community's failure to prevent the genocide in Rwanda in 1994. They likely saw Libya and the extension of its precedent throughout the region, under a clear UN Security Council mandate, as a historically unique opportunity to establish an effective global norm against impunity in killing civilians. Critics of humanitarian intervention, who often saw the "Responsibility to Protect" as an open-ended invitation for foreign meddling that caused more problems than it solved, denounced the intervention for the same reason.

The intervention in Libya, led by the United States, France, the U.K., and NATO worked, though not as quickly as many had hoped. The no-fly zone and bombing of Qaddafi's positions saved the rebels in Benghazi from a near-certain massacre. NATO warplanes had now entered into what had previously been an indigenous Arab uprising. Qaddafi did not back down, and airpower alone could not immediately tip the balance. Libya soon degenerated into a difficult, violent stalemate—a warning to others in the region, an invitation to would-be rebels, but also an obstacle to Western interventions elsewhere. It took long, tense months before Qaddafi finally lost Tripoli. But in the end, none of the worst-case predictions made by skeptics materialized. The reports of massive civilian casualties inflicted by NATO were wildly exaggerated. There was no stalemate, no partition of the country, no collapse of the opposition into bickering tribes. Certainly there would be many difficulties to come in reconstructing Libya, but the intervention itself accomplished its goals.

The Libya intervention clearly affected the dynamics of the unfolding struggle in Syria. The Syrian protests began to gain momentum almost immediately on the heels of the NATO intervention in Libya. That intervention had clearly emboldened protestors, giving them hope that Assad might restrain from the worst violence, fearing international action. Online activists out of Syria openly sought to emulate the Libyan model, highlighting regime atrocities and placing their struggle within the unfolding, collective, hashtagged Arab narrative, even if conditions on the ground did not quite fit the model. It also likely encouraged Assad to crack down hard, for fear of exactly such momentum building. But if Assad unleashed violence against protestors, some believed, he would actually be helping activists abroad to attract meaningful international intervention. This is not to say that the almost unbelievably courageous protestors on the ground brought the violence upon themselves intentionally, as some have claimed, but rather that the integration of the Arab public sphere was so tight by then that lessons could not help but be drawn from one country and applied to the next.

The uprising in Syria, whatever its outcome, had strategic ramifications far beyond those of any other major theaters, even Egypt. It shattered one of the contending narratives of the Arab uprisings, which was that they targeted pro-American regimes. Until Syria fell into turmoil, the main challenges had been directed at the pro-Western regimes that dominated the regional order. Syria's uprising turned the tables on Iran and the "resistance" axis, transforming the geopolitical significance of the uprisings. While Iran had little success in exploiting the changes, it could at least claim that blows against the axis of moderates were, by default, gains for the resistance. But the new Arab divide between revolution and counterrevolution rejected such binary logic. Much of the Arab public now refused to accept brutality against citizens even by the forces of resistance. Standing up to Israel and America could no longer trump internal repression in the new regional calculus.

The Syrian uprising therefore came to be seen through the lens of regional power politics: a struggle among Iran, Saudi Arabia, and Turkey for the center of the Arab world.[3] Syria had always been the "beating heart" of the Arab nation, at least in its own mind and propaganda, and its geographic centrality ensured that any dramatic changes there would resonate broadly. It remained technically at war with Israel, it continued to play a role in Lebanese politics and served as the bridge between Iran and Hezbollah, and its long borders with Iraq and Turkey allowed its conflicts to easily spill over into its large neighbors. Where Libya remained on the margins, a matter of general Arab consensus but of little core strategic significance, Syria's fate touched on both of the great cold wars of this period—the one between Iran and the Sunni Arab states, and the one between the Arab public and its rulers. The outcome, whether the flight of the Assad regime or its survival as a wounded and shunned pariah, would profoundly weaken Iran's regional position.

But, ironically, as important as Syria was to American interests in the region, the U.S. had few policy instruments to bring to bear on its outcome. Years of sanctions had left it with few economic levers. It had only recently returned an ambassador to Damascus, against great domestic opposition from conservative critics of the Syrian regime—though Ambassador Robert Ford would become one of the most effective American advocates for the Syrian opposition during his brief tenure. Everyone, including the Syrian regime and its adversaries alike, understood that the U.S. had no interest in intervening militarily. Indeed, the U.S. repeatedly warned Syrian protestors publicly that it should not count on international intervention. While hawks fumed at Obama's alleged missed opportunities in Syria, the truth was that the most America could realistically do was to offer moral and rhetorical support, help build regional consensus against Assad, and shepherd international sanctions through the United Nations.

Whatever the result of the Syrian and Libyan struggles, they fundamentally shifted the nature of the Arab uprisings. Questions of international intervention took priority over the agency of Arab citizens. Peaceful protest fell before severe state violence, forcing some to take up arms and others to cling desperately to a peaceful protest strategy against all provocations. At the same time, both Syria and Libya proved that direct violence against protestors backfired. In Libya, Qaddafi's brutal march to Benghazi consolidated unprecedented international support for intervention. In Syria, Assad's casual cruelty triggered a cascade of defections that would not likely have otherwise materialized. American and international efforts to build a global norm against impunity for such violence, through the United Nations and the International Criminal Court, could ultimately be one of the most durable achievements of the Arab uprisings.

LIBYA

Libya emerged from nowhere to jar the Arab uprisings into a radically new direction. Its protests began in familiar ways. The #feb17 hashtag marked an enthusiastic, peaceful protest in Benghazi calling for democratic reforms. The language of the protestors, their rhetorical style, their youthful composition, and their grievances all fit perfectly within the unfolding narrative. But Qaddafi was the first of the Arab leaders to immediately unleash the full brutality of his military apparatus against the protest movement. The regime attempted to cut off information about the repression, jamming al-Jazeera's satellite feed and blocking Facebook and other sites. Its own media verged on the surreal, broadcasting delusional speeches by Qaddafi and regime officials alongside bizarrely disconnected news. But the unblinking al-Jazeera cameras, fed a constant stream of videos from inside Libya posted online or sent to Doha through its "Sharek" video-sharing portal, captured the horrific bloodshed of something that was suddenly entirely different.

The protests rapidly spread in spite of Qaddafi's troops' brutality. Indeed, most likely they spread so rapidly precisely because of the violence, in a classic example of the violence-mobilization dynamic where brutality that touches upon ever more families and tribes pushes the previously uncommitted parts of the public off the fence. Hundreds of people were killed in the first week by regime military forces. Those deaths, publicized on the Internet and on al-Jazeera, shocked even those who expected the worst of Qaddafi's regime. Each death touched on a family or tribe that demanded vengeance, shut down the possibility of a negotiated resolution, and increased international condemnation. The stakes of the escalating violence grew even higher as the extent of Qaddafi's violent intent became evident. His was not the selective repression of the typical Arab autocrat determined to make an example of some challengers. Qaddafi's rhetoric and the behavior of his troops signaled an eagerness to do far more. As he threatened to hunt down traitors house to house, he warned that "there will be no mercy. Our troops will be coming to Benghazi tonight." It is impossible to know whether Qaddafi would have actually followed through on his threats, as critics of the intervention often argue. But few Libyans or those watching abroad doubted his intentions.

The timing of the Libyan bloodbath and its interpretation in the Arab public sphere are absolutely essential for understanding what followed. Qaddafi's brutality came at the highest point of the integration of the Arab public. Flush with victory after the fall of Ben Ali and Mubarak, the Arab public largely identified with the Libyan protestors as another chapter in the same unfolding story. Partly for that reason, the bloodshed was not seen as a calamity afflicting distant strangers. Arabs everywhere saw it as an attack on themselves, and immediately sensed that the outcome in Libya would have direct and major implications for their own struggles: Should Qaddafi's cruelty succeed in maintaining his hold on power, other Arab leaders would be emboldened to follow his example. If he failed, it would encourage other Arab protest movements to rise up.

On February 19, Saif al-Islam, Qaddafi's son, gave a particularly bizarre interview on Libyan state television that became a focal point for the emerging narrative. Saif's speech blamed Facebook, Arab satellite television channels spreading lies and misinformation, foreign merce- naries, Islamists, and drug-laced Nescafé for the violence. Like most Arab leaders, he warned that Libyans should not see themselves as Tunisians or Egyptians and that the situations were totally different. His appear- ance was roundly mocked throughout the new Arab public sphere. The uncompromising rhetoric also quickly crushed any hopes for a political solution to the growing conflict. The harsh line taken by Saif al-Islam, whom the West had held as the "good" Qaddafi and architect of a reformed and globalizing Libya, shattered hope for a transition within the family.

Following his speech, massive protests immediately broke out across Libya. These were met with extreme violence. Almost immediately, the Libyan protest movement turned into an alarmingly bloody civil war, dramatically changing the media narrative. On al-Jazeera and the social media networks, the war was suddenly very real, graphic, and bloody. This coverage resembled Iraq in 2003 or Lebanon in 2006 more than it did the reports from Tahrir Square. Moreover, with few journalists on the ground in Libya, it was difficult for anyone to make sense of frightening reports of military aircraft bombing and strafing protestors, of tanks deployed against unarmed civilians, of groups of thugs set free to rape and pillage protesting neighborhoods. Libya's Ambassador to the United Nations Abd al-Rahman Shalgam resigned in protest over the reported killing of civilians, delivering a highly emotional—and influential— speech denouncing Qaddafi. On February 21, the influential Islamist face of al-Jazeera, Yusuf al-Qaradawi, gave religious sanction on live tele- vision for someone to end Libya's misery by killing Qaddafi.

Events moved very fast. Violence spread and the media blackout generated tremendous uncertainty and fear. By February 20, the rebels had taken control of Benghazi, which had long been the epicenter of resistance to Qaddafi and had a history of resisting Tripoli's control. Within a short time, Benghazi had become a haven for an emerging new Libya, with nascent proto-state institutions, a transitional council, and a campaign for international recognition. But for all of the initial enthusiasm, that early success could not be replicated in other cities. Over the coming weeks, Qaddafi's military relentlessly crushed opposition across the country with its superior firepower. Qaddafi's forces bombarded the oil port of Ras Lanuf, brutally seized control of Brega, and pushed toward Benghazi.

Spokesmen for the newly formed rebel leadership frantically pleaded their case for a no-fly zone and military help to the UN and to the international community. Their calls were taken up by a cascade of Libyan officials who resigned their posts in protest, by British and French intellectuals and politicians, and by prominent Arab public figures. Qaddafi's speeches, beginning on February 22, were absolutely uncompromising, calling the opposition "terrorists" and demanding that his people hunt them down. Three days later, he declared that "the people who don't love me don't deserve to live." By March 4, human rights organizations placed the death count at over 6,000. On March 12, a spokesman for the Libyan rebels warned that if no action were taken soon, Qaddafi's forces could kill half a million people.[4] Dennis Ross, a senior White House official, told a small group of experts in a private meeting that the administration feared that the coming assault on Benghazi would be "Srebrenica on steroids"—a preventable massacre that would be a permanent blot on the conscience of the world.

The brutality of Qaddafi's advance was all too real. The international community could not ignore this unfolding catastrophe. Partly, this was simply because of the near certainty of a horrific massacre that could be prevented at relatively low cost. But it was also crucial because of its central place in the narrative of the Arab uprisings that had consumed international media attention. It *mattered* that the Libyan horrors unfolded in the shadow of Tunis and Cairo, with the whole world as well as every Arab protest movement watching and interpreting events through that lens of popular peaceful protest. The response was too slow and too weak for many activists, but the move toward a no-fly zone and military intervention was almost unbelievably quick by diplomatic standards. On March 1, the U.S. Senate passed a resolution favoring a no-fly zone, and on March 7, the GCC also issued an unprecedented statement endorsing one. On March 16, with his forces closing in on Benghazi, Qaddafi warned the rebels in a radio broadcast, "It's over. We are coming tonight. We will find you in your closets." After a month of Qaddafi's grinding, bloody campaign against the rebels, NATO and U.S. officials took this threat seriously. On March 18, UN Security Council Resolution 1973 authorized the use of "all necessary means" to stop the killing. Qaddafi immediately announced a cease-fire and offered to negotiate for the first time. Bombing began the next day.

There has been an enormous amount of debate about the motivations for the NATO intervention. Britain and France pushed early for international action to prevent the killing, while the Obama administration hesitated over the likely costs and risks of military intervention. Perhaps the French took a hard line to distract attention from their embarrassing stance on Tunisia, where they had offered military assistance to Ben Ali. Maybe the British saw an easy way to show their flag. Quite probably, the Qataris and Saudis supported the intervention to get personal revenge on the despised Qaddafi.

Some of the objections to the intervention are frankly absurd. One popular line among self-proclaimed realists, who traditionally oppose humanitarian interventions, was that no massacre was in fact imminent, because Qaddafi would not have carried through on his threats. This suggests a touching, if not particularly "realist" faith in the goodwill of a dictator who had just survived the worst challenge of his life, ruled through fear and repressive power, and had just publicly declared his intent. The U.S. intelligence community agreed with most Libyans and Arabs that Qaddafi's threat was real. So do I.

Another popular line on the left suggested that the U.S. sought to seize Libyan oil fields. Again, this makes no sense: Qaddafi had been happily selling his oil for years. Nor did a somewhat tortured argument on the left that the intervention was driven by an interest in preventing a flow of Libyan refugees and migrant laborers into Europe make much sense, given that the conflict made such flows more rather than less likely. The popularity of such generic anti-imperialist arguments on both the Arab and Western Left has more to do with their own predispositions than with anything happening on the ground.

A more plausible, but still unsatisfactory, objection is that the NATO military intervention preempted the prospects for a peaceful resolution. By this argument, Qaddafi might have accepted a cease-fire and negotiated a transition had he been given the chance following the passage of the Security Council resolution. The intervention, by this argument, unnecessarily militarized the situation and irrevocably tainted the Libyan national fate. But while it is impossible to know with certainty, this argument is ultimately unpersuasive. The far more likely outcome, based on the trends on the ground in Libya and on the patterns seen in Syria and Yemen, is that Qaddafi would have quickly broken the agreement as soon as the threat of intervention receded and that the bloodshed would have continued. I see no reason whatsoever to believe that Qaddafi's regime would have voluntarily surrendered power or undertaken serious reform in the absence of an intervention.

The NATO intervention did not exactly disguise its motives. It was most likely driven by the impending bloodbath, the calculations of regional and international players, and the context of the Arab uprisings. Qaddafi's threats were certainly the most urgent factor. Obama and his NATO allies simply could not accept the slaughter of Libya's rebels under the watchful eyes of the international media. Another Rwanda, another Srebrenica, would be an eternal mark of shame—a massacre unfolding in real time that the U.S. had the power to stop. In my conversations with administration officials at the time, I found those concerns about an incipient bloodbath to be by far the most urgent factor on their minds. The effects of Qaddafi's victory on the rest of the Arab world would be catastrophic, encouraging all other dictators to resort to whatever violence they needed to hold on to power. Stopping Qaddafi, on the other hand, could help to reinforce an international norm on crimes against humanity. It could empower the International Criminal Court and potentially deter others from resorting to such violence out of fear that international responses would doom rather than rescue their regimes.

The Obama administration very clearly was not seeking out a war with Libya. Obama had repeatedly emphasized that the changes in the Arab world were driven from within, not by Washington, and the president did not want to impose American military intervention onto the unfolding Arab Spring. But the administration saw clear signs of impending massacre, as Qaddafi's forces closed in on Benghazi and the colonel gave public speeches calling for the extermination of fighters like rats. For all the subsequent criticism of the U.S. intervention, inaction would have also carried deep costs. I have no doubt that the same people who lambasted Obama for the intervention would have blasted him for the massacre that followed his inaction: *the promises of Cairo,* they would almost certainly have written, *died in the streets of Benghazi.*

The official Arab demand for an intervention in Libya was a bit more complex, driven by several factors. It is not plausible that Saudi Arabia, profoundly undemocratic at home and in the process of intervening to crush Bahraini democracy protests, particularly cared about such things in Libya. Quite simply, by 2011, Qaddafi had no allies in the region. He had systematically alienated every major leader: humiliating the emir of Qatar at the 2009 Doha Summit; allegedly conspiring to kill the king of Saudi Arabia; and lambasting the entire Arab order in his rambling speeches to assorted Arab gatherings. These personal animosities reinforced cold-blooded, strategic interests on the part of some key Arab states. Saudi Arabia in particular was content to see the West intervene in Libya, if this meant diverting the West's gaze from unsavory happenings in Bahrain, where the crackdown began at almost precisely the same time as the GCC move to endorse action in relatively faraway Libya.

For the Arab public, however, there was little ambiguity: the Libya uprising was part of its own struggle. The outcome there was seen as fundamentally, organically tied to the fate of the entire region. Al-Jazeera's saturated coverage of the fighting put the Libyan conflict squarely at the center of regional attention. Qaddafi's brutality against unarmed protestors struck most Arabs as an assault on "us," an act of violence that directly affected their emerging identity as a collective Arab uprising and—if it succeeded in crushing the rebellion—would provide a model for other Arab dictators to follow. Allowing Qaddafi to survive and prosper would doom not only the Libyan people, but the entire region's hopes.

The Libyan massacres dominated al-Jazeera's screens and Arab social media sites for weeks, with rawer demands for their own governments and for the international community to stop the killing. When Obama condemned the violence on February 24 and called for a meeting of the UN Human Rights Council, the response was overwhelmingly to demand more forceful American action. Almost none wanted an American military intervention on the ground, but almost all wanted the U.S. to enforce a no-fly zone.[5] It is not clear that most of those demanding a no-fly zone fully understood the military measures that would be needed to enforce one, including significant bombing of Libyan targets—a tension that would appear when the NATO intervention began.

That Arab public opinion could have been so supportive of Western intervention is remarkable, deserving much more attention than it has received. Memories of the invasion of Iraq remained raw, and skepticism of Western intentions could hardly be higher. The Israeli-Palestinian conflict, often considered to be the primary issue by which Arabs judge American policy, remained deeply stalled and had little relevance to the Libya debate other than perfunctory demands that a no-fly zone also be extended to Gaza. Given the deeply ingrained suspicion and hostility toward the U.S., how is it that the new Arab public quickly and overwhelmingly moved to demand an American military intervention? Simply because the Libyan upheavals were now widely viewed through the lens of the great Arab revolt, and not as part of a Western war against Islam or imperialist thirst for oil. The terms of debate had changed.

The Arab support for the NATO intervention in Libya provoked one of the more fascinating debates of the entire season. The Arab public sphere has for decades been virtually defined by its deep hostility to Western interventions. The lion's share of Arab opinion opposed not only the 2003 invasion of Iraq but also the 1990–1991 intervention to reverse Iraq's occupation of Kuwait. It tended to view Western foreign policy through the lens of its support for Israel and, in the previous decade, of what many saw as a war against Islam.

Al-Jazeera enthusiastically embraced the Libyan uprising from the start. Shortly before the intervention began, I asked Al-Jazeera's director, Wadah Khanfar, how long his station's support for an intervention would last if Western bombs began killing Libyan civilians. He shook his head, amazed that it had come to this, but then assured me that al-Jazeera shared the Arab public's conviction on the urgency to act. That night in mid-March, one of the station's cameramen in Libya was killed, making the issue even more personal to Khanfar and his staff. Some, however, point to Qatari foreign policy as the driver of the station's coverage. Whatever the reason, al-Jazeera flooded the zone, covering every twist and turn in the battle for Libya with fevered, twenty-four-hour determination that kept it in the center of Arab public debate for months.

What about the intervention itself? The NATO intervention did indeed stop Qaddafi's forces in their tracks and almost certainly prevented a bloodbath in Benghazi. It produced a rare moment of applause from the activist voices of the new Arab public, who for a moment saw the West finally stepping forward to do what they considered the right thing. Meanwhile the Transitional National Council (TNC) racked up an impressive list of diplomatic accomplishments, including recognition as the legitimate government of Libya by a growing roster of states. But it did not lead to Qaddafi's rapid fall.

The war then settled into an uneasy stalemate. Qaddafi had sufficient funds and support to resist both domestic and international assault. The rebels had NATO air strikes to protect them and soon received a grab bag of help from external supporters: Qatari purchase of oil vouchers and military advisers on the ground, French communications equipment, and so forth. The rebels began to establish a proto-state in Benghazi, expanding the Transitional National Council to represent all regions of Libya and to include respected, independent bureaucrats who promised not to seek future political office in a free Libya.

As the war dragged on, critics of the intervention came to dominate the public debate, and tensions predictably began to surface in this uncertain new polity. The dominance of Benghazi rankled other regions of Libya, which had long been divided by competition and mutual mistrust. The inclusion of prominent regime defectors aroused suspicions among rebels about double agents. In August, the sudden killing of the rebel military chief, seemingly at the hands of the political leadership, ripped apart the political elite of the Libyan rebels. While all the trends ran in favor of the rebels, the drawn-out process rubbed raw nerves and disappointed those who had hoped that international consensus and support could bring down the hated dictator.

Libya's role in the new Arab public also began to change. As the war dragged on, the conflict looked far less like a chapter in the peaceful Arab protest movements than like a slightly tawdry slide show. War reporting took the place of protest coverage, as the news focused on day-to-day movements in the frontlines. Al-Jazeera broadcast endless grainy footage of firefights and explosions, as its critics began to complain about its heavy focus on Libya at the expense of other countries, such as (especially) Bahrain. Meanwhile, anti-imperialist groups grew more vocal in rejecting the NATO intervention, even while offering little love for Qaddafi. Days after the fall of Tripoli, *al-Akhbar* editor Ibrahim al-Amin was already calling on Libyans to rise up against the (non-existent) NATO occupation of their country.[6]

The sense of possibility and hope for an escape from one of the region's worst tyrants gave way to fears about chaos, stalemate, and civil war. Few thought that Qaddafi could win, with the international forces arrayed against him. But simply by surviving, he drained the campaign of its moral and strategic purpose and kept alive his hopes for the internal fissures of his opponents to bring on collapse.

Yet Libya was never actually a stalemate. The trends were clearly against Qaddafi. Nation after nation recognized the TNC in the place of Qaddafi's government. A regular stream of defectors went from Qaddafi toward the rebels, with almost no examples of movement in the other direction. In mid-May, the rebels broke the siege of the city of Misrata. Finally, in mid-August, the dam finally broke and Qaddafi's regime quickly collapsed. Most analysts expected that Ramadan would slow the rebels, but instead there was a sudden collapse in the pivotal oil town of Brega. When it fell, the entire Libyan regime seemed to follow suit. Tripoli's sudden fall in August took most casual observers by surprise, but in fact had been carefully planned for months by the rebels and their supporters inside Qaddafi's capitol city. In October, Qaddafi himself was captured and killed, allowing Libyans to turn a symbolic page and reducing the prospects of an organized insurgency cohering around the old regime.

The fall of Tripoli and Qaddafi's death forced Libyans and the outside world to now confront many profound questions that were deferred during the long fighting. The unity of the new Libyan rulers would be tested quickly, as they struggled to establish authority over the many armed groups. Islamist groups who had played a role in the fighting expected to be represented in the new Libyan regime. Western observers were shocked to hear NTC head Mustafa Abdul Jaliil declare his support for Islamist shari'a law and polygamy during his speech declaring Libya's liberation, and by images of the al-Qaeda flag appearing in Tripoli. But for all those fears and concerns, Libyans now had a real chance to create a better political system—and at least in the early days following the end of the war had not succumbed to the many risks.

The Libya intervention did not produce the rapid cascade effects for which some had hoped, mainly because it could not meet exaggerated expectations of a rapid and easy victory. But it did transform the strategic calculations of actors throughout the region. The deterrent effect the Obama administration had wanted did not fully materialize, in part because the counterexample of Saudi Arabia's tacitly tolerated intervention in Bahrain undermined the message. While military action might have increased the credibility of American and NATO intentions in the rest of the region, it decreased its available military and diplomatic resources. Potential adversaries, from Tehran to Damascus, looked at the stalemate in Libya and calculated that they now had less to fear from a West bogged down in a controversial war in North Africa. And at least some fence-sitters across the region looked at Libya as a cautionary tale of what might await them, should they join in protests against their regimes.

At the same time, both regimes and protestors did take note of the new reality that blatant violence against civilians nonetheless might trigger such intervention. Some protest movements might have toyed with the idea of provoking violence in order to invite intervention, though there are no known instances of this actually happening. Most had learned the lesson of *silmiyya* from Cairo, that peaceful movements had a better chance of winning international support and of attracting fence-sitters in their own countries. They did pay careful attention to how international attention might inhibit action against them and how they might exploit violence to their advantage. Regimes, for their part, attempted to calculate how much violence they could risk and carefully eyed the International Criminal Court referrals, the targeted sanctions, and the military action that Qaddafi had brought upon himself. It is impossible to know how much any of these factors weighed in each case, but they were indisputably present. When Qaddafi finally fell, protest movements across the region were galvanized into renewed efforts as they regained some of their flickering hope, especially in forgotten Yemen.

But it was Syria that became the bloodiest, most vexed battlefield of the Arab uprisings.

SYRIA

Syria is stable because you have to be very closely linked to the beliefs of the people. This is the core issue. When there is divergence between your policy and the people's beliefs and interests, you will have this vacuum that creates disturbance.

—BASHAR AL-ASSAD[7]

Few expected the uprisings to spread to Syria. Assad himself clearly felt that the protests were a challenge to the regimes allied with the United States and Israel, and felt protected by their resistance identity and popular foreign policy. He rather smugly believed that his own reforms had already anticipated popular anger, telling the *Wall Street Journal* that "if you didn't see the need of reform before what happened in Egypt and Tunisia, it's too late to do any reform." He had preemptively increased subsidies for heating oil and delayed plans to cut other subsidies. In reserve, the regime had a massive repressive force at its disposal, the support of key sectors in the business community, and a population genuinely fearful that any uprising might lead to an Iraq- or Lebanon-style sectarian war.

There was not much of an opposition movement in Syria. Its particularly intense breed of authoritarianism had eviscerated any form of independent civil society or political opposition. Organized political opposition, including the Muslim Brotherhood, existed only in exile. Nor was there a robust, thriving cadre of young Internet activists or bloggers, as in Egypt or even Tunisia. Syria had nothing like the freewheeling independent Egyptian press. People broadly lived in fear of the security forces, and the smothering control of the public realm left Syria a "kingdom of silence."[8]

Yet Syrians had as many grievances as any other Arab population. Over the previous years, the country had seen serious pressure on the business community and ever-greater economic problems. Rising trade with Turkey had flooded the country with cheap goods, helping consumers but hurting many Syrian businesses. Pervasive corruption had only gotten worse, while intra-regime infighting had intensified in the years since the forced retreat from Lebanon and the ongoing UN Special

Tribunal's investigation of the 2005 murder of then-Prime Minister Rafik Hariri that had often been blamed on Damascus. Migration to the cities had created an ever-growing urban underclass desperate for work and poorly integrated into existing social and civil networks. And promises of political reforms never materialized, undermining confidence in the regime's credibility and any hope for change through normal institutional channels. Assad's "resistance" foreign policy and constant invocation of foreign conspiracies could only go so far to distract and deter political opposition.

As was the case elsewhere in region, such structural and endemic grievances could probably have festered for quite some time. Syria's repressive apparatus was strong, pervasive, and loyal to the regime. The military was deeply intertwined with the ruling regime through tribal and sectarian ties and massive crony capitalist corruption. The population was largely depoliticized and atomized through decades of fierce repression and enforcement of public red lines against political dissent. And many Syrians deeply feared that their country could become another Iraq or Lebanon—very real fears in a country divided along sectarian lines and with direct experience of the horrors of civil war in both neighbors. Syria was not Egypt or Jordan, where the regime could tolerate a critical press or demonstrations that stayed below a certain threshold. It relied on total suppression of any public dissent, a pervasive security and intelligence presence, and the enforcement of fear. It took courage for Syrians to challenge this system of control.

In short, it seemed that Assad could afford his confidence. And, indeed, Syria was quiet for the first few months of the Arab uprisings. Assad even felt confident enough to lift the ban on Facebook and other social media at a time when other Arab rulers were cracking on down on what they considered the source of their problems. Protests called by online organizers for February 3 fizzled, in part because of the massive deployment of security forces at the designated rallying points. Protests against the alleged beating of a young man broke out on February 17 but were forcefully put down by a wary security establishment the following week. In early March, Assad offered a general amnesty for those accused of crimes before March 7, seemingly offering a way forward for those who had risked protesting in the early days.

It was not until mid-March that the first signs of popular mobilization appeared in the margins of Syrian society. Demonstrations were
still rare, however, with the vast majority of Syrians opting for caution.
Online activists attempted to create a sense that Syria was joining in the
regional uprising, but very little was actually happening on the ground.
What changed the situation in Syria was the momentum from the rest of
the regional ferment—particularly the example of Libya, where the
NATO intervention almost exactly coincided with the return of
protests—and the regime's inability to restrain itself from using violence
against the few protestors who did materialize.

Had Assad refrained from violence and offered deeper reforms
early in the game, he likely would have been fine. But instead his
speeches seemed to mock the concerns of his people, violence against
protestors created a predictable dynamic of escalating rage, and his
regime found itself trapped by its own choices. It's fair to say that Assad
did to himself what his external enemies had failed to bring about for
a decade.

The demonstration effect in Syria was powerful. Syrians were deeply
embedded within the Arab public sphere, even more so because of
the state-enforced silence of their own media, and they could see what
was happening all around them in the first few months of 2011. The
sense of empowerment, spur to action, shattering of red lines, and
overcoming of fear that characterized the regional movement could
have the most significant effects in an arena that depended on complete
control and intimidation. The inspiration of the other Arab uprisings
and identification with those struggles clearly drove the early moves in
Syria. A young Damascene activist reflected, "It's just time to be free.
We learnt from other [Arab] revolutions not to remain silent, and that
if we don't take advantage of this opportunity we will remain cowards
forever."[9]

Syrian youth proved to be as engaged, competent, and fearless as their
regional counterparts. Longtime Syrian dissident Michel Kilo marveled
that the new generation was "better, much better" than his generation.
"What the youth have managed to do is really enormous," Kilo argued.
"They have managed to form a popular revolution. . . . These young
people are less ideological and they have a bigger vision about society

and freedom."[10] Their new attitudes manifested not just in street demonstrations but in the telltale signs of an emergent public sphere. One perceptive analyst described the first months of the year, even before demonstrations picked up steam: "In what had long been—or forced to become—a depoliticized society, casual discussions suddenly assumed a surprisingly political tone. What the regime used to do and get away with came under intense and critical public scrutiny. Subtle expressions of insubordination surfaced. Previously routine and unchallenged forms of harassment and extortion by civil servants met unusual resistance on the part of ordinary citizens."[11]

The tight control over the domestic public sphere meant that, as with France-based activists in Tunisia, external activists had to take a leading role in Syria. Those activists were often largely unknown inside of Syria, creating some tensions and doubts about their real identities and intentions (some at least were known to be members of the long-banned Syrian Muslim Brotherhood). Outside activists had been trying since early in the year to build support for protests through Facebook organizing, the distribution of videos, and the other tools of the Arab Spring. The initial call that went out on Facebook for March 15 demonstrations was not qualitatively different from those in February. Protestors anywhere in the Arab world had to be brave, but it took exceptionally extraordinary courage to begin protesting in Assad's Syria. Political protest in Syria meant almost certain arrest and likely torture, long-term harassment, and retaliation against family and friends. Memories of the destruction of Hama in 1982 by then-president Hafez al-Assad's military in order to crush an uprising linked to the Syrian Muslim Brotherhood remained vivid across the country as a lesson. One of the great ironies of the Arab uprisings of 2011 is that its bloodiest battlefield was one where only a tiny number of extraordinarily brave protestors actually initially challenged the regime.

An energetic media campaign organized outside Syria pushed a narrative of protest and challenge largely divorced from realities on the ground, raising uncomfortable questions that have never been fully engaged about the line between information and activism. Twenty-seven-year-old dissident Rami Nakhle became one public face of what was described as a network of about twenty activists dedicated to disseminating videos and information about the unfolding Syrian opposition movement.[12] Typical of the materials distributed was a YouTube video featuring a young woman named Mawa.[13] But these online activists raised many questions, particularly as their videos began to heavily influence international and Arab media coverage. The near-total absence of foreign journalists increased the importance of such sources, while also making it more and more difficult to assess their credibility.

The beginning of the Syria protests in March resembled the process in Tunisia more than in any other comparable Arab country. Tunisia and Syria had similar levels of domestic repression, including control of the media and total domination of civil society. The protests began on the periphery, in a distant agricultural area. The initial protests in the isolated Syrian town of Deraa began for idiosyncratic, local reasons; they were prompted by the arrest of a student for writing graffiti. On the ground, youth activists began "began with small acts of solidarity with Egypt and Tunisia, in particular candlelight vigils in which a few dared to gather in public places despite the menacing presence of security personnel."[14] But one lesson that the regime had learned from Egypt and Tunisia was that it should not allow any small protests to gain momentum, and that it should allow none to occupy a public space. As a result, the regime's violent response transformed this local challenge into a massive societal convulsion.

When protests began to take hold after the police beatings of some youth scrawling graffiti in the southern town of Deraa, the regime struck hard, fast, and brutally in an effort to prevent any revolutionary momentum from building. Rather than allow protests in Deraa to play out, Assad's regime chose to deploy massive force on March 21 to send a message to other would-be challengers. The violence was indiscriminate, poorly timed, and captured on video to be uploaded to the Internet. It generated more outraged protestors than it deterred and triggered a highly destructive cycle of repression and resistance that swamped any possibility of a top-down reform initiative. And it helped to turn the Arab world, and much of the international community, away from engagement with the Assad regime and toward increasingly open confrontation.

Context matters. Perhaps in another era, this kind of overwhelming repression could have worked, as it did for Assad's father in 1982 in Hama. But no local protest met with such overt regime violence could remain strictly a local affair three months into the Arab uprising, especially with an online contingent determined to publicize the events. International and regional norms against such abuses had begun to evolve, the attention of online activists and of al-Jazeera shined a glaring spotlight on them, and both Syrians and other Arabs consciously placed the unfolding events within the broader Arab story. In that story, Assad was the villain, regardless of his "resistance" foreign policy. This of course suited those Gulf states that had long been hostile to Assad, and whose media had spent most of the previous decade criticizing the Syrian regime.

The Assad regime in very real ways brought its fate upon itself. Had it shown restraint, the regime likely would have avoided serious challenges from the small and carefully monitored opposition. But the deaths set off a chain reaction. Opposition websites used the bloodshed to drum up anger at the regime, while the violence began to touch more and more families and tribes. Anger began to snowball. There are few more clear examples of this violence-mobilization dynamic than Syria during these early protests. Rather than intimidating would-be dissidents, regime brutality instead created a self-fulfilling prophecy of rolling defections. On March 27, Assad deployed the army for the first time. His officers had none of the Egyptian or Tunisian qualms about shooting on their own people, which may, in the end, be what doomed their regime. By the end of the summer, there were nearly 2,000 confirmed deaths, while protests had grown to touch almost every part of Syria.

There were limits to the snowball, however. For months, Damascus and Aleppo remained quiet, while protests and violence raged in peripheral areas. In June, leading Syrian intellectual and later the nominee to head the Syrian opposition coalition, Burhan Ghalyoun, advised leaders of the revolution in an open letter that "this is a new stage in the development of the revolution, the stage of winning over the silent public."[15] As late as July 29, desperate protest leaders used Friday's demonstrations to tell those key cities that "your silence is killing us." Minority communities remained quiet, fearing what might come, with

their anxieties stoked by lurid regime-fueled tales of the role of deceased
Iraqi insurgency leader Abu Musab al-Zarqawi's jihadist cadres filling the
ranks of the opposition. Many, even most, Syrians remained deeply fearful of official retaliation and tried to keep their heads down. Absent
reason to believe that there was a good chance the regime would fall,
most ordinary people simply were not going to risk their lives and repu-
tations to express their anger.

There was a difficult international debate about the value of dialogue
with the Assad regime and its ability to reform itself. In his May 19
speech at the State Department outlining America's position in the
region, President Obama said,

> [T]he Syrian people have shown their courage in demanding
> a transition to democracy. President Assad now has a choice.
> He can lead that transition, or get out of the way. The Syrian
> government must stop shooting demonstrators and allow
> peaceful protests. It must release political prisoners and stop
> unjust arrests. It must allow human rights monitors to have
> access to cities like Deraa; and start a serious dialogue to
> advance a democratic transition. Otherwise, President Assad
> and his regime will continue to be challenged from within and
> will continue to be isolated abroad.

This proved a prescient guide to how the coming months would
unfold.

Not only the United States but also many Arabs and even Syrians
saw the value of dialogue and political reform from above, for without
such a process, the only option was violent regime change.[16] Assad made
a number of reform proposals in this period to try and blunt the
momentum of the opposition. He accepted the resignation of his
government in March and in June proposed constitutional changes that
would in principle end the Ba'ath Party's monopoly on power. But by
this point in the cycle of violence, such offers had little credibility.
Opposing groups could hardly trust in the good faith of the regime when
it was actively slaughtering them.

This is where the regime's brutality became self-defeating, as indiscriminate violence caught up even these "ostriches" who had tried to

avoid trouble by laying low in its net and demolished their sense of personal security through silence. As Ghalyoun mused in late July,

> I believe that there actually is a significant, not-so-small group of Syrians who remain silent. One of the main reasons for their silence is their concern for stability. Here, we are speaking of businessmen, professionals, manufacturers, and economists. The livelihoods of these people require stability, and they believe that the Asad regime secures this stability. Now . . . we are moving towards a new phase during which the silent group is becoming convinced that it is impossible to guarantee stability by return-ing to the old system. Such a return is impossible after three months of bloody struggle that has resulted in a large number of dead and injured persons, including martyrs.[17]

Abroad, too, the indiscriminate violence caused the regime to shed support. There was a palpable tipping point in the early summer as the Arab public's instinctive identification with a popular protest movement and outrage over regime violence began to overwhelm any residual sup-port for its foreign policy. This feeling was captured by the influential Egyptian columnist Fahmy Howeydi, who confessed in June that the killing of (at that point) more than 1,200 citizens had caused him to lose sympathy for Syria's regime despite his longtime admiration for its foreign policy.[18] As the death toll passed 2,000, it had become clear that even if Assad somehow survived at home, Syria's regional role and influ-ence would not recover for a long time.

The regime apologized for the violence and offered progressively broader political and economic reforms to head off the increasingly organized and politically driven protest movement. The government pre-pared a draft law to open up some limited media freedoms. On July 23, Vice President Farouq Sharaa outlined a road map for political reform to the Arab daily *al-Hayat*.[19] On July 24, the government presented a new law legalizing political parties, but did not touch the "leading role" of the Ba'ath Party in the constitution. Indeed, the reforms on offer by the end of the summer would have been nothing short of revolutionary, had they actually been implemented. But Assad's response was poorly received. People met his speeches with derision, while immediately dismissing the promises of reform as transparent efforts to buy time and break the opposition's momentum. They discounted offers of political reform as both insufficient and lacking credibility, since the proposals did not touch the core security apparatus that underpinned the regime.

Syria used the means at its disposal to prevent media coverage of the protests, hoping to maintain a façade of normality and block the cycle of anger over televised images of brutality. It complained bitterly about al-Jazeera. It expelled most foreign journalists and even more ruthlessly monitored its own press. The media blackout actually made online activist communities more powerful, since the international media came to rely on them for videos and testimonies and had little ability to independently verify what they received. Official Syrian discourse and reporting lost credibility, even when it may have been closer to the truth on the ground than the activist-fueled narratives.

The violence also emptied the possibility of any other reforms being acceptable. Over the course of the summer, the regime repeatedly called for national dialogue, promised cease-fires, and proposed a number of far-reaching reforms, including legalizing political parties and holding free elections by the end of 2011. But with activists being hunted down and tanks shelling cities, few Syrians found such offers sufficient or credible. As U.S. Ambassador Robert Ford told me on July 15, "I have seen no evidence yet in terms of hard changes on the ground that the Syrian government is willing to reform at anything like the speed demanded by the street protestors. If it doesn't start moving with far greater alacrity, the street will wash them away."

As the violence expanded, the international community and the Arab League all stood by helplessly. Where Libyans begged for international assistance in the face of near-certain defeat, the Syrian opposition was overwhelmingly against any form of external military intervention. They would not have found a receptive audience had they asked. The conditions that had made intervention plausible there simply did not exist in Syria. Russia and China blocked any Libya-style UN mandate for intervention. There was no Arab consensus in support of intervention, even when the Arab League finally delivered a peace plan and call for ending violence in November. Syria retained powerful external allies such as Iran and the powerful Lebanese Islamist movement Hezbollah, able and willing to step forward to protect its interests. Syria's location at the heart of the Levant made any military intervention geopolitically explosive. The rebels held no liberated zones of the country that could become the base of an alternative government.

The absence of any clear opposition leadership complicated international efforts to engage in Syria and also left many Syrians uncertain about the proposed alternative to the hated but at least well-understood Assad regime. Even sympathetic observers mused that the Syrian revolution may have "begun before its time," and might have been better served by a longer period of formation and preparation (as if such a thing were possible in the context of the mad rush of the Arab uprisings, or in the Syrian context at any time).[20] As Ghalyoun warned, the silent majority could not rally to the side of the opposition when there was no clear leadership, no unified message, and no program for what might come after.[21]

Where the Libyans had quickly formed an inclusive Transitional National Council, the Syrian opposition in exile remained fragmented and incoherent. Nobody really knew the relative strength inside Syria of the competing opposition groups, and the groups themselves lacked any acceptable process for making decisions. Internal and external opposition forces disagreed on core issues. The Syrian army and business community remained on the fence. Leftists and liberals mistrusted the role of the Muslim Brotherhood, while many had concerns about the neoconservative and pro-Israeli ties of many U.S.-based activists. The opposition could agree on some basic points of consensus—no taking up of arms, no sectarianism, no foreign intervention—but little beyond that. In a series of meetings, opposition figures—in Antalya (June 2), in Damascus (June 28), in Istanbul (July 16, August 19)—failed to overcome these obstacles despite the growing urgency. The emergence of local coordination committees established to guide protests in each city and town further complicated views of the opposition.[22] These highly decentralized, largely anonymous youth movements had a sometimes uneasy relationship with the older activists and exile politicians with whom the international community and Syrian government preferred to engage.

The role of exiles in promoting the Syrian uprisings also created vulnerabilities in the war of narratives. Many of the Syrian activists in the

West enjoyed the support of pro-Israeli or neoconservative groups, dating back at least a decade. Others in Europe, especially, had ties to the Syrian Muslim Brotherhood. Each kind of affiliation created opportunities for attacks on their legitimacy, integrity, or nationalist credentials. Frustrated activists vented their own anger at their external supporters: "the outside opposition lives far from the harsh internal conditions, in hotels and comfortable homes, outbidding the opposition of the interior who suffer from harsh repression. Some of the external opposition call on the Western states to intervene militarily, and some sit side by side with Zionists and refuse dialogue with the regime."[23] Regime propaganda relentlessly pointed toward foreign conspirators, highlighting alleged Israel and American ties while simultaneously pointing to hard-line Salafi jihadists returned from Iraq to stir up trouble.

Syria's unique place in regional politics complicated the regional response. As the only fully fledged Arab member of the "resistance" bloc, Syria stood as potentially the greatest prize in the regional game of thrones. After the assassination of Lebanese Prime Minister Rafik Hariri in February 2005, Syria had been the target of a major, coordinated pressure campaign combining the United States, Lebanon's March 14 movement, France, Saudi Arabia, and most of the "axis of moderates." That campaign had forced Syria, alleged to have participated in the assassination, to withdraw its troops from Lebanon, had put key members of the Syrian regime under the scrutiny of the UN's Special Tribunal for Lebanon, and led to significant international sanctions.

Few regional players expected that Assad would actually fall, leaving them cautious about going beyond bland statements urging restraint. They only showed their hand in August after the regime's survival seemed to be seriously in question. Their caution also reflected several years of attempted engagement with Damascus, not only by Washington and European capitals but also by the Saudis, the Turks, and others. Assad had only quite recently repaired Syria's relationship with Saudi Arabia, after years of open cold war, and Riyadh hesitated to abandon that painfully negotiated entente. Turkey had made its new relationship with Syria a centerpiece of its energetic Arab policy. Iraq, which two years earlier had been demanding that Assad be brought to the International Criminal Court for harboring insurgents, had warmed to Syria.

Prime Minister Nuri al-Maliki made his first visit to Damascus in years, accusing Israel of fomenting the instability. Lebanese leaders had been flocking to Damascus, especially after the fall of the Saad Hariri government in March.

But for all those efforts, one did not have to scratch deep to find a reservoir of hatred for Assad. What is more, almost every regional power worried about the possible consequences of his fall. Israel may have despised the Damascus regime, but could hardly complain about decades of absolute quiet on the Golan Heights compared to the persistent problems elsewhere. A new regime in Syria would mean unpredictability and uncertainty, of which Israeli leaders hardly needed more. All of Syria's neighbors worried about the kind of instability and chaos that could follow a regime collapse—flows of refugees, sectarian violence, and an open regional proxy war to claim the prize of the throne. Nobody wanted to see an Iraq-style Western intervention with all that would entail.

Syria's allies struggled with its sudden problems. Iran offered support to Assad's regime, including promises of financial and military support, but could do little of practical value. Hezbollah found itself trapped in an iron vise, unable to reconcile its attempts to align with the broad Arab public with its strategic dependence on Syrian support. Its position on Syria deeply undermined its long-cultivated image of "resistance" in the name of the Arab people, probably fatally. The spiraling situation in Syria put the resistance axis decisively on the opposite side from the Arab public for arguably the first time in a decade.

The U.S. would certainly have welcomed a regime change in Syria, and its own standards laid out in Obama's May 19 speech seemed to dictate action to stop the violence and push for political reform. But on its own, it had virtually no leverage. It had no relationship with the Syrian military, as it had enjoyed with Egypt. Years of sanctions because of Syria's actions in Lebanon had left the U.S. without significant trade or financial relations that might be disrupted with new sanctions. Other weapons had been tarnished by misuse, most notably the Special Tribunal for Lebanon, which had lost credibility with its endless leaks and had only recently shifted its gaze from Damascus toward Hezbollah at a politically convenient moment. Any serious U.S. action would require regional and international cooperation to have any real impact on Syria, so the Obama administration set out to actively work with its regional partners and European allies to build such a coalition.

Those efforts revealed real differences from the situation in Libya. Where Qaddafi had alienated virtually everyone in the region and world, Assad at least initially enjoyed strong support from Iran and Turkey, as well as Russia and China. Syria had the ability to stir up major trouble in Lebanon and even Iraq, should it feel threatened. And, like North Korea, its own weakness became a source of strength, as everyone in the region—including Israel—worried that Assad's fall might lead to a bloody sectarian civil war like Iraq's that could spill out into the region.

Were a military option desired, Syria's terrain was far less favorable to air power than Libya's. Urban fighting was far more likely than convoys of trucks in the desert. And absolutely nobody had any interest in invading and occupying Syria after the long years in next-door Iraq. Key regional actors preferred to give Assad more time to repent and reform, and lead the political transition.

Ambassador Ford's visit to Hama on July 9 to protect that population from an impending regime assault signaled a more aggressive American posture, galvanized international attention, and gave heart to the Syrian opposition. In response, regime thugs attacked the American and French embassies. The real point of no return was the regime's August 1 assault on Hama, with no U.S. ambassador to stand in the way. Assad seemed to believe that crushing resistance in this key city before Ramadan would demoralize the opposition and diffuse pressure ahead of the coming month. Instead, the violence badly backfired on him. The images of the assault on Hama, followed by a succession of ever more brutal military assaults around the country—including a shocking naval bombardment of Latakia—seemed to push the world over a threshold.

In this context, international intervention became a frequent topic of debate, despite the many obstacles to such action. The Obama administration had clearly laid out a policy demarcating violence against peaceful protestors as a red line. The NATO and UN intervention in Libya, including an International Criminal Court referral and sanctions along with the no-fly zone, had established a clear precedent for similar reactions to Assad's campaign. But the U.S. and its allies took pains to warn Syrian protestors that they should not expect such a military intervention. In November, America's ambassador to NATO Ivo Daalder said that its leadership was not even thinking about such an intervention.[24] NATO's Secretary General Anders Fogh Rasmussen said bluntly in the same week that NATO would not intervene in Syria.[25]

In the Arab world, the shift had more to do with long-standing competition with Assad than with any moral qualms. It is difficult to believe that the GCC felt particularly upset by Assad's brutality toward his own people after its own very similar moves in Bahrain. It is far more likely that the Saudis and others in the Gulf saw Assad's weakness as an opportunity to strike a major blow against Iran. Whether Assad fell or remained in power, comprehensive sanctions and international isolation would badly damage Syria's value to Tehran. If the move against Syria also won a few points with empowered Arab publics, so much the better. Saudis could hardly contain their glee when the protests came to Syria, as its columnists rushed to crow that the "resistance" foreign policy hadn't protected Assad after all.[26] The growing campaign against Syria fit well with the old "moderate/resistance" axis in which they had invested so much energy during the 2000s, and the Saudis fell comfortably back into old habits and old rhetoric.

And so the Arabs moved in early August. First, the Arab League issued an unusually blunt condemnation of Damascus that fell short of the activists' hopes but nevertheless sent a strong signal. On August 8, King Abdullah redeemed that signal in a televised statement calling for an end to Syria's bloodshed. Kuwait recalled its ambassador, while Qatar's enthusiasm for the rebellion could be seen every day on al-Jazeera. Other Arab countries followed the Gulf's lead, with varying degrees of caution. Even the Muslim Brotherhood came out against the Syrian regime, breaking the traditional "resistance bloc" decisively. That Hezbollah and Iran, along with Iraq, remained committed to Assad fueled a sectarian narrative that pitted those Shi'a powers against the Sunni mainstream in troubling ways.

As for Turkey, the violence put its "no problems with neighbors" foreign policy under a cruel spotlight. The growing violence deeply undermined President Recep Erdoğan's strategic efforts to cultivate positive Arab opinion and put growing pressure on Turkey to act. Few other countries had Turkey's leverage over Syria, making its calculations perhaps the most important. It vacillated, trying to use its influence to convince Assad to begin serious reforms, while resisting international and Syrian popular calls for it to exercise more direct pressure. What influence had its engagement actually purchased? It made a last-ditch effort to reach out to Assad, in a tense six-hour meeting with Foreign Minister Ahmet Davutoglu. But after a clear and forceful Turkish warning that violence must cease, Assad instead escalated his attacks.

By the time Obama called on Assad to step down on August 17, the conditions were far more suitable to such a policy than they had been two months before. A call for regime change in June would have been propaganda gold for Assad, evidence that the so-called uprising was really just another American-Zionist plot. By August, Assad's gambit blaming the Americans fell on deaf ears with the Syrian and wider Arab public, who understood perfectly well that Syria's brutality had brought its problems onto itself. What is more, by August, regional and international partners were prepared to join in with rigorous sanctions and political isolation in far more serious ways than in the earlier days of the uprising.

At the time of this writing, the outcome in Syria is impossible to discern. But a few things are clear. Assad did cling to power—and seemed more likely to survive over the coming years than to fall. The limits on international action combined with his regime's ability and willingness to use deadly force. By October and November, dozens of citizens were reported killed every day. Assad's forces pushed into opposition strongholds, arresting or murdering thousands of suspected opponents. The military did not divide, the business community did not splinter, and significant parts of the population remained on the side of the regime.

But even in the most brutally repressive Arab state, the indiscriminate use of violence proved to be self-defeating. As the Egyptian columnist Fahmy Howeydi reflected in August, Syria had enjoyed every opportunity to repair its relations with its own people but had made the wrong choice at every turn and thus isolated and ultimately doomed itself.[27] And even in such an environment, empowered Arab publics refused to be deterred. A resistance foreign policy was no protection from such dynamics.

And what did all of this mean for America?

CHAPTER 8

AMERICA'S CHALLENGE

O N MAY 19, 2011, Barack Obama delivered a sweeping speech at the State Department outlining his administration's approach to the Arab upheavals. After months of dealing with cascading crises on a case-by-case basis, the administration now hoped to lay out a clear, overarching vision for America in the new Middle East. What, in America's view, was driving the upheavals? How did it affect America's interests? How should the United States respond?

The president's vision that day came down firmly in support of the proposition that the uprisings represented a fundamental change in the region that would ultimately benefit both the people of the region and the United States. He rejected any suggestion that an easy return to the old status quo would be possible, or desirable. The president unequivocally declared that support for political reform and democratic transitions would be a top priority of his administration. But that sweeping declaration almost immediately ran into the complicated realities of conflicting American interests and its limited capabilities.

Obama demonstrated he understood that the Arab protest movements neither needed nor wanted American leadership: "We must proceed with a sense of humility. It's not America that put people into the streets of Tunis or Cairo—it was the people themselves who launched these movements, and the people themselves who must ultimately determine their outcome." But Obama also understood that America could play a vital role in supporting their aspirations—in restraining regimes from violence, in offering economic assistance, in coordinating international and regional responses, and in crafting exit strategies for dictators. Providing such help served American interests as well as ideals, he suggested. A more democratic Middle East, one that provided opportunities for its citizens and offered space for open political competition and public debate, would be more difficult for the U.S. to navigate but would ultimately be a region better aligned with America's vision of a liberal international order. Obama's embrace of this rising Arab public fit comfortably with the vision outlined in his June 4, 2009, speech in Cairo that had called for a renewed relationship with the Muslims of the world based on mutual interests and mutual respect.

Obama laid out key principles to guide American action: a rejection of the use of violence against civilians; a commitment to what he called universal rights, including basic freedoms of speech, assembly, and religion along with the rule of law and gender equality; advice to regimes to initiate "political reform that can meet the legitimate aspirations of ordinary people." He signaled that America would not rule out the participation of peaceful Islamist movements in new democracies and would judge them by their actions rather than by their identities. He focused on empowering and supporting Arabs in their own efforts rather than imposing American models and emphasized multilateral diplomacy over American leadership. Obama argued that the NATO intervention in Libya should have broader meaning to the leaders of the region, that the use of excessive violence would cost them their legitimacy with their people and with the international community. But he would tailor these principles to specific local conditions, even if that meant tolerating in Bahrain what he condemned in Syria. But he resisted articulating a single doctrine—each case, it seemed, would be judged on its own merits and policies adapted according to a prudent balance of interests, options, and opportunities.

When the remarks had concluded, I joined NPR's new media guru Andy Carvin and the Deputy National Security Adviser Benjamin Rhodes for an innovative Twitter dialogue about the speech. Carvin and I selected questions from thousands submitted online to pose to Rhodes, tweeted out his answers, and attempted to monitor the feed for follow-up questions. The latter soon became impossible, as the #MESpeech hashtag became one of the top trending items on Twitter and thousands of messages per second blew past my MacBook Air's screen. (I was only able to keep up at all thanks to a last-second assist from Twitter through the mediation of State Department Internet policy leader Alec Ross.)

The online dialogue revealed both the opportunities and the challenges to the United States in this new world. The skepticism and suspicion of Obama's speech came through clearly. For all the U.S. had tried to do to reach out to the Arab public sphere, its response was underwhelming. Again and again, the same sentiment returned: Obama was a nice man who gives beautiful speeches, but with no follow-through.

Tweeps participating in the dialogue honed in relentlessly on the inconsistencies and perceived hypocrisies of the new strategy. Why was there no mention of Saudi Arabia? Were Palestinian lives worth less than the lives of other peaceful protestors? How could the principles laid out in the speech be reconciled with American silence in Bahrain?

The online debate captured some of the most important questions surrounding America and the Arab uprisings. Moreover, they did so far better than the often-insular American public discourse. The Middle Eastern participants had little patience for American pieties or circumlocutions. They demanded answers: What was the administration's *real* position in this rapidly changing Middle East? Was the empowerment of the Arab public actually compatible with U.S. regional interests? Was America actually conspiring with the counterrevolution to thwart the Arab popular will? Why did the U.S. intervene in Libya but not Syria, Egypt but not Bahrain?

But as important as the suspicion and the challenge was the fact that Rhodes and, through him, the president were there in the discussion. They were listening, trying to engage and explain, and recognizing through their actions the importance of this new public sphere. This has not always been the case, alas. American public diplomacy has struggled to keep up with the dramatic changes in the Arab world. From U.S. Embassy officials in Cairo watching the events in Tahrir taking place two blocks away on television to the paucity of high-ranking officials on Arab television stations, the administration often fell short of meeting the demands of this restless new public. In fact, dealing effectively with the emerging Arab world is going to require a revolution in how the State Department and the White House think about engagement—

who they talk with, what they say, where they go, and ultimately which policies they pursue.

The difficult truth is that any American strategy will be consistently trapped between competing demands. The president instinctively sided with the aspirations of the Arab people for change and understood how excessive American intervention could backfire against protestors. He was genuinely shocked that Egyptians might not see him as on the side of the people. "We have the chance," he argued in that speech in May, "to show that America values the dignity of the street vendor in Tunisia more than the raw power of dictators." An America that successfully formed new bonds with an empowered Arab public, he wagered, would no longer have to make the tortured compromises with dictators that had long been the hallmark of its place in the region.

Yet, at the same time, the president had to keep a careful eye on America's strategic position and core interests. The dignity of protestors in Bahrain or Yemen seemed to hold less value. But this was rooted in rather obvious strategic realities. No American administration could ignore Israel's security needs, the military bases that made up the U.S. security architecture in the Gulf, the flow of oil, the continuing struggle against al-Qaeda, or the Iranian challenge. And Obama, of all presidents, knew the urgency of carefully managing the drawdown of troops from Iraq without that tortured country relapsing into civil war. Every adjustment to the U.S. posture alarmed key allies such as Israel and Saudi Arabia, each of which had the ability to put real pressure on the president.

Amid all of this was the painful reality that few Arabs trusted or liked American policy, no matter what the president said. The Obama administration had to fight an uphill battle after eight years of American troops in Iraq, memories of Arab prisoners abused in Iraqi prisons and Guantanamo Bay, and perceived bias toward Israel. Even those who found Obama personally sincere doubted his ability to meaningfully change American behavior. How could Obama convince Arabs of a change in American priorities when America continued to back Israel, focus on containing Iran, leave Guantanamo open, escalate drone strikes, and wage an ongoing campaign against al-Qaeda?

Characteristically, Obama's responses to the Arab uprising ended up frustrating all sides. He refused to indulge in the kind of moral posturing and empty rhetoric so beloved of the Bush administration, opting instead for a measured tone and deference to Arab agency that left his neoconservative critics cold. Neocons raged that Obama was always too slow and too timid, the phrase "leading from behind" capturing the thrust of their critique.

This pragmatic approach also angered Arab activists, for whom American moves were always too little, too late, and for whom tactical flexibility amounted to deep hypocrisy. When he worked quietly behind the scenes and avoided taking credit, as with his pressure on the Egyptian military, he successfully avoided charges of American interference but at the same time failed to get credit for what he had done. Meanwhile, Arab regimes were infuriated at being abandoned by their primary international patron, while Israel fumed about the likely empowerment of Islamists or of broader anti-Israeli publics.

This won't be the last time that American policy frustrates most and satisfies few. America will inevitably struggle to find its feet in the emerging Middle East. But if its relationship with the changing region is to improve, it must come to understand the shifting logic of the regional balance of power, the new lines of cooperation and conflict, and the new sources of power. It must decide how to reconcile its enduring strategic interests with the very different priorities of the rising new Arab public.

This is why it is so crucial to understand the new lay of the land in the changing Middle East. The major approaches to regional politics do not offer a useful guide to the emerging region. This concluding chapter details the responses of the major regional powers to these new realities and lays out a strategy for dealing properly with the ramifications of the Arab uprising. Already, the Obama administration has made some promising initial steps and has acted far more effectively than most of its critics will acknowledge. But if it continues to act as a status quo power, changing only its rhetoric and making fatal compromises on a case-by-case basis, it will fail.

THE OLD MIDDLE EAST MEETS THE NEW

The United States and Arab states aren't the only regional powers frantically trying to recalibrate in the face of these regional changes. Turkey thrived, with its calculated appeals to Arab public opinion earning Prime

Minister Erdoğan hero status when he came to the region in the autumn. Israel, Iran, and al-Qaeda, by contrast, have struggled to reposition themselves. Israel has retreated ever further into a self-protective shell, squabbling with the Obama administration and declining any thoughts of a peace process, while finding itself more isolated in the region and the world. Iran has found itself almost entirely irrelevant and increasingly consumed with its own domestic problems and growing international isolation. And al-Qaeda suffered multiple blows even before the death of its leader at the hands of the United States. But even as these traditional powers struggle, they continue to shape the future of the region, post-upheaval.

The new Arab politics will see a continuing struggle for power among key regional actors within a political arena defined by the new Arab public sphere. Both aspects must be integrated into our under-standing of regional politics: the independent aspirations of the public, and the power politics of regimes. Sometimes these will work at cross-purposes, sometimes they will coincide. But it will be difficult for the United States to effectively engage both realms, of power and of the people, without new approaches to core regional issues.

The highly integrated regional public sphere will reinforce the importance of regional issues such as Palestine. The shift to domestic politics will not cause such issues to decline in salience, as many expected; the broader Arabist worldview is too deeply rooted in the new Arab public. The connections are too strong and the possibilities for political gamesmanship too great. The lessons of the past are clear; a shared identity and normative framework will likely make regional politics more rather than less competitive, as more players vie for the same ideological positions. What will most likely emerge is a period during which politicians attempt to outbid one another, as all try to prove themselves as the most revolutionary or the most pro-Palestinian.

The media and political space will be ever more tightly linked in the coming years, but the systems of government across the region will likely be much more heterogeneous. For decades, Arab regimes had increasingly come to resemble one another. As presidents handed power to their sons and kings chose parliaments with limited power, the distinctions between regime types blurred. The long tenure of most leaders, and their constant interaction, created a deep comfort level and familiarity even among the bitterest rivals.

The new Arab world will feature a much wider array of political systems. Some, such as Egypt and Tunisia, may make a full transition to democracy. Others, like Yemen and Syria, may be stalled in near-endless civil war. Some will successfully undertake limited reforms, while others will remain tightly controlled. Variations are growing more profound: the states of the GCC have proven thus far to be more resilient, the states of North Africa have experienced the most change, while the Arab heartland from Palestine to Iraq remains unstable, open, and contested.

This much-greater variation in regime type will introduce new turbulence and opportunities. As in the days of the Arab Cold War, the balance of control over the domestic sphere will be an important aspect of regional power. A country such as Qatar with few internal problems will be a more effective player than a sectarian-divided and succession-focused Saudi Arabia. States with deep internal challenges will be arenas for proxy struggles between the powerful, as the new "struggle for Syria" or the nearly decade-long proxy war in Iraq demonstrates. Whether Libya becomes a player or an arena in which regional powers compete for influence will depend heavily on how quickly the new regime establishes central control and legitimate government.

Will more democratic states such as the new Egypt be more or less vulnerable to external meddling? My hunch is that democratization will multiply the points of potential intervention, as political parties can be funded and media outlets established. The political system as a whole will become more resilient and resistant. Saudi Arabia will likely try to promote Islamist movements and America will try to promote liberal ones, but both are likely to find unexpected resistance. More democratic systems will be more transparent, politicians will be more accountable, and the system will be more legitimate, all reducing the ability of outside players to pull strings. But in most cases, leaders will have to be more attentive to public opinion and less able to conceal unpopular policies.

Traditional military capabilities will of course still matter. The participation of Qatar and the UAE in Libya or the burning questions of how to deal with stalemates in Yemen and Syria suggests that specific kinds of military means such as special forces and airpower may become even more potent in a new age of intervention. Whether Iran gets a nuclear weapon will matter in the military balance, but likely only at the margins, as its challenge has always been more political than military in the narrow sense. The greater question is whether popular sentiment in countries such as the new Egypt or even a new Syria might lead to a renewed push to seek military parity with Israel or drive crises of brinksmanship over Israel's likely increasing problems with Palestinians.

Economic power will matter more as well. The shift of power and attention toward the GCC states during the Arab uprisings has been palpable. This is partly because of their relative domestic calm, but it is more obviously because of their ability to throw huge amounts of money at problems. The GCC states have dedicated billions of dollars to Egypt's and Tunisia's transitions, spent billions propping up monarchies in Jordan and Morocco, supported international operations in Libya, and played a key diplomatic role throughout. With Western countries battling through their own crippling financial problems, the wealth of the Gulf will be an appreciating diplomatic asset. Saudi money will likely buffer it from the unpopularity of many of its policies, at least to a point.

But only to a point. Media and ideological power will also increase in utility. Al-Jazeera has become a major weapon in Qatar's arsenal, allowing that tiny state to play an outsized role in shaping the Arab agenda. Saudi Arabia has for a while devoted huge resources to its media empire, particularly the television station al-Arabiya and a variety of newspapers. The Lebanese television arena has long been an extension of its political wars, and Egypt's will likely go in that direction as contending political factions seek useful weapons. Iran and Hezbollah have both done well, especially with Arab Shi'a, with stations such as al-Manar and al-Alam.

Media outlets alone will not be enough, however. The ability to credibly align with and to shape the new Arab public will be a core part of the balance of power. Qatar and Turkey, for instance, have done exceedingly well over the last decade in crafting foreign policies appealing to Arab public opinion and have been rewarded with greater diplomatic power. Saudi Arabia and the "moderate bloc" of American allies usually found themselves pushing against the stream of public opinion in the 2000s, trying to create a reality that did not exist on its own. Their policy had its effects, as in the relentless campaign against Hezbollah in the latter half of the decade, but was never as natural or easy. In the coming period, expect ambitious states to try to tailor their foreign policies to popular narratives and causes wherever possible. Expect them to try to score against their rivals by pointing out their hypocrisies and defections from that normative consensus. And expect the media wars to be more central to the real political conflicts of the region.

Some potentially powerful states will likely emerge as "swing votes" in the new Arab politics. Postrevolutionary Egypt could be such a power if it manages to complete its revolutionary transition and formulate a stable political order with an independent foreign policy. So might Libya, if it makes a transition to a stable and legitimate government and can rationally use its oil resources and new ideological appeal. Qatar is already playing a disproportionate role in the region's politics, in part because few other Arab states have been able to match its energy, resources, or ambition.

Another plausible candidate to be such an independent actor is Iraq after the American withdrawal, completed in December 2011. The removal of Iraq from the regional balance of power shaped the international relations of the last decade; its return is likely to shape those of the next decade. Its oil wealth, geographic position, and size could make it once again a major player; but its internal weakness, ties to Iran, increasingly Shi'a identity, and marginal status in the new Arab public could likewise condemn it to the sidelines. Will Baghdad consolidate control over its national space and push back the proxy wars, or will it remain an arena for regional battle? Will Shi'a identity and growing economic and cultural ties to Iran drive Iraqi foreign policy, allowing Tehran to compensate for the loss of Syria? Or will prickly Iraqi nationalism put limits on the ability of Iran to dictate Baghdad's new direction? A more independent Iraq would be well placed to play the role of the swing vote that is likely to be effective in the emerging Middle East, a bridge between Iran and the Arab world that could maintain good relations with the U.S., as do Qatar and Turkey. But the more that it identifies and acts as a Shi'a power, the less such soft power it will enjoy, particularly in the Gulf, where the prejudices of the Saudi leadership have long blocked any chance of rapprochement.

If such "swing states" are the likely winners of the new Arab politics, what about the losers? Israel and Iran currently look to be the greatest losers from the new regional environment.

The Arab uprisings, and the fall of Mubarak in particular, threaten to overturn the key pillar of Israel's strategic position during nearly forty years. Earlier Israeli governments, especially in the 1990s, had dreamed of peace and a new, integrated Middle East in which Israel could finally be a normal state. The Israel that confronted the Arab uprisings, by contrast, had written off Arab publics as irredeemably hostile and counted on its relationship with autocratic Arab regimes to protect it. Israel had developed very comfortable working relations with most Arab leaders over the previous decade, while pursuing policies that infuriated the vast majority of the Arab public. That easy cooperation on issues such as the containment of Iran or the isolation of Hamas even without progress toward peace encouraged Israeli leaders to largely give up on efforts to reach out to or persuade Arab publics of the potential for peace. With the failure of the 2000 Camp David summit and the outbreak of the violent Al-Aqsa Intifada, Israeli policy took a hard shift to the right both at home and abroad. The Arab public complained bitterly about this increasingly transparent cooperation on a wide array of issues, but autocratic regimes easily brushed aside their protests.

The Arab uprisings came in the context of the near death of the peace process and the fading hopes on any side for a peaceful, negotiated two-state solution to the Israeli-Palestinian conflict. There had not been any meaningful negotiations for over ten years. Over that period, Israel had dramatically increased the size and scope of its settlements in the West Bank and built a security wall on Palestinian territory that looked suspiciously like a final status border. It had unilaterally withdrawn from Gaza in 2005, only to go back to war against Hamas in the final days of the Bush administration. Israel's war with Gaza in the weeks before Obama came to office galvanized intense international criticism. The last few years have seen Israel consumed with battles over its ethics and its legitimacy, fighting against the UN's Goldstone Report on alleged war crimes during the Gaza war, and stumbling badly with its harsh treatment of the Turkish "freedom flotilla," the *Mavi Marmara*, when its security forces boarded the ships, killing eight Turkish citizens and one Turkish-American. In short, the empowerment of the Arab public could not have come at a worse time for Israel.

The Obama administration's efforts to restart peace talks when it came to office in 2009 responded directly and admirably to the hopes of the new Arab public. As time passed, those efforts appeared increasingly quixotic. In speech after speech, Obama laid out a vision of peace based on two states for two peoples, which would have once been profoundly appealing. But by 2009, no basis for such talks existed. His failed effort to convince the Israeli government to freeze settlements destroyed Arab confidence in his administration while roiling Israeli-American relations. Cooperation between the U.S. and Israel continued, of course, and in most ways became even closer, especially on Iran. But the public relationship became sharply politicized, as Netanyahu repeatedly sought to mobilize Republicans against the Democratic president and Israel's supporters waged a scorched-earth media campaign against him.

The transformed region deeply challenges Israel's grand strategy for the region. Israelis are right to worry. Its carefully nurtured relationships with Arab regimes were suddenly less valuable in an era of empowered public opinion. The changes in Egypt threw into question the Camp David treaty, and instability in Jordan perennially raised doubts about its eastern border. In late August 2011, a terrorist attack provoked an Israeli response in the Sinai that killed several Egyptian soldiers. An angry protest in Cairo outside the Israeli embassy demanded the expulsion of the Israeli ambassador and got the withdrawal of Egypt's ambassador to Israel. A few weeks later, a protest outside the Israeli Embassy turned violent, as angry Egyptians broke through its security measures and ransacked the embassy. These are likely only the first of many challenges to come to Israel's presence in Egypt and across the region. Israelis must now confront the harvest of years of calculated refusal to engage or respond to Arab public opinion.

By 2011, the only real question that remained seemed to be whether the coming Palestinian uprising would be peaceful or violent. After the failure of the Obama administration to force Israel to accept a settlement freeze, the Palestinians moved to a new strategy: going to the United Nations to seek recognition as a state, combined with a nonviolent protest movement pushing for independence. Both moves had real limitations. The UN strategy could not deliver an actual state, no matter how many votes the bid gained in the General Assembly. The Security Council would never approve it, given America's firm disapproval. Without the Security Council, the recognition would remain symbolic and have little more effect than the 1988 recognition of a Palestinian state by the same body. The move to the UN did outrage the Israelis, however, who claimed to see it as a Palestinian abandonment of negotiations. But the Palestinian leaders would never have gone to the UN to request a vote on statehood or taken the route of popular mobilization, had there been a negotiations track available.

The Palestinian issue still has the power to galvanize the empowered Arab public at a moment's notice. Palestine is central to the Arab identity narrative at the heart of the new public sphere. Arab regimes will likely find it ever more difficult to cooperate openly with Israel, and events on the ground in the West Bank and Gaza could inflame regional instability with little advance notice. Political competition, both between Arab states and within more democratic ones such as Egypt, may encourage rhetorical outbidding and the embrace of extreme, but popular, positions. In the post-upheaval Arab world, the prognosis for relations with Israel was, to put it mildly, grim.

Iran, perhaps surprisingly, is also emerging as a clear loser. The Islamic Republic had reasonably expected to be a primary beneficiary of the Arab upheavals as regimes hostile to its interests struggled and sometimes fell.[1] Key advisers around Mahmoud Ahmadinejad and Ali Khamenei at first saw themselves working from a position of increasing strength.[2] Scholar Farideh Farhi notes that "Iranians judged that the sentiment of the Arab public will ultimately be more along the lines the Iranians have taken in terms of their positions on the Arab/Israeli conflict."[3] Indeed, Khamenei sought to brand the uprisings as an "Islamic awakening," and seemed to see them as a vindication of his foreign policy. Few in the region agreed.

But, in fact, Iran has turned out to be deeply challenged by the unfolding events. It is difficult to identify a single arena other than Iraq where Iran has played a major role in 2011. It had little do with the uprising in Yemen, and any role it had in the Bahraini catastrophe came only after the crackdown had devastated the protest movement and some angry Shi'a sought refuge in external support. Even worse, when the turbulence spread to Syria, Iran risked losing its only Arab ally. Hezbollah's struggles undermined the power of another key regional partner. At home, its domestic politics became more contentious as the economy struggled, infighting consumed the competing conservative camps, and the dormant Green Movement continued to smolder. Only its closer hold on Baghdad could offer comfort.

Iran's botched 2009 elections are the single greatest reason for its declining appeal to an Arab public that defined antidemocratic regimes as the enemy. The violent repression of the Green Movement was widely covered on al-Jazeera and other satellite television stations, disgusting an Arab public largely sympathetic to democracy movements. This is particularly important, given the empowerment of Arab publics by the recent wave of uprisings. As one Arab commentator put it, Tehran struggled with "the contradiction between its open support for the Egyptian protestors . . . and its harsh position towards the demands raised by the protest movement against the election results in June 2009."[4] This statement is a very common refrain across much of the Arab media. Many go even further, speculating whether the Arab uprisings will inspire Iran's own opposition to renew its challenge to the Islamic Republic.[5] Some go so far as to warn that "if Iran is not able to control the course of the Egyptian revolution, then the Iranian regime itself will be in danger."[6]

Tellingly, Tehran's regional influence peaked in the middle of the Bush administration's tenure. With Saddam gone, Iraq devastated, and America increasingly bogged down in a ferocious insurgency, there was no power to check Iranian power in the region, other than Israel and America's Arab allies.[7] Iran defined itself by its resistance to the American-dominated regional order. The United States, Israel, and most Arab regimes accepted that frame for regional politics, to Tehran's advantage. The focus on Iran had the paradoxical effect of highlighting Iran's position, allowing Tehran to benefit from and take credit for any real or perceived setback faced by its rivals. But the new regional environment has little time for such polarized frames or outdated appeals. As one pundit complained, "Khamenei's speaking of an 'Islamic New Middle East' is a clear attempt to revive through the intifadas the victory of the Iranian project over the late lamented George Bush's project!"[8]

There is little sign among either regimes or newly empowered publics of any regional attempt to jump on the bandwagon with Iran.[9] Quite the contrary. Gulf states became even more hawkish and aggressive, choosing to team up against Iran rather than to join it in a challenge to U.S. policy. They have also intensified their military relations with the United States, including massive arms purchases and military coordination. While independent-minded states such as Qatar and Turkey have built solid working relations with Iran and sought a role as mediators, few states in the region show any signs of actually aligning with Tehran.

This does not mean, as is often suggested, that the Gulf states would support an American-led military attack on Iran. As much as they fear and detest Iran, they also fear the consequences of such a war, including Iranian retaliation and the response of their own people, and would prefer the problem be solved short of war. Fears of popular uprisings will likely increase this caution about potentially destabilizing adventures. Saudi Arabia may continue to hate and fear Tehran, but most regimes will be less keen to cooperate with an America whose new policies they detest and fearful of anything that might trigger popular protests.

Even the U.S., usually prone to exaggerate the Iranian threat, acknowledged Iran's weakness. Chairman of the Joint Chiefs of Staff Admiral Michael Mullen put it bluntly: "Iran is the real loser here."[10] Iran barely rated a line in Obama's 2011 speech to the UN General Assembly, and hardly anyone noticed its absence. Its nuclear program continued apace, of course, which meant that it could recapture international attention in a heartbeat. Regional moods could change again, reviving Iran's flagging fortunes. But politically, the Arab uprisings at least temporarily put Iran's regional appeal on ice.

THE NEW POLITICS OF ISLAMISM

On July 29, 2011, I stood in a jam-packed Tahrir Square with nearly half a million Egyptian Islamists of all varieties. Muslim Brothers, the Gama'a al-Islamiyya, and Salafis from all over the country joined to demand the application of shari'a (Islamic law) and overt definition of the nation's identity as Islamic. The secular protestors who had been occupying Tahrir for weeks, and who laid claim to the mantle of the revolution, could only stand by helplessly as Tahrir became Islamist for one day.

Furious, many protestors left. By the time the square cleared that evening, new fears had been implanted in Egypt and around the world that the Islamists would emerge the victors of the revolution.

The images of bearded men screaming for God's law touched sensitive nerves worldwide. For a decade since 9/11, American popular discourse was consumed with the notion that radical Islam was sweeping the Middle East. President George W. Bush had said, presumably seriously, that America must fight the global war on terror in order to prevent al-Qaeda from creating a global caliphate.

This was an absurd notion. Al-Qaeda was and had always been an ideological fringe, able to attract broad support only by masking its extreme ideology in favor of a generic political critique of the West. The Bush administration aided al-Qaeda enormously. Its apocalyptic rhetoric and confrontational policies helped to fuel a self-fulfilling prophecy driving toward bin Laden's vision of a clash of civilizations between the West and Islam. By the mid-2000s, al-Qaeda's core arguments enjoyed widespread support, and its jihad in Iraq placed it at the center of popular fury.

But al-Qaeda could not escape the limitations of its own extremism. Most Arabs opposed American empire and took Islam seriously, but few wanted a Taliban-style Islamic state, accepted suicide bombings, or tolerated the killing of Muslims declared to be nonbelievers. Al-Qaeda never really had the ability to motivate large-scale Arab or Muslim support without help from foolish Western policies.

Al-Qaeda's own actions destroyed its image with most Arabs. The carnage in Iraq, from the beheading videos beloved by Abu Musab al-Zarqawi to the intra-Sunni conflict of 2006–2007 to the indiscriminate attacks on Shi'a Iraqis, all turned ordinary Arabs against al-Qaeda. Terrorist attacks in Muslim or Arab countries invariably galvanized public opinion against them rather than rallying support. The Bush administration in its final years and then the Obama administration got much smarter in rhetoric and practice, abandoning the most controversial policies and rhetoric of the early war on terror. By 2010, al-Qaeda was on the ropes.

When the Arab uprisings broke out, al-Qaeda struggled to place itself at the center of events with very limited success. Ayman al-Zawahiri, who took over as head of al-Qaeda after the killing of Osama bin Laden, made repeated efforts to claim the uprisings as in line with Al-Qaeda's own rejection of the Arab order; his words fell on deaf ears, rarely even generating mainstream Arab media coverage or stimulating any significant discussion across the Arab public. What was far more frequently remarked was that the peaceful changes in Egypt and Tunisia fatally undermined the al-Qaeda argument that only violent jihad could accomplish such change.

Even before bin Laden's death, al-Qaeda had lost the ability to galvanize mass publics in the Arab world. This did not mean that it was impotent. It could still organize terrorist attacks, especially close to home, and its branches in places like Yemen increasingly targeted the U.S. homeland. But a terrorist group is no mass movement, and only the latter could truly challenge core Western interests in the Middle East or the world. Al-Qaeda by 2010 had retreated from aspiring to the latter to holding on as the former. These groups had little to contribute to the emerging Arab public sphere, and virtually nobody outside their tiny subculture cared.

But at the same time, the confusion and even collapse of some Arab security services undoubtedly relaxed the pressure on these groups' activities. In Egypt, Libya, and Yemen, aggressive counterterrorism efforts collapsed, at least temporarily. Some prisons emptied. Attention was directed elsewhere. Few of the radicalized jihadist subculture are likely to change their minds in response to these uprisings, or to decide to lay down arms and rejoin society. They will try to turn to the only means they know to restore their prospects—terrorism and violence.

The Muslim Brotherhood and the newly politicized Salafis, on the other hand, have thrived in the new environment. Tunisia's el-Nahda party won an impressive plurality in the first free elections. Morocco's Islamist Party of Justice and Development won over 100 seats, the largest by far of any party, in its elections. Egypt's Freedom and Justice Party, the political arm of the Muslim Brotherhood, and several Salafi parties were poised to win big as Parliamentary elections began at the end of November. Wherever free elections were held, it seemed, Islamists proved the most popular and the best organized.

To say that al-Qaeda suffered while Islamists gained is no contradiction for those who understand the Islamist milieu. The Muslim Brotherhood may have provided some of the intellectual foundations for al-Qaeda, but the two organizations were mortal enemies locked in fierce, hostile public battles during the 2000s. The Brotherhood condemned al-Qaeda's terrorism and embraced democratic participation. It preached patient transformation of society from below and rejected the logic of *takfir*, by which extremists declared their adversaries to be non-Muslims. Brothers viewed themselves as part of a society that they hoped to change, not as the only true Muslims standing outside a den of vice that they hoped to destroy. The depth and intensity of the enduring conflict between the Brotherhood and al-Qaeda, despite their shared blanket ideology, are not only an important reminder of the reality of divisions among Islamists but also a useful lesson for the coming competition in the broader Arab public sphere.

A popular initial take on the Arab uprising was that the relative absence of Islamists showed that a silent majority would overwhelm any role for Islam in public life. But this view was quickly debunked. Yusuf al-Qaradawi, al-Jazeera's star Islamist, the Muslim Brotherhood–affiliated populist icon, shocked liberals by drawing a crowd a million strong to his sermon in Tahrir Square the first Friday after Mubarak's fall This should come as no surprise. Islamism has been transforming Arab public culture for generations. It was never going to simply disappear. An empowered public will include Islamist voices, almost by definition. After all, such groups had spent decades cultivating strong popular organizations, opposing the unpopular authoritarian regimes, and working to transform public culture in a conservative direction. They enjoyed financial and political support from the Gulf and from well-organized diaspora communities. They could not help but benefit from the opening of political space or to do well should elections be organized. They are generally the most well-organized, best-funded, and most politically savvy political movements, and are able to tap into the deeply held Islamic sentiment that they have been helping to cultivate for decades.

The question is whether their participation will ultimately be constructive or destructive. For the most part, their participation will be a good thing. It is good that Salafis who spent decades denouncing democracy as an affront to god's law now race to form political parties. The move from the violent margins into the mainstream of democratic political life will normalize Islamist movements. But it will also tempt them to attempt to push for goals that frighten and alienate their secular-minded citizens. Some will pass that test, as Tunisia's Rached Ghannouchi did with his ideological moderating influence and efforts to reassure in the days following el-Nahda's electoral victory. But others will not, and this will pose great challenges to each new democratic transition.

But the new landscape also poses real challenges to these Muslim Brotherhood–style movements. Islamist movements had evolved in response to a distinct political environment marked by repression and clear political limits. The newly opened political arenas posed both opportunities and challenges that have left them in ferment. While all Islamist groups agree on the generic need to create Islamic societies and to follow shari'a, they sharply disagree on what that means in practice. They compete for the same constituencies and the same legitimization. The illusion of Islamist unity in Tahrir that day was only that—a politically useful illusion, soon to be exposed in the bitter cut and thrust of daily political combat. Islamists will be changed by the political openings and new challenges they face. In Tunisia, the long-banned el-Nahda Party had to figure out how to navigate as the leading political force within a largely secularized and Western-looking nation. In Egypt, the Muslim Brotherhood found itself joined on the stage by a veritable rainbow of new Islamist parties and movements, from more liberal breakaway Muslim Brotherhood groups to hard-line Salafis and even reformed jihadists.

Meanwhile, the political involvement of Salafi groups introduced a new factor into the Islamist field. The younger generations are tempted by a Salafi movement that rejects the Muslim Brotherhood as insufficiently Islamic and overly political, too much of a creature of the urban middle classes. Across the Arab world, these Salafis preached an austere form of Islam defined by rigid dress codes, a simplified religious doctrine, and extremely conservative societal norms. Well financed by Saudi Arabia and other wealthy Gulf donors, and through workers who made money in the Gulf, these Salafi movements reshaped entire neighborhoods. They may share a common agenda in the abstract of "creating an Islamic state," but in practice they mean very different things by an "Islamic state," to the point where neither would recognize the other's ideal as an authentic example of one. In practice, the Salafis are fiercely competitive. Those tensions are already emerging in the new regional environment. Some will fade away, as the Salafis join the political process and leave behind their fervent attacks on the Brotherhood's "idolatry." Other tensions will intensify, as the different groups form political parties and find themselves competing for the same voters and battling for the same religious legitimacy.

Islamists' common agenda masks deep, profound, and intense internal divisions and disagreements between groups. Salafi jihadists see the Muslim Brotherhood as corrupt sellouts who place temporal power and comfort over the call of God. The Muslim Brotherhood sees Salafi jihadists as extremist fanatics who commit atrocities against fellow Muslims and irrationally condemn the society around them. Pious Muslims shudder at backward Salafis and worry about the political calculations of the Muslim Brotherhood.

These divisions are important to keep in mind. There is no Islamist monolith, and when Islamists are goaded into extreme statements to fend off competition on their right flank, they increase suspicion and resistance among the mainstream public. Islamists will be a part of the evolving Arab political scene but are unlikely to dominate. Some Islamists are truly radical and will be unable or unwilling to adapt to the norms of electoral competition. Others will join governments and grapple with the compromises of political life. But few will remain unchanged.

Islamists themselves are deeply sensitive to the fears they provoke in others. While they resent their exclusion from political power and mutter angrily about the denial of power to the majority, they also recognize that the West and their own secularists view their political activities with great unease. Islamist leaders speak forcefully about the need to avoid a replay of Algeria in the early 1990s, when too-great victories by the Islamic Salvation Front triggered a military coup and a bloodbath. They also fret about the fallout of the Hamas electoral victory in 2006, which led to international sanctions and a deep divide in Palestinian politics. They point approvingly to Turkey's Justice and Development Party, a mildly Islamist party that has proven wildly successful electorally by appealing to the rising conservative, pious Anatolian merchant class. In short, they want to be included as legitimate players in the emerging Arab order. That would be a major positive achievement, should they be brought in from the cold, committed to democratic norms, and conclusively abandoned violence.

In short, Islamism is a major trend within the mainstream of the new Arab public sphere that has been building for decades and will not disappear any time soon. It takes many forms, some deeply incompatible with each other. Islamists do not share common goals except in the most abstract way; they disagree about tactics and compete for the same constituencies. Their full participation in emerging democracies should be encouraged, not banned, since no meaningful democracy can exclude a sizable portion of its population from full citizenship. A decade ago, Salafi groups denounced democracy and provided a nurturing environment for jihadist subcultures. Today, major Salafi groups are rushing into the democratic political game and falling over themselves to reassure the West and their own people of their moderation. Such participation will change these movements. But while Islamist participation in politics should be encouraged, liberals should have no qualms about fighting to defeat them in the political realm. Islamists have no monopoly on authenticity and very rarely enjoy even plurality (much less majority) support.

The new public sphere itself has consequences for Islamism. Islamists who participate in these new public spheres really do think and behave differently than their elders. The Muslim Brotherhood leadership was profoundly shaped by the harsh repression of the Nasser era of the 1950s and 1960s. Secretive, elusive, and cautious, these leaders shied away from public scrutiny or from taking risky political gambits that might endanger the survival of the organization. But its youth activists were fully of the Kefaya generation.[11] Many maintained blogs and participated in an individual capacity in the protest movements over the course of the decade. They identified more with the restless impatience of their secular peers than with their cautious organization.

The Muslim Brotherhood struggled with such independent behavior, however. In 2009, its internal elections tipped the balance of power within the organization toward conservative, religion- and organization-focused leaders. Key political reformists such as Abdel Moneim Aboul Fotouh and Mohammed Habib lost their seats in the Guide's Office. A cascade of defections and resignations followed, as the young activists found themselves no longer at home in the organization. Brotherhood leaders minimize the significance of these departures (one told me that there were 300,000 to 400,000 youth in the Brotherhood, so they could hardly be threatened by the loss of a few dozen). But the ones leaving were the best and the brightest, the most politically engaged and the leaders of the future. Aboul Fotouh told me in September 2011 that 6,000 former Brotherhood youth were now volunteering for his presidential campaign.

Many of these youth activists left the Brotherhood after the revolution to form their own splinter movements and political parties. Others were expelled for their independent political activity. Over the summer of 2011, I talked with almost two dozen former Muslim Brotherhood youth activists. Only three or four remained with the organization. The rest had left. One became a spokesman for Mohamed el-Baradei and then helped form a new centrist political party, al-Adl, for which he won a seat in Parliament. One became an anonymous administrator for the "We Are All Khaled Said" Facebook page. Several helped form the Egyptian Trend political party. Many had become independent activists, unaffiliated with any group. Their departure demonstrates the extent to which the changed political conditions will challenge and reshape the Muslim Brotherhood in unpredictable directions.

U.S. GRAND STRATEGY

So where does the United States fit in this new Middle East? How can it best adapt to the new regional realities in ways that both advance its interests and align with its values? Is it even possible to align itself with a public opinion that largely opposes its foreign policies and distrusts its intentions? The Obama administration has not pleased many with its modest, careful approach to realigning America in the new region. Yet with a few key exceptions—notably the Israeli-Palestinian conflict and Bahrain—it has done reasonably well in responding to the torrent of developing events, protecting core U.S. interests while rhetorically embracing the democratic transformation.

But this pragmatic approach will not be enough in the years to come. The United States is desperately in need of a new doctrine to make sense of its position in the Middle East, and none of the major existing approaches will do. The two most robust, overarching American theories of how to deal with the Middle East during the last two decades have been realism and neoconservativism. Neither offers a useful guide to the new period. Realism does not adequately appreciate the disruptive force of an empowered Arab public and how this will change regional dynamics. And neoconservativism badly misunderstands that new Arab public.

Realism for many years seemed uniquely well adapted to the Middle East. The region's anarchic, violent, competitive environment, coupled with the absence of democracy, made it seem plausible that regimes would pursue their self-interest in survival rather than follow ideology or domestic politics. Certainly, the region's leaders have shown every inclination to play dirty, to ignore their public commitments, and to act aggressively to advance their own ends. Authoritarian Arab regimes have been insulated against domestic political pressure, and their leaders prone to assume *l'etat c'est moi.*

The region has never been as perfect a fit for realism as it appeared, however. The overarching American military presence and alliance network meant that the regional international system of the mid-2000s was not quite as "anarchic" as it seemed. Almost every regime in the region other than Iran and Syria was part of the American alliance system. This meant that whatever their distrust or hostility, most of these regimes were unlikely to go war with one another—and certainly not without American foreknowledge. Arab leaders were often as vulnerable to regional public opinion as they were impervious to the demands of their own people. Then there's the consistent power of ideological appeals; Nasserist pan-Arabism was an instrument of Egyptian state power and interest, but not in any form typically prioritized by realist theories.

The Arab uprisings have made the realist position even less tenable. Most realists simply throw up their hands at the sudden focus on democracy, popular upheavals, or an administration looking to be on "the right side of history." Such realists warn that the U.S. should not give in to wishful thinking about either the prospects for change or the alignment of democratic states in the region with the United States. They are likely right about the second (democracy will not likely strengthen alignments if public opinion is sharply hostile), but wrong about the first. Whether or not Arab countries succeed in making transitions to democracy, the empowerment of the public is a long-term trend that is unlikely to fade from the concerns of Arab leaders any time soon. The more that Arab publics matter, the less realists have to offer either for theory or for foreign policy advice. Realists may have a stronger case to make that the embattled dictators are better allies to America than newly emerging democracies that give greater weight to those who demand independence from American hegemony and oppose Israel. But if those changes are real, as I believe that they are, then there is no choice other than to adapt both theory and policy to the new situation. The Arab uprisings were not made in America. Their fate is not up to us, and preferring an authoritarian region will not make it so.

Realists are on stronger ground with their calls to reduce America's strategic commitment to the Middle East. Since the invasion of Iraq, which almost all realists opposed, the dominant trend among realists has been against interventionism and toward a reallocation of American resources away from the Middle East toward Asia. Realists therefore almost universally opposed the U.S. intervention in Libya as tangential to American interests. They saw it as unlikely to affect broader trends in the region, consistent with a general dismissal of the power of ideas or of diffusion effects. They rejected the idea that humanitarian concerns, rather than national interests, should drive U.S. military action. And they warned of the distraction from what they saw as truly vital interests elsewhere. All of these form a consistent worldview, but one that misunderstands the vital trends shaping the new Middle East.

The neoconservatives who dominated the Bush administration, for their part, might have seemed thoroughly discredited by their failures. The Bush administration managed American strategic interests in the Middle East in an almost uniquely bad manner. It behaved not like a status quo power managing an effective system but as a revisionist power determined to change the rules of the game. It abandoned any pretense of seeking Israeli-Palestinian peace, thereby removing the curtain that allowed Arab governments to cooperate with the U.S. and Israel. Its invasion of Iraq destroyed the region's strategic equilibrium, embroiling the U.S. in a grinding military counterinsurgency, while fueling anti-Americanism and empowering Iran. Its global war on terror made a mockery of international law, normalized torture and illegal surveillance, enhanced the standing of the most violent and extreme groups within Islamism, and fueled a narrative that the United States was at war with Islam itself. But the neoconservatives retain a strong position in the American political debate about the Middle East and are championed by almost all Republican presidential candidates. They will be a key part of the coming debate about how America should respond to the new region.

There is little evidence for the vindication of neoconservativism beyond the fairly self-evident truth that Arabs want democracy. The Bush administration saw the need for Arab democracy in the abstract, but shied away from its implications when Islamists made gains in Egyptian and Palestinian elections. After raising expectations in 2005 with a series of speeches promising new support for democracy over stability, its rapid reversal in the face of Islamist electoral gains in Egypt and Palestine shattered its credibility. And virtually all of the Arab public that might be empowered by democracy deeply, passionately, and viscerally hated the Bush administration's policies. While some appreciated American pressure on their governments, this did not translate into alignment with America on other issues.

The Bush administration's broader strategy of mobilizing Arab fears of Iran while ignoring the Israeli-Palestinian peace process actually *depended* on the suppression of Arab public opinion. While America's regional standing collapsed, Iran's rose and Iraq descended into an inferno, Israel and most Arab regimes aligned ever more publicly against the so-called "resistance" bloc of Iran, Syria, and nonstate actors such as Hezbollah and Hamas. The consolidation of this new organizing framework of "moderates" against "resistance," without engaging in any serious way on the Israeli-Palestinian front, was in some ways the Bush administration's greatest success. This is why Secretary of State Condoleezza Rice famously saw "the birth pangs of a New Middle East" in the carnage of Israel's war with Lebanon. This is why Egypt, Saudi Arabia, and most other Arab regimes quietly supported Israel against Hezbollah for some ten days before the public outrage grew too great.

But this "success" is also why the Bush administration's embrace of the promotion of democracy was always its oddest choice. The Bush administration's Freedom Agenda rested on a gamble that global trends would eventually bring freedom to the region, and that such freedom would create a situation more favorable to the United States (and Israel) than the authoritarian status quo. Those beliefs were normatively attractive and, in my view, broadly right. But they simply did not make much sense within the rest of the Bush administration's grand strategy. The Arab uprisings in fact directly challenged the core of the neoconservative American grand strategy.

The only way that a strategic framework aligning Arab regimes with Israel against Iran, while ignoring the peace process, could possibly work was by keeping public opinion out of the picture. Virtually every U.S. policy went against the expressed preferences of the Arab public. The more that Arab regimes embraced the alliance with Israel against Iran in the name of "moderation," the more that public opinion flocked toward the opposite pole of "resistance." Indeed, by almost every measure, the *suppression* of public opinion rather than its empowerment was a *necessary* part of Bush's grand strategy for the region. It's no small wonder, then, that Bush backed away from the Freedom Agenda as soon as the first open elections produced victory for the resistance, in the form of Hamas's triumph in the 2006 Palestinian legislative elections.

Over the course of the 2000s, most Arab regimes found that they agreed with Israel—at times more than with the U.S.—on a few big things. They feared Iran. They didn't care much about the Palestinian issue or expect much from the peace process. And they didn't want democracy intruding on their realpolitik. This was the region that the Bush administration helped create and that by 2009 was hardwired into the strategic logic of the Middle East and the base foreign policies of most of the region's leaders. The region's leaders wanted a tough line against Iran. They wanted to keep the Palestinian issue quiet, but didn't much care about solving it. They wanted moderate Islamist opposition movements tarred as terrorists and to thus have license to crush them. And they wanted to ignore their publics.

This is why the Bush administration and other neoconservatives tended to slip away from caring about the public when it proved inconvenient. They frequently claimed that Arab leaders in private were far friendlier toward U.S. objectives such as the invasion of Iraq or the containment of Iran than they let on in public. This was true. But their ability to act on those private convictions depended almost entirely on the extent to which they were insulated from public opinion, either at home or in the region. They badly misjudged Arab politics in part because they assumed the irrelevance of public opinion and prioritized their personal interactions with regime officials or a small set of local interlocutors. Such conversations may reflect the private views of officials hoping to influence American policy, but they are not necessarily either "truth" or a reliable guide to future behavior. More to the point, their systematic refusal to say the same things in public as they do in private—or to act on their avowed preferences—should have long since been a signal. If the privately expressed opinions of these Arab leaders were what really mattered, one might ask, then why did those regimes so rarely do what they had privately promised? The rise of the new Arab public will bring more and more of politics into the public realm and make it far more difficult to conceal such policies behind closed doors. Leaders will have to be more responsive to their publics.

The fetishizing of the use of force when dealing with the Arab world was another central pillar of neoconservativism. Obsessed, for unclear reasons, with Osama bin Laden's dictum that "Arabs will follow the strong horse," neoconservatives adopted a comprehensively hawkish policy agenda. Iraq was only the most obvious example of this. It extended to the rejection of engagement with Syria or Iran, the hardball treatment of Hezbollah in Lebanon, and so on. This also led them to demand that the U.S. insert itself into the center of all events, to be seen as doing something even when prudence would suggest otherwise.

The Obama administration's preference to remain in the background, assembling coalitions for action in places like Libya and Syria is anathema to the neoconservative sensibility. But in the era of the new Arab public, and one of declining American power, it will likely be far more effective. Arab protestors certainly do not seem to be "following the strong horse" as they risk their lives to battle powerful dictators against all odds. They are not calling for American leadership and, indeed, are more likely to bristle at anything associated with U.S. policy than to embrace it.

The Arab uprisings also fundamentally challenge the neoconservatives' conception of friend and enemy. As George Bush famously declared, the world was to be divided into two camps: "Either you are with us or you are against us." At the level of grand strategy, this translated into a stark division of the Middle East into radicals and moderates. Thus, Saudi Arabia emerged as a moderate because of its role supporting

Israeli preferences and combating Iran, despite the deep illiberalism of its domestic system and its role in spreading religious conservatism across the region. Turkey and Qatar, strong American military allies that appealed broadly across the Arab world but were critical of Israeli policies, were demonized and treated like enemies. The Arab uprisings reject these divides directly and completely. The new Arab public brings together Islamists and secularists, leftists and liberals, and all sectors of society in pursuit of shared goals. It demands both democracy and independence from American domination in the same breath.

In short, neoconservativism offers a terrible guidebook for dealing with the empowered publics of the Middle East. A return to realpolitik is no better advised, in a world where leaders are more constrained by the demands of their restless publics. What usually lies in the middle is a conventional liberalism focused on long-term reform and the cultivation of Arab civil society. This is an admirable agenda, but woefully inadequate to a period of rapid, urgent, ferocious change. What then remains?

The academic field of Middle East studies offers far better analysis than others of what is happening in the region. But most specialists in Middle East studies are handicapped in any effort to construct a new doctrine by a broad mistrust of American intentions. Most identify closely with the protestors challenging authoritarian rule and could at times fall into the temptation to take sides as advocates or cheerleaders for the protests rather than offer dispassionate analysis. Their deep suspicion of American empire did battle with their hope for meaningful international pressure on behalf of Arab protestors. Many pushed for fundamental change in America's posture in the region—to abandon Israel, to completely withdraw support for allies—without fully thinking through either the consequences or the political possibilities. They were unwilling to make concessions to the real pragmatic challenges of policy.

Indeed, their mistrust of American intentions often blinded them to what the Obama administration was actually doing. They doubted reports of Obama's efforts to remove Mubarak and to restrain the military in Egypt, and were exceptionally quick to assume the worst about American intentions. Their lowest moment, I fear, was their opposition to the intervention in Libya, which would have allowed many thousands of Libyans to be slaughtered before the eyes of a horrified Arab public out of vague fears about possible future NATO imperialism. I remain satisfied that NATO intervened to stop this tragedy from taking place, and that ultimately the removal of Qaddafi, the assistance in creating a new Libya, and the strengthening of global norms against brutalizing citizens will justify that decision. But more broadly, a left-leaning academic tradition focused primarily on countering America's imperium cannot offer—and likely does not want to offer—useful advice on how the U.S. can most effectively respond to the Arab uprisings.

CALLING AMERICA'S BLUFF

I believe that it is possible for the United States to play a constructive role in shaping the Arab uprisings in directions that support the aspirations of most Arabs, protect U.S. interests, and align with American values. I do not think that this will be easy. I have spent enough time with Obama administration officials to believe that they deeply and sincerely want to see Arab democracy take root and to forge new, positive relations with the new Arab public. But I also have seen little willingness or ability to make the policy adjustments that this will require. America does not need to abandon Israel or acquiesce to Islamist hegemony to effectively meet the challenge of a new region. It does, however, need to match its actions with its words across the region and be willing to accept the costs of a turbulent transition.

The Obama administration has adopted a pragmatic, case-by-case approach to the Arab uprisings. It has embraced the argument that change is inevitable, that a more democratic Middle East would advance American interests, and that it must be "on the right side of history." Obama insisted that the changes in the region were neither driven by nor about America itself. At the same time, Obama proved cautious toward changes in the Gulf and resistant to formulating a single, coherent doctrine that might compel action in places such as Bahrain or Syria. And its approach to the Israeli-Palestinian conflict badly undermined its standing with both the old powers of the regional status quo and with the newly empowered Arab public.

Obama's response to the Arab uprisings began from the broadly realist instincts in the first two years of his administration. In his earliest moves on the Middle East, he demonstrated his desire to repair America's relations with the Arab and Muslim worlds by moving beyond Bush's controversial policies and rhetoric. He vowed to withdraw from Iraq, and largely kept that promise. He engaged forcefully on the peace process, pressuring Israel to freeze settlements and pushing for negotiations to resume, but he failed on both counts. He prioritized the Iranian nuclear challenge, but focused on diplomacy and multilateral engagement as the way to influence Tehran's behavior and to undermine its regional appeal.

Obama oriented American public diplomacy from the start toward the broad mainstream of the Arab world rather than to the narrow slice of extremists who had dominated the Bush administration's concerns. In his major address in Cairo to the Muslim communities of the world in June 2009, Obama focused not only on these issues of high politics but also on the concerns of ordinary people about jobs, security, dignity, and opportunity.[12] He spoke the language of "mutual interest and mutual respect," promising an engagement between equals rather than American tutelage. The speech firmly stated a commitment

> to governments that reflect the will of the people. Each nation gives life to this principle in its own way, grounded in the traditions of its own people. America does not presume to know what is best for everyone, just as we would not presume to pick the outcome of a peaceful election. But I do have an unyielding belief that all people yearn for certain things: the ability to speak your mind and have a say in how you are governed; confidence in the rule of law and the equal administration of justice; government that is transparent and doesn't steal from the people; the freedom to live as you choose. These are not just American ideas; they are human rights. And that is why we will support them everywhere.
>
> Now, there is no straight line to realize this promise. But this much is clear: Governments that protect these rights are ultimately more stable, successful and secure. Suppressing ideas never succeeds in making them go away. America respects the right of all peaceful and law-abiding voices to be heard around the world, even if we disagree with them. And we will welcome all elected, peaceful governments—provided they govern with respect for all their people.

The Obama administration spoke frequently about the constituent elements of democracy in this period—human rights, political freedoms, civil society, and universal aspirations for freedom. The administration understood the deep, pervasive problems across the region and the threat those underlying trends posed to stability. It was particularly worried about Egypt, but the concerns extended to the entire region. Indeed, over the course of fall 2010, the White House had been crafting a document assessing the likelihood of regional turbulence and the urgent need for political reform.[13]

But Obama was pragmatic. He came to office frankly recognizing the age of authoritarian retrenchment that had taken root in the last two years of the Bush administration. Obama backed away from bold rhetoric, placing the U.S. at the center of the democracy struggle, and instead focused on longer-term capacity building and civil society. Engagement replaced democracy promotion as the overarching strategic framework for dealing with Arab publics. The concept was one that, if more clearly articulated, would have been quite resonant with what actually happened in 2010 and 2011: that empowered and capable Arab publics would push for democratic change on their own, without U.S. prompting, and that the main American role was to quietly give them the political space to move.

But clearly Obama's bid for engagement on these terms was too little and too late to make up for decades of a foreign policy that largely depended on autocratic rulers working against the preferences of their people. The high expectations raised by Obama's election were followed by a steep crash, as disappointed Arabs saw him unable to deliver on his promises. Everywhere I went in the Arab world in 2011, the conversation quickly went to the same place: "Obama is a good man who means well and speaks beautifully, but he doesn't deliver."

The Arab uprisings in a very real sense called a long-standing American bluff about democracy. For decades, Americans had called for democratic reform in the region, while enjoying the practical benefits of cooperation with dictators. Whatever the long-term benefits of a democratic Middle East or the normative value of the liberation of Arab publics, in the near term, the Arab upheavals clearly challenge the U.S.-dominated status quo.

Americans generally fail to recognize how little credibility the U.S. has on the question of democracy. The U.S. has almost always spoken about the value of Arab democracy, but Arabs know that its support has almost always faded in the face of its actual outcomes. The first Bush administration punished democratizing Jordan and Yemen for siding with pro-Iraqi public opinion during the Gulf War, while handsomely rewarding Mubarak for ignoring Egyptian preferences. It quietly backed the Algerian military's coup against democracy in 1991. The Clinton administration went along with King Hussein's retraction of democratic changes in the mid-1990s in order to sustain Jordan's peace treaty with Israel, and generally prioritized the peace process and the dual containment of Iran and Iraq over democracy. George W. Bush's administration gave bold speeches on democracy and devoted significant funds to promotion programs, but quickly backed away when Hamas won Palestinian elections in 2006 and left behind a region less democratic than it inherited.

Where the U.S. did push for democratic reforms, this was primarily to increase the legitimacy and stability of its allied regimes in order to prevent more radical change, or else to destabilize and weaken hostile regimes. The calculation has long been that the concrete benefits of Arab dictators' cooperation on counterterrorism, on the Israeli-Palestinian peace process, or on confrontation with Iran and Iraq far outweighed any benefits that a democratic change might offer. The Arab upheavals directly challenged that calculation of costs, as change began to seem unavoidable and the benefits of collaboration with dictators no longer seemed a safe bet.

The U.S. has a massive semipermanent military presence in the Gulf and maintained robust alliances with almost all of the authoritarian regimes in the region. Its primary interests have been consistent for decades and have generally enjoyed robust bipartisan support. The U.S. has sought to maintain the predictable flow of oil at what it considers to be reasonable prices, not through direct ownership but through alliances with oil producers and the military presence to prevent regional or international competitors from disruptions. It has sought to protect Israel, not for strategic reasons but because of a deeply felt, bipartisan identification with the Jewish state. Its deep investment in the peace process since 1973 has been primarily meant to bridge the innate contradiction between its alliance with Israel and its interests in the Arab world—an urgent need that helps to explain why the peace process lumbers on many years after most observers thought it dead.

The U.S. has become more deeply and intimately involved in the region over the years. Before 1990, it had more of an "offshore" presence, relying on local allies to protect its interests, while avoiding significant direct involvement—a role epitomized, perhaps, by its simultaneous support for both Iran and Iraq during their devastating eight-year war. This began to change in 1990, when the U.S. took advantage of the changes in the Soviet Union to obtain UN authorization for a massive military intervention to liberate Kuwait from Iraq. After Operation Desert Storm, America maintained an ever-growing architecture of military bases and alliances in the Gulf to enforce the sanctions on Iraq and to simultaneously contain Iranian power. It convened the Madrid Peace Conference in 1991 and then spent the next decade consumed by the micromanagement of peace talks among Israel and the Palestinians and Syria. It is difficult to forget the image of Aaron Miller, a top White House official, on his hands and knees measuring the distance between lampposts in Hebron as a metaphor for how fully America had inserted itself into every intimate detail of Arab political life.[14]

After 9/11, the U.S. became even more deeply present in the Middle East. It deepened its security cooperation with most Arab regimes in the global war on terror, sending those regimes everything from cash and equipment to detainees for torture. To fight what it viewed as a "war of ideas," the Bush administration inserted itself into every corner of the Arab media and public culture, almost always in deeply unpopular ways. Its pressure on Arab governments to revise their textbooks and remove radical interpretations of Islam may have made sense from the perspective of combating al-Qaeda, but it was an unprecedented intrusion into the deepest, most intimate parts of Arab culture guaranteed to stoke resentment (try to imagine Americans' reaction to China stepping in to remove passages from our textbooks deemed offensive to Asian sensibilities). And then, of course, there was the invasion and occupation of Iraq, which brought hundreds of thousands of troops and contractors into an Arab country along with the images from Abu Ghraib prison and the descent into a bloody hell of civil war and insurgency.

No U.S. administration has fully confronted the contradiction inherent in simultaneously relying heavily on Arab governments for security cooperation, alienating and enraging public opinion, and pressuring the friendly governments to open up the system to hostile publics. From its support for Israel to the war on terror and the sanctions on and invasion of Iraq, the U.S. has consistently pursued deeply unpopular policies across the region. More democracy would only mean more problems. While unhappy about its unpopularity and fitfully engaging in public diplomacy to try and repair its image, the U.S. generally considered its low standing with publics an acceptable price to pay. The terrorist attacks of 9/11 sent America down the wrong path in its engagement with the region, toward an overwhelming focus on extremism and radicalization. The Arab upheavals should be an opportunity to devote the same level of resources and urgency to a far broader engagement with the new real Arab public. As Arab publics matter more, the U.S. will need to decide whether it will continue paying higher costs or whether it will make unpopular adjustments to its core foreign policies. The latter seems unlikely, and public diplomacy alone is unlikely to bridge the gap.

The Arab uprisings clearly destabilized the status quo that America had shaped and within which it prospered, no matter how much Americans sympathized or identified with their aspirations. Most of the threatened leaders were American allies. The publics surging into the streets overwhelmingly opposed American policies, such as the occupation of Iraq, support for Israel, or even the containment of Iran. The uprisings badly worried Israeli security officials, who saw their carefully constructed relations with Arab leaders and treaty-protected borders to the east and south threatened. As the turbulence moved into the Gulf, it threatened the predictable flow of oil, and even the U.S. military base structures (especially in the pivotal case of Bahrain).

The Arab uprisings pushing for democratic change threaten the very foundations of the American-backed regional order. The protestors may not burn American flags, but they are a direct challenge to the American-led status quo. While the protests themselves focused on domestic issues of governance, corruption, and poverty, those complaints are part of a broader narrative of resistance. As the Egyptian activist Ibrahim Houdaiby eloquently puts it, the January 25 revolution in Egypt sought to liberate Egypt not just from Mubarak but from the shackles of the foreign occupation that Mubarak cultivated.[15]

In the short term, the uprisings have weakened traditional allies without building new ones. The public that indisputably matters more has been conditioned to mistrust and dislike American foreign policy by long years of experience. The uprisings are aimed directly at the U.S.-backed status quo, no matter how many times the administration tries to align itself with them. Nor is it in America's power to stop the uprisings even if it wanted to. No administration could possibly adapt to their aspirations without harming the existing network of alliances. As one senior administration official muttered ruefully to me over coffee in the late spring, "the truth is that right now we don't have a single friend in the region."

It is therefore remarkable how quickly the Obama administration saw the changes in Tunisia and Egypt as an opportunity rather than as a threat. Where the Bush administration talked about democracy but abandoned it at the first sign of progress, the Obama administration acted on its belief that democracy would serve America's long-term interests. It chose to place itself "on the side of history" and to identify with the aspirations of the protestors and their demands for change. The consequences of this decision will have long-reaching but poorly understood implications for America's place in the region. Aligning itself with those aspirations for change will be quite a trick, but it is not impossible.

The Arab world is changing. The United States can't stop it. The changes will have major implications for the foreign policies of Middle Eastern states, many of which will challenge the status quo that the U.S. has long maintained.[16] The common delusion in Washington that these Arab revolts were only about domestic issues and had no interest in the Palestinian cause or American foreign policy will not long survive the Egyptian election system. One of the best moves by the Obama administration has been to recognize that the Arab upheavals did not depend on or want American leadership, and to seek ways to align the U.S. with the rising Arab public without claiming authorship.

The Cairo speech of June 2009 was a distant memory by the time Mohammed Bouazizi set the Arab uprisings in motion. There is therefore little reason to believe, as some would like, that Obama in any way inspired the Arab uprisings.

But Obama did contribute in both passive and active ways. First, by simply not being George W. Bush, he made American support for Arab aspirations conceivable. There were still reservoirs of hope within the pervasive disappointment, which led activists to demand that he act at times when Bush would have been told to stay far, far away. When he pushed for an international intervention in Libya, he did not carry Iraq's baggage. And his temperament and willingness to allow America to take a backseat, which so enraged neoconservatives, proved to be an asset at a time when Arabs were taking their fates into their own hands. Precisely because Obama was not filling the airwaves with empty rhetoric about American visions of Arab democracy, the Arab activists had space within which to act. The fundamental fact, which Obama understood better than most of his critics, was that America could not be the driving force in the Arab uprisings. These were popular uprisings by Arabs and for Arabs, and not something made in Washington.

Then, Obama actively took a number of steps that not every administration would have taken. For all the Bush administration's talk of Arab democracy, it rapidly backed away from the implications of confronting Mubarak after the crackdown midway through the 2005 parliamentary elections and essentially abandoned democracy promotion after Hamas won the 2006 Palestinian elections. Perhaps the Bush administration would have seized the moment in January 2011 to push Mubarak to step down and empower Arab democracy, but would it really have followed through with Israel and Saudi Arabia firmly opposed, counterterrorism stakeholders pushing for the essential role of Omar Suleiman, and the boogeyman of Iran lurking over the horizon? Perhaps. Would Mubarak have been more successful at blaming foreign conspirators for the protests if the demonized Bush had been available to single out? Maybe.

We will never know. But we do know that under George W. Bush, not a single Arab country began a transition to democracy on its own. Only Iraq came close, in the context a horrific military adventure whose consequences we still suffer today. Under Obama, by the end of the summer of 2011, Egypt, Tunisia, and Libya had already begun such a transformation; Morocco had introduced serious constitutional reform; and several other Arab countries had a fighting chance for change. That is not a bad record for an administration that supposedly did not care about Arab democracy.

The administration's response to the uprisings developed in stages. It viewed Tunisia as an intriguing test case for democratic change, one that did not fundamentally touch on any core U.S. interests. On Egypt, the administration went into full crisis mode. The president quickly recognized the power of the unfolding protests and seized the opportunity to push for peaceful change. Indeed, the rapidly unfolding crisis—experienced in the hyper-speed of "Twitter time"—made moves look slow and reactive that by any reasonable standard were shockingly fast for Washington. Obama called on Mubarak to step down six days after protests began, but for Egypt's protestors, that wasn't fast enough. An unprecedented international coalition authorized by a Security Council resolution stopped Qaddafi's forces on the outskirts of Benghazi and prevented a massacre, but for interventionists, this was too slow.

By February, the administration was well into the process of formulating a doctrine making sense of America's position in the region. But then Bahrain and the Saudi-led counterrevolution threw a major wrench into the works. The American position on Bahrain is not difficult to understand. The administration had been working hard on nudging the Bahraini palace toward a deal on political reform with the opposition, and seemed close to accomplishing that goal. But when things went wrong, the U.S. found itself unable to reconcile its competing needs. The U.S. Fifth Fleet based in Bahrain, intense Saudi interest, and concerns about Iran make it overdetermined that the U.S. would back away from demanding change in Manama. No call that King Hamad had lost legitimacy and must leave would be forthcoming. Realpolitik generated an absolutely unavoidable hypocrisy, which then fatally crippled the administration's broader regional stance, especially with the young activists who saw the entire Arab uprisings as a unified narrative.

What about Libya? The NATO intervention in March baffled critics on both left and right. Few were satisfied with the argument that the intervention had prevented a likely massacre in Benghazi, a "Srebrenica on steroids," or that the outcome in Libya would have major implications for the process of change throughout the region. For the left, this was Obama reinvented as Bush, or, at best, as the Clinton who bombed Serbia in 1999 over Kosovo. Surely, according to the left, the NATO intervention was aimed at grabbing Libyan oil or some other nefarious scheme. On the right, Obama failed to lead by having NATO rather than U.S. forces run the operation and by refusing to consider ground troops or a post-Qaddafi occupation. Many in the middle were puzzled at a non-war launched without formal congressional approval that the president refused to either fully own or disown.

The Libyan intervention took far longer to be resolved than the administration had hoped and, by the end, had few public backers. But it did succeed. The intervention did prevent Benghazi from falling. NATO air power and a better trained and armed rebel force slowly pushed toward Tripoli. An alternative Libya government came into shape and gained growing international recognition. All of this was accomplished at very little cost to the United States—just over $1 billion in six months, according to calculations by the Council on Foreign Relations' Micah Zenko, or barely a rounding error in Pentagon budget calculations.[17] And it did have effects beyond its borders, including helping to advance the Syrian uprising. And it helped to create a new regional norm against regimes using violence against their people that would come into play again and again, from Yemen to Syria.

In May, as described in the opening to this chapter, the president finally decided to roll out his major speech on the region. It laid out a coherent vision of America's role, firmly aligning America with the democratic transformations across the region, while always putting an Arab rather than American face on the changes. The speech even brought up Bahrain, recognizing the damage done to the U.S. image by its silence on that crackdown. But it also included a fairly standard appeal for movement on the Israeli-Palestinian front that immediately became the primary focus for postspeech controversy over the 1967 Israeli-Palestinian borders. But this speech failed to resolve the controversy over America's true intentions. Arab activists increasingly viewed the U.S. as part of the counterrevolution, despite all of Obama's efforts to align himself with their struggle.

The leftist activists in Egypt campaigned against World Bank and IMF loans that Washington saw as crucial for creating the economic context for a successful democratic transition but that the activists denounced as an attempt to protect neoliberal hegemony. When the SCAF unleashed a ferocious campaign against alleged U.S. funding of activist groups such as the April 6 Youth Movement, activists complained about their own honor but almost never rose to the defense of America. Indeed, even as Americans saw democracy assistance as one of the key ways in which it could help Egypt's transition, virtually nobody in Egypt was willing to publicly defend that democracy assistance. What was meant to consolidate positive views of America instead became a shameful burden to hide from view.

The turmoil in Syria that escalated over the summer introduced new challenges to the American position. Unlike most of the countries where the U.S. had grappled with change, Syria was a hostile regime and Iran's key Arab ally. For neoconservatives, it made no sense to show restraint toward the Assad regime. They urged forceful condemnation and a push for regime change very early in the Syrian protests, though this perhaps should not be surprising since most had been pushing for regime change in Syria for a decade. Many activists pushed as well for a more forceful American position toward Assad and savaged U.S. statements that Assad might still have a chance to lead a reform process. But Obama here was again well within the regional consensus and was content to allow Assad's brutality to drive the process of his alienation. Obama understood, correctly, that forceful American intervention too early would change the dynamic toward one of nationalist rejection of foreign conspiracies.

Obama's approach to the regional transformations was in the end about as effective as could have been hoped for. He could not satisfy everyone, but he did manage to protect core American interests while pushing for reforms and change. Under his watch, at least three dictators fell, replaced by better regimes with a hope of more fundamental transitions to come. Still, questions remain as to what direction the U.S. should take after the turbulence, and what kind of Middle East it should try to help shape.

This is not to say that the Obama administration's strategy has been perfect. Far from it. Its approach to the Israeli-Palestinian conflict has been frankly disastrous, though what other approach would have worked better is not clear, given the rightward trend in Israeli politics and the changes on the ground undermining any possible two-state solution. It fumbled Bahrain badly and was overly deferential to Saudi concerns.

It failed to effectively engage the new Arab publics in such a way as to gain their appreciation or support for its efforts, a failure of public diplomacy that will haunt America for years.

But overall it has gotten some big things right. It understood very quickly the significance of an unstoppable wave of Arab popular mobilization. It worked very effectively to help facilitate a transition in Egypt that could have been far bloodier or stalemated for an extended period. It prevented an appalling massacre in Libya and eventually helped remove Qaddafi and bring in a more democratic, representative regime. It avoided major mistakes, such as a counterproductive early escalation in Syria. And it has worked effectively with international and regional institutions, avoiding the kinds of unilateral adventurism that marred the Bush administration and effectively mobilizing multilateral action across multiple theaters.

THE NEW MIDDLE EAST
AND AMERICA'S CHALLENGE

If the U.S. hopes to navigate the new Arab world, it needs to make fundamental changes. Above all, it must recognize the reality that the empowerment of the Arab public forces it to do things differently. The rise of the Arab public should be seen as a challenge as massive and essential as counterterrorism after 9/11. It should drive a fundamental reorientation of bureaucratic and policy priorities.

The U.S. should treat the rise of the new Arab public as an existential issue for American foreign policy, one that should drive a fundamental reorientation of its approach to the region. A good place to begin is to accept that Arabs are not stupid. Arab publics have long experience in decoding the propaganda of their own regimes and have a well-earned skepticism of virtually anything that the United States proposes. The Arab public sphere has been relentlessly dissecting American policy for many years and has fairly well-fixed notions that are not easily changed, whether through public diplomacy or through even the most beautiful presidential speeches, unless America's policies match its words. Arab publics have a hypersensitivity to double standards, particularly on the Palestinian issue. Why do all peoples have the right to democracy except Palestinians, they ask, and why is there a responsibility to protect

Libyans but not Gazans? They understand America's place in the region, better than most Americans do, and have no patience with the pleasantries of American political discourse. Americans may believe that they can keep the same basic regional policies while winning over Arab publics. Arabs do not.

Real public diplomacy has never been more strategically essential for the United States in the Middle East. The phenomenon of American diplomats watching on television the Tahrir Square protests unfold three blocks away should never happen again. A senior embassy official should never ask what good it would really do to be out talking to people in upper Egypt, as I heard in the summer of 2011. The empowerment of publics means that America cannot hope to succeed without systematically listening to, engaging with, informing, and communicating with the new Arab publics. This engagement should be considered as seriously now as the "war of ideas" was after 9/11.

America also needs to take seriously the deep and fundamental linkages between issues. A vast industry has been devoted to convincing American policy makers that there is no real relationship between the Israeli-Palestinian conflict and wider strategic issues in the region. This is poppycock. The unification of Arab political space and the crystallization of a new Arab collective narrative has ratcheted up the already real interconnections among issues in the region. The impact of one country's struggles on another's politics will grow. The indexes through which Arabs judge American policy will multiply. Core Arab issues like Palestine will be impossible to avoid—but so will urgent new crises such as Syria's uprising.

Democracy may or may not take hold, but domestic politics will be more open and turbulent in most places. There will likely be more focus on distinct national concerns as countries turn toward democratic competition and domestic reform. With luck, each country will develop a strong local media of its own dedicated to the urgent functions of any fourth estate—transparency, accountability, and public debate. But it would be wrong to assume that this will reduce the attention to broader regional issues. The pan-Arab consciousness of the rising generation is impossible to miss. Social media connections remain much denser within countries than at the pan-Arab level, but the trend has been in the latter direction. The Arab uprisings have imprinted on them the deep shared identity and narrative that had perhaps faded from the minds of their elders in the face of the dismal reality of Arab state competition.

All of this means that a serious rethinking of America's relationship with Israel cannot be avoided. American support for Israel is bipartisan, deeply held, and unlikely to change any time soon. The United States should support Israel and help it as a real friend. But this must go in both directions. The Israeli government of Benjamin Netanyahu aggressively cultivated Republican support against President Obama and has helped to turn Israel into an increasingly partisan issue in the United States, undermining decades of bipartisanship in the pursuit of short-term gain. More worrying is that his approach has been popular, not idiosyncratic, and broadly in line with the trends in Israeli public opinion. Put bluntly, it has never been more important to America that Israel solve its Palestine problem, but it has never been less likely that Israel will be able or willing to do so.

This does not mean that the U.S. should abandon Israel. Even if this were possible, given American domestic political realities, it would not be advisable. America's ties to Israel are deep, at the societal level as well as at the military and intelligence levels. Israel is a closely identified ally of the United States, for all the turbulence in the relationship, and friends are not to be abandoned lightly. But the relationship will have to change if the U.S. hopes to navigate the new Arab public. The old dodges and workarounds simply will not work anymore. Decades of American policy have been based on the ability to manage the tension between its alliance with Israel and its alliance with the Arabs through the pretense of a peace process and reliance on dictators to crush public opposition. When President Mahmoud Abbas brought a bid for Palestinian state-hood to the UN, the Obama administration could respond only by calling yet again for a return to negotiations. It is playing defense on Israel's behalf in international institutions and around the world, deploying ever greater diplomatic capital to ever less effect. This will no longer work. With the peace process dead and rising public power, the U.S. must be willing to listen to new ideas and approaches, act multilaterally, and encourage Israelis and Palestinians alike to overcome their short-term interests and fears.

The U.S. will also have to do better in grappling with the challenge posed by Islamist groups. As Arab arenas open to political competition, Islamist movements will be powerful competitors in most and will make strong bids to take power through the ballot box in some countries. Even where such movements credibly commit to democratic rules, they are still profoundly antiliberal. The U.S. will no longer be able to fudge the gap between an abstract commitment to democracy and the reality of what Arab majorities may choose to vote for.

Fortunately, America has come a long way since the dark days after 9/11 when ignorance ran rampant. The U.S. government now understands Islamic movements far better than before and appreciates their variety, internal rivalries, and doctrinal differences. The government will be more likely to respond rationally to the public participation of Islamist movements. The Obama administration has admirably laid out a position that accepts their democratic participation, while also advocating for core liberal values. Its senior officials have declared their willingness to engage with Islamists who commit to democratic participation and nonviolence, and such meetings with Islamist party leaders in places such as Egypt and Tunisia have begun. There are even more resources upon which to draw, not least the fact that America itself is a land of deep religious faith mediated by a shared civic contract and could be a model for Arab societies in that vein.

Inside the United States, however, there is virulent anti-Islamic populism, its exponents barely tempered by the backlash against the Oslo anti-Islam terrorist who drew heavily on their writings. The campaigns of the lunatic anti-Islamic right fuel resentment of America in the Muslim world and could conceivably shape the policies of a future Republican administration in disastrous ways. Combating this anti-Islamic trend at home has never been a more urgent national security priority. America cannot engage effectively with a region struggling to peacefully incorporate Islamists through democracy if it is dominated by ideologues who demonize and attack them at every turn. Nor can it continue its effective campaign to marginalize and defeat al-Qaeda if its own public feeds a narrative about a clash of civilizations that does not exist.

Finally, the U.S. will need to accept the limits of its ability to control the Middle East. Washington has long been accustomed to the habits of empire. In no other part of the world does that label fit more comfortably. But the rise of the empowered Arab public marks the end of those days when America could enforce an unpopular regional order. The powers that drive Arab politics in the coming years will be those like Turkey, Qatar, and the new Egypt that maintain good relations with America even while pursuing popular and independent foreign policies. And the U.S.'s struggling economy and a war-weary population put clear limits on its ability to engage again in foolish, expensive wars of choice. The days of browbeating allies to be with us or against have passed. We should now expect to deal with the states of the region as partners and allies and even rivals.

This is not a counsel of despair or decline. It is a counsel of hope. It is a vision of an America that takes seriously its own ideals and values, even as it protects its vital national interests. It is an approach to foreign policy that acknowledges other states and publics as equals and partners, not as objects or obstacles to overcome. The Arab uprisings are only the beginning of these changes, and the world they are making will not be as familiar, comfortable, or predictable as the world we have come to know. But we cannot stop it. We should not want to stop it. We should embrace a region moving at last toward what its people always knew it could be. That is America's challenge.

ACKNOWLEDGMENTS

I HAVE BEEN BLESSED in my efforts to understand and to engage with the Arab uprisings by an incredibly talented and supportive community of scholars, analysts, colleagues, and government officials. Since the beginning of the Arab uprisings, I have had the opportunity to interact on a regular basis with a wide variety of Obama administration officials. My reconstruction of U.S. thinking about the changes in the Middle East draws heavily on those ongoing interactions, interviews, consultations, and discussions. Since most of those discussions were not meant for attribution, I do not quote from them or thank individuals here. But I am grateful for the opportunity to have helped.

I launched the Project on Middle East Political Science (POMEPS), a collaborative network of such scholars, in early 2010 with the generous support of the Carnegie Corporation of New York and the Social Science Research Council. When the Arab uprisings began, POMEPS helped the academic community step up to the challenge of making sense of these developments for Washington and the world. As a perusal of the footnotes to this book should make clear, I have learned an incredible amount from my colleagues and could not have written this book without them. I would like to thank Hillary Wiesner and Tom Asher, the POMEPS steering committee, and my assistants, Maria Kornalian and Mary Casey.

One of the key initiatives of POMEPS was the May 2010 launch of the Middle East Channel on ForeignPolicy.com, where I had been blogging since the site's relaunch in January 2009. With the support of the Middle

East Task Force at the New America Foundation and the editors of *Foreign Policy*, the Middle East Channel quickly became the premiere online site for the informed discussion of regional politics. In my role as editor, I worked to bring academics into the policy debate—and they responded. I would like to thank Susan Glasser for her constant support, along with Blake Hounshell, David Kenner, Daniel Levy, Amjad Atallah, Tom Kutsch, and Jon Guyer.

Thanks also to the Center for a New American Security for their support since taking me on as a Non-Resident Senior Fellow in 2009. I have gained great respect for the rigor and intellectual integrity of the CNAS team over the course of producing three policy reports. Thanks to Kristin Lord, John Nagl, Nate Fick, Andrew Exum, and the entire CNAS team for everything—it's been an honor.

An ongoing research project supported by the US Institute for Peace has also been important for shaping my thoughts on these issues. Sean Aday, Henry Farell, and John Sides have been fantastic collaborators, and I am grateful for the enthusiastic support of Sheldon Himmelfarb and his team.

I am even more profoundly grateful for the many relationships with Arab bloggers and online activists that I have formed over a decade of such research and through my own blogging about the Middle East. I have had the good fortune to meet many of the activists at the center of the Egyptian revolution and other Arab uprisings, or to form relationships with them through online interactions. They have profoundly shaped my understanding of the region, even where we disagree. I will always be awed by their courage, creativity, and integrity.

My day job, of course, is at George Washington University, where I took over the Middle East Studies Program and the Institute for Middle East Studies in 2009. I have enjoyed a wonderful intellectual community, as well as great institutional support for my activities since coming to GW. I would particularly single out Nathan Brown and Edward Gnehm for setting an example for what it means to be a good colleague—it would be hard to imagine smarter, harder working, or more gracious partners. Dean Michael Brown has been consistently supportive. Doug Shaw has worked tirelessly to shepherd through grants and programs, and has been flexible and gracious in dealing with my entrepreneurial ways. Thanks also to Suzanne Stephenson, Emily Voight, Rhea Myerscough, and many other GW colleagues.

I hesitate to list the many friends and colleagues whose intellectual engagement has helped shape my ideas over the years, because I would inevitably leave some out. I will therefore limit myself only to a few who directly helped on this manuscript. I would like to particularly thank Nathan Brown (again), Steven Cook, and Colin Kahl for reading this entire manuscript; Lisa Anderson for working with me on editing a book on the uprisings and organizing a conference at the American University of Cairo; Jillian Schwedler and Curt Ryan for keeping alive the legacy of the Jordan Mafia; Gideon Rose for pushing me to think big; and Lauren Bohn for her tireless reporting energy and assistance during research trips to Tunisia and Egypt.

Finally, Brandon Proia, my editor at PublicAffairs was a pleasure to work with throughout the process of writing this book.

My deepest thanks and eternal love and gratitude go to my family, to whom I dedicate this book: Lauren, Sophia, Alec, and even Jack—the most annoying dog alive, perhaps, but who accompanied me on the long early morning walks where I formulated many of the ideas in this book. While I alone am responsible for any errors of fact or interpretation in this book, I reserve the right to blame them on Jack.

NOTES

INTRODUCTION

1. F. Gregory Gause III, "Why Middle East Studies failed," *Foreign Affairs*, June 2011, http://www.foreignaffairs.com/articles/67932/f-gregory-gause-iii /why-middle-east-studies-missed-the-arab-spring.

2. The Abu Aardvark blog was at http://abuaardvark.typepad.com until January 2009 and then moved to http://lynch.foreignpolicy.com.

3. My comments at that time can be found at http://abuaardvark.typepad.com /abuaardvark/2008/09/democracy-in-eg.html.

CHAPTER 1

1. Faisal al-Qassem, episode of The Opposite Direction, al-Jazeera, "The Arab People and Revolutions," December 23, 2003, http://www.aljazeera.net/channel /archive/archive?ArchiveId=92550.

2. http://mideast.foreignpolicy.com/posts/2011/01/06/obamas_arab_spring.

3. Marc Lynch, *Voices of the New Arab Public* (Columbia University Press, 2006).

4. Jill Crystal, "Authoritarianism and its adversaries in the Arab world," *World Politics* 46 (2004), p. 277.

5. Lisa Wedeen, *Ambiguities of Domination* (University of Chicago Press, 1999).

6. Riyadh Agha, "The Youth in the Arab revolutions," *Al-Ittihad*, July 15, 2011, http://www.alittihad.ae/wajhatdetails.php?id=60260.

7. http://twitter.com/#!/Daloosh/status/115471018746847233, September 18, 2011.

8. http://www.demdigest.net/blog/2011/10/yemeni-activist-dedicates-nobe
l-prize-to-youth-of-arab-spring/; http://www.reuters.com/article/2011/10/07
/us-yemen-nobel-idUSTRE7961CH20111007.

9. Hani Nasirah, "The Tunisian revolution," Al-Jazeera, February 7, 2011.

10. http://www.whitehouse.gov/the-press-office/2011/05/19/remarks-president-
middle-east-and-north-africa.

11. Simon Henderson, http://www.foreignpolicy.com/articles/2011/04/14
/outraged_in_riyadh.

12. Michael Hudson, *Arab Politics: The Search for Legitimacy* (Yale University Press,
1979).

13. Mustafa al-Zayn, "On the Arab Intifadas." *Al-Hayat*, March 19, 2011,
http://international.daralhayat.com/print/245823.

14. Eva Bellin, "The Robustness of Authoritarianism in the Middle East,"
Comparative Politics 36, no. 2 (2004): 139–157.

CHAPTER 2

1. For other comparisons to this period, see Morton Vjalborn and Andre Bank,
"Signs of a New Arab Cold War: The 2006 Lebanon War and the Sunni-Shi'a
Divide," *Middle East Report* 242 (Spring 2007).

2. Michael Barnett, *Dialogues in Arab Politics* (Columbia University Press, 1998);
Marc Lynch, *Voices of the New Arab Public.*

3. Malik Mufti, *Sovereign Creations: Pan-Arabism and Political Order in Syria and Iraq*
(Cornell University Press, 1996).

4. Malcolm Kerr, *The Arab Cold War* (Oxford University Press, 1971), p. 4.

5. Steven Heydemann, *Authoritarianism in Syria* (Cornell University Press, 1999),
p. 51.

6. Mufti, *Sovereign Creations*, p. 93.

7. Kerr, *The Arab Cold War*, p. 16.

8. Mufti, *Sovereign Creations*, p. 96; quotes from Sadat's 1977 autobiography, *In
Search of Identity* (HarperCollins, 1978), p. 152.

9. Nasir Aruri, *Jordan: A Study in Political Development* (Springer, 1972) p. 9.

10. Betty Anderson, *Nationalist Voices in Jordan: The Street and the State* (University of Texas, 2005), p. 162.

11. Anderson, *Nationalist Voices in Jordan*, p. 162.

12. Uriel Dann, *King Hussein and the Challenge of Arab Radicalism: 1955–1967* (Oxford University Press, 1991), pp. 62–63.

13. Dann, *King Hussein and the Challenge of Arab Radicalism: 1955–1967*, p. 56.

14. Michael Oren, *Six Days of War* (Oxford University Press, 2004).

CHAPTER 3

1. See Larbi Sadiki, "Popular uprisings and Arab democratization," *International Journal of Middle Eastern Studies* 32 (2000): 71–95.

2. Fouad Ajami, *The Arab Predicament*, 2nd ed. (Cambridge University Press, 1991).

3. Ellen Lust-Okar, "Competitive Clientalism in the Middle East," *Journal of Democracy* 20, no.3 (2009): 122–135.

4. Jim Paul, "States of Emergency: The Riots in Tunisia and Morocco," *MERIP Reports* 127 (October 1984): 3–6.

5. Mark Tessler, "The Origins of Popular Support for Islamist Movements" (1997), in *Public Opinion in the Middle East* (University of Michigan, 2011).

6. See Ann Lesch, *Sudan: Contested National Identities* (Indiana University Press, 1998).

7. Larbi Sadiki, "Bin Ali's Tunisia: Democracy by Non-Democratic Means," *British Journal of Middle Eastern Studies* 29, no.1 (2002): 57–78; Mark Gasiorowski, "The Failure of Reform in Tunisia," *Journal of Democracy* 3, no.4 (1992): 85–97; on the political economy foundations, see Clement Henry Moore, "Tunisia and Bourguibisme: Twenty Years of Crisis," *Third World Quarterly* 10, no. 1 (1988): 176–190.

8. Joost Hilterman, *Behind the Intifada* (Princeton University Press, 1991), pp. 3–4.

9. Wendy Pearlman, *Violence, Non-Violence and the Palestinian National Movement* (Cambridge University Press, 2011).

10. Michael Hudson, "After the Gulf War: Prospects for Democratization in the Arab World," *Middle East Journal* 45, no. 3 (1991): 407–26.

11. Tessler, "The Origins of Popular Support for Islamist Movements."

12. Rex Brynen, "Economic Crisis and Post-Rentier Democratization in the Arab World: The Case of Jordan," *Canadian Journal of Political Science* 25 (1992): 69–97; Glenn Robinson, "Defensive Democratization in Jordan," *Middle East Journal* (1999): 387–410.

13. Marc Lynch, *State Interests and Public Spheres: The International Politics of Jordan's Identity* (Columbia University Press, 1999).

14. Laurie Brand, "The Effects of the Peace Process on Political Liberalization in Jordan," *Journal of Palestine Studies* 28, no. 2 (1999): 52–67.

15. Lamis Andoni and Jillian Schwedler, "Bread Riots in Jordan," *Middle East Report* 201 (1996): 40–42.

16. Hugh Roberts, "Moral Economy or Moral Polity? The political anthropology of Algerian riots," London School of Economics Development Research Center, Working Paper 17 (October 2002), p. 1.

17. Daniel Brumberg, "Islam, Elections and Reform in Algeria," *Journal of Democracy* 2, no. 1 (1991): 58–71.

18. Luis Martinez, *The Algerian Civil War, 1992–1998* (Columbia University Press, 2003).

19. Lahouari Addi, "Algeria's Army, Algeria's Agony," *Foreign Affairs* 77, no. 4 (1998): 44–53.

20. Paul Silverstein, "An Excess of Truth: Violence, Conspiracy Theorizing and the Algerian Civil War," *Anthropological Quarterly* 75, no. 4 (2002): 643–674.

21. *Martin Evans and John Phillips, Algeria: Anger of the Dispossessed* (Yale University Press, 2007); Michael Willis, *The Islamist Challenge in Algeria* (University of California, 1996).

22. Dirk Vandewalle, "From the New State to the New Era: Toward a Second Republic in Tunisia," *Middle East Journal* 42, no. 4 (1988): 602–620.

23. Robert Burrowes, "The Republic of Yemen," in Michael Hudson, *The Middle East Dilemma* (Columbia University Press, 1991), p. 191.

24. Burrowes, "The Republic of Yemen," p. 192.

25. Stephane Lacroix, *Awakening Islam* (Harvard University Press, 2011); Madawi Rasheed, *Contesting the Saudi State: Islamic Voices from a New Generation* (Cambridge University Press, 2007).

26. Fred Lawson, "Demands for Political Participation in the Arab Gulf States," *International Journal* 49, no. 2 (1994): 378–407.

27. Asef Bayat, "Activism and social development in the Middle East," *International Journal of Middle East Studies* 34 (2002): 1–28. See, also, Jill Crystal, "Authoritarianism and its adversaries in the Arab world," *World Politics* 46 (1994): 262–289.

28. http://abuaardvark.typepad.com/abuaardvark/2005/05 /kifaya_in_a_jor.html.

29. Burhan Ghalyoun, Michel Samaha, and Essem el-Erian, Open Dialogue, Al-Jazeera, May 17, 2003.

CHAPTER 4

1. Marc Lynch, "Tunisia and the New Arab Media Space," *Foreign Policy*, January 15, 2011, http://mideast.foreignpolicy.com/posts/2011/01/15 /tunisia_and_the_new_arab_media_space.

2. Hugh Miles, "The Al Jazeera Effect", *Foreign Policy*, February 8, 2011, http://www.foreignpolicy.com/articles/2011/02/08/the_al_jazeera_effect.

3. Oraib Rentawi, "From Tunis to Cairo: who are the new revolutionaries?" *Al-Dustour* (Jordan), January 29, 2011.

4. http://www.jordantimes.com/?news=33187.

5. Kristin Diwan, "Kuwait: Too much politics or not enough?" Foreign Policy, January 10, 2011, http://mideast.foreignpolicy.com/posts/2011/01/10 /kuwait_too_much_politics_or_not_enough; Marc Lynch, "The Wages of Arab Decay," *Foreign Policy*, January 5, 2011, http://mideast.foreignpolicy.com/posts /2011/01/05/crumbling_arab_moderate_regimes.

6. Hugh Roberts, "Algeria's National Protesta," *Foreign Policy*, January 9, 2011, http://mideast.foreignpolicy.com/posts/2011/01/09/algeria_s_national_protesta.

7. Rasha Moumneh, "A young man's desperation challenges Tunisia's repression," *Foreign Policy*, January 3, 2011, http://mideast.foreignpolicy.com/posts/2011/01/03/a_young_man_s_desperation_challenges_tunisia_s_repression.

8. Christopher Alexander, "Tunisia's Protest Wave," *Foreign Policy*, January 2, 2011, http://mideast.foreignpolicy.com/posts/2011/01/02/tunisia_s_protest_wave_where_it_comes_from_and_what_it_means_for_ben_ali.

9. *Al-Hayat*, January 25, 2010.

10. Bassem Bounneni, "The limits of silencing Tunisia," *Foreign Policy*, January 12, 2011, http://mideast.foreignpolicy.com/posts/2011/01/12/the_limits_of_silencing_tunisia.

11. Ethan Zuckerman, "The First Twitter Revolution?" *Foreign Policy*, January 14, 2011, http://www.foreignpolicy.com/articles/2011/01/14/the_first_twitter_revolution.

12. Personal conversations with Nawaat.org organizers, Doha, March 2011; see interview with Sami Ben Gharbia, Al-Jazeera English, July 11, 2011.

13. For a similar argument, see Laryssa Chomiak and John Entelis, "The Making of North Africa's Intifadas," *Middle East Report* 259 (Summer 2011): 8–15.

14. Marc Lynch, "Tunisia's New Al-Nahda," *Foreign Policy*, June 29, 2011, http://lynch.foreignpolicy.com/posts/2011/06/29/tunisias_new_al_nahda.

15. See Yasmine Ryan, "How Tunisia's Revolution Started," Al-Jazeera English, January 26, 2011, http://english.aljazeera.net/indepth/features/2011/01/2011126121815985483.html.

16. Moumneh, *Foreign Policy*, January 4, 2011, http://mideast.foreignpolicy.com/posts/2011/01/03/a_young_man_s_desperation_challenges_tunisia_s_repression.

17. Full-length programs on December 27, 2010, and January 9, 10, 11, 18, 2011.

18. Chomiak and Entelis, "The Making of North Africa's Intifadas," p. 13.

19. http://www.npr.org/2011/01/26/133224933/transcript-obamas-state-of-union-address.

20. Mohamed Krishan, *Al-Quds al-Arabi*, January 4, 2011.

21. Mohamed Krishan, *Al-Quds al-Arabi*, January 12, 2011.

22. AbdelWahhab al-Effendi, *Al-Quds al-Arabi*, January 14, 2011.

23. Steven Cook, "The calculations of Tunisia's military," *Foreign Policy*, http://mideast.foreignpolicy.com/posts/2011/01/20/the_calculations_of_tunisias_military.

24. Ibrahim Eissa, in *al-Dostor*, January 14, 2011.

25. Hazem Saghieh, in *al-Hayat*, January 18, 2011.

26. Mohamed el-Baradei, quoted in *The Guardian*, January 18, 2011.

27. http://www.aawsat.com//leader.asp?section=3&article=603341&issueno=11732.

28. Sultan al-Qassemi, "Twilight of the Arab Republics," *Foreign Policy*, January 17, 2011, http://mideast.foreignpolicy.com/posts/2011/01/17/twilight_of_the_arab_republics.

29. http://aljazeera.net/NR/exeres/DC13D82E-94BC-4200-94CE-34049F1CDFE6.htm.

30. Arwa Abdulaziz, http://twitter.com/#!/arwa_abdulaziz/status/26358617888260096, quoted in http://globalvoicesonline.org/2011/01/16/arab-world-after-tunisia-whos-next/.

31. http://twitter.com/#!/JinanAlrawi/status/32116271562625024, quoted in http://globalvoicesonline.org/2011/02/01/arab-world-a-revolution-time-table/.

32. Amal Bouebakr, "Algeria's protests in the shadow of Tunisia," *Foreign Policy*, January 17, 2011, http://mideast.foreignpolicy.com/posts/2011/01/17/algeria_rages_on.

33. See translation at http://globalvoicesonline.org/2011/01/17/libya-gaddafi-wages-war-on-the-internet-as-trouble-brews-at-home/.

34. Sean Yom, "Jordan Between Contagion and Consent," *Foreign Policy*, February 2, 2011, http://mideast.foreignpolicy.com/posts/2011/02/02/don_t_forget_about_jordan_a_regime_caught_between_contagion_and_consent.

35. Monira al-Qadari, http://twitter.com/#!/moniraism/status
/30554070775234561, quoted in http://globalvoicesonline.org/2011/01/27
/yemen-thousands-protesting-against-saleh-rule/.

36. Mona el-Ghobashy, "The Praxis of the Egyptian Revolution," *Middle East
Report* 258 (2011), http://www.merip.org/mer/mer258/praxis-egyptian
-revolution.

37. Sheila Carapico, "What al-Jazeera shows and doesn't show," *Foreign Policy*,
February 4, 2011, http://mideast.foreignpolicy.com/posts/2011/02/04/what_al
_jazeera_shows_and_doesn_t_show.

38. Quoted in *New York Times*, May 11, 2011, http://www.nytimes.com/2011/05
/12/us/politics/12prexy.html.

39. http://pewglobal.org/2011/04/25/egyptians-embrace-revolt-leaders
-religious-parties-and-military-as-well/.

40. http://www.abudhabigallupcenter.com/147896/egypt-tahrir-transition.aspx.

CHAPTER 5

1. http://twitter.com/#!/dia_assada/status/39789823103344640.

2. "Kings don't fold," *This American Life*, April 11, 2011, http://www.thisamericanlife
.org/sites/all/play_music/play_full.php?play=432&podcast=1.

3. http://twitter.com/#!/Brian_Whit/status/33066145300873216.

4. http://globalvoicesonline.org/2011/02/11/yemen-protests-continue-away
-from-international-media-eyes/.

5. Sheila Carapico, "Best and Worst Case Scenarios for Yemen," *Foreign Policy*,
March 24, 2011, http://mideast.foreignpolicy.com/posts/2011/03/24/worst
_and_best_case_scenarios_for_yemen.

6. Gregory Johnsen, "See Ya Saleh," *Foreign Policy*, March 23, 2011, http://www
.foreignpolicy.com/articles/2011/03/23/see_ya_saleh.

7. http://www.guardian.co.uk/world/2011/jan/23/yemen-arrests-protest-leader.

8. http://www.guardian.co.uk/world/2011/feb/03/yemen-protesters-day-rage.

9. Hugh Roberts, http://mideast.foreignpolicy.com/posts/2011/01/09/algeria_s
_national_protesta.

10. Andrew Lebovic, "Will February 12 bring revolution to Algeria?" *Foreign Policy*, February 9, 2011, http://mideast.foreignpolicy.com/posts/2011/02/09/will_february_12_mark_a_revolution_in_algeria.

11. Quoted in http://globalvoicesonline.org/2011/02/25/will-algeria-follow-tunisia-and-egypt/.

12. http://themoornextdoor.wordpress.com/2011/03/01/notes-on-algeria/.

13. Luke Schleusener, "From blog to street: the Bahraini street in transition," *Arab Media and Society* 1, no. 1 (2007), http://www.arabmediasociety.com/?article=15.

14. Toby Jones, "The siege of Bahrain," *Foreign Policy*, http://mideast.foreignpolicy.com/posts/2011/02/18/the_siege_of_bahrain.

15. http://www.demworks.org/blog/2011/08/libya-back-online-sort.

16. Angus McDowall, "Oman Protests Fizzle," *Wall Street Journal*, March 3, 2011, http://online.wsj.com/article/SB10001424052748703409904576174571884664378.html.

17. Hisham Miraat, "Showdown in Morocco," *Foreign Policy*, May 26, 2011, http://mideast.foreignpolicy.com/posts/2011/05/26/showdown_in_morocco.

18. Avi Spiegel, "The Unknown Moroccan Islamists," *Foreign Policy*, June 13, 2011, http://mideast.foreignpolicy.com/posts/2011/06/13/the_unknown_moroccan_islamists.

19. As described by Laila Lalami, February 20, 2011, http://www.thenation.com/blog/158751/rocking-casbah-moroccos-day-dignity.

20. Madawi al-Rasheed, "Yes it could happen here," *Foreign Policy*, February 28, 2011, http://www.foreignpolicy.com/articles/2011/02/28/yes_it_could_happen_here.

21. Toby Jones, "High Anxiety," *Foreign Policy*, March 23, 2011, http://www.foreignpolicy.com/articles/2011/03/23/high_anxiety.

22. Nour Odeh, "Palestine's Youth Revolt," *Foreign Policy*, March 23, 2011, http://www.foreignpolicy.com/articles/2011/03/23/palestines_youth_revolt.

23. Sean Yom, "Don't Forget About Jordan," *Foreign Policy*, February 2, 2011, http://mideast.foreignpolicy.com/posts/2011/02/02/don_t_forget_about_jordan_a_regime_caught_between_contagion_and_consent.

24. http://www.7iber.com/2011/01/photos-sound-angryjordan/.

25. Curt Ryan, "The King's Speech," *Foreign Policy*, June 17, 2011, http://mideast
.foreignpolicy.com/posts/2011/06/17/the_kings_speech.

26. Taher al-Udwa, "After Tunisia, whose turn?" *Al-Arab al-Yom*, January 17,
2011, http://www.alarabalyawm.net/pages.php?articles_id=14375.

27. Laurie Brand, "Why Jordan is not Tunisia," *Foreign Policy*, January 18, 2011,
http://mideast.foreignpolicy.com/posts/2011/01/18/why_jordan_isn_t_tunisia.

28. Sean Yom, "Jordan's Stubborn Regime Hangs in the Balance," *Foreign Policy*,
March 31, 2011, http://mideast.foreignpolicy.com/posts/2011/03/31/jordans
_stubborn_regime_hangs_in_the_balance.

29. Marc Lynch, "An Odd Calm in Beirut," *Foreign Policy*, March 10, 2011,
http://lynch.foreignpolicy.com/posts/2011/03/10/an_odd_calm_in_beirut.

30. Michael Barnett, *Dialogues in Arab Politics.* (Columbia University Press, 2000).

31. Fahmy Howeydi, July 6, 2011, http://www.shorouknews.com/Columns
/column.aspx?id=497326.

32. Lauren Bohn, "Tunisia's Forgotten Revolutionaries," *Foreign Policy*, July 11,
2011. http://www.foreignpolicy.com/articles/2011/07/13/tunisia_s_forgotten
_revolutionaries.

CHAPTER 6

1. See Matt Reed, "The GCC: How much for stability?" August 15, 2011,
http://middleeastprogress.org/2011/08/the-gcc-how-much-for-stability/.

2. Hazem Saghiye, "Revolution and Counter-Revolution," *al-Hayat*, April 5, 2011.

3. Burhan Ghalyoun, "Civil strife and aborting the democratic revolution,"
al-Ittihad, April 6, 2011, http://www.alittihad.ae/wajhatprint.php?id=58453.

4. Bilal al-Hassan, in *al-Sharq al-Awsat*, July 11, 2011.

5. Toby Jones, "Bahrain: Kingdom of Silence," Carnegie Endowment for
International Peace, May 4, 2011; Joost Hilterman and Toby Mathiessen,
"Bahrain Burning," *New York Review of Books*, August 18, 2011, http://www
.nybooks.com/articles/archives/2011/aug/18/bahrain-burning/.

6. Testimony of Joe Stork before the Tom Lantos Human Rights Commission, Human Rights Watch, May 13, 2011, as quoted by International Crisis Group, "Bahrain's Rocky Road to Reform," June 28, 2011, p. 4.

7. Quoted in http://globalvoicesonline.org/2011/06/03/morocco-pro -democracy-movement-faces-state-repression/.

8. Al-Sayid Walid Abah, "The constitutional revolution in Morocco," *al-Ittihad*, June 6, 2011, http://www.alittihad.ae/wajhatdetails.php?id=59813.

9. Abdel Meguid, "Arab democracy without revolutions," *al-Ittihad*, July 7, 2011, http://www.alittihad.ae/wajhatdetails.php?id=60113.

10. For instance, the National Dialogue Committee, appointed March 13, 2011, http://www.ammonnews.net/article.aspx?articleNO=82666.

11. Sean Yom, "Jordan's stubborn regime hangs in the balance," March 31, 2011, http://mideast.foreignpolicy.com/posts/2011/03/31/jordans_stubborn_regime _hangs_in_the_balance.

12. http://www.aawsat.com//print.asp?did=630515&issueno=11913.

13. Arabi Sadiq, "Tunisia: a roadmap to democracy," al-Jazeera, January 20, 2011.

14. Marc Lynch, "Tunisia's New Al-Nahda," *Foreign Policy*, June 29, 2011; also see Hazem al-Amin, al-Hayat, March 19, 2011.

15. Murad Bin Mohammed, "Tunisia discusses its identity," al-Jazeera, March 20, 2011.

16. http://www.abudhabigallupcenter.com/148391/Confidence-Government -Divides-Yemenis.aspx.

17. http://www.nytimes.com/2011/04/04/world/middleeast/04yemen.html?_r =2&ref=world.

18. Stacey Yadav, "Opposition to Yemen's Opposition," *Foreign Policy*, July 14, 2011, http://mideast.foreignpolicy.com/posts/2011/07/14/opposition_to_yemen _s_opposition.

19. @noonarabia, August 22, 2011, http://twitter.com/#!/NoonArabia/status /105905135099711488.

20. Rabab el-Mahdi, "Where are we with the events in Syria?" *Al-Shorouk*, August 9, 2011.

21. Lindsey Stephenson, "Ahistorical Kuwaiti Sectarianism," *Foreign Policy*, April 29, 2011, http://mideast.foreignpolicy.com/posts/2011/04/29/ahistorical_kuwaiti _sectarianism.

22. Asad AbuKhalil, *al-Akhbar*, July 23, 2011.

CHAPTER 7

1. Hazem Saghiye, "The Intifadas and the participation of the outside world," *al-Hayat*, August 6, 2011, http://international.daralhayat.com/print/294861.

2. Ragheda Dergham, "The Arab revolutions and exit strategy for regimes," *al-Hayat*, July 15, 2011, http://international.daralhayat.com/print/288124.

3. George Sama'an, *al-Hayat*, April 18, 2011, http://international.daralhayat.com /print/256554.

4. http://www.guardian.co.uk/world/2011/mar/12/gaddafi-army-kill-half -million.

5. For a taste of the online debate, see http://globalvoicesonline.org/2011/03/08 /libya-debating-the-no-fly-zone-video/.

6. Ibrahim al-Amin, *Al-Akhbar*, August 21, 2011, http://www.al-akhbar.com /node/19628.

7. Bashar al-Asad, interview, *Wall Street Journal*, http://online.wsj.com/article /SB10001424052748703833204576114712441122894.html.

8. Syrian activist Suhair Attasi, quoted on al-Jazeera English, February 9, 2011, http://english.aljazeera.net/indepth/features/2011/02/201129103121562395 .html.

9. Rania Abouzeid, "Dissent in Damascus' Shadows," *Time*, August 12, 2011, http://www.time.com/time/world/article/0,8599,2088366,00.html.

10. http://www.npr.org/2011/07/08/137680644/syrias-best-known-dissident -reflects-on-uprising?ft=1&f=1009.

11. International Crisis Group, "The Syrian Regime's Slow-Motion Suicide," July 6, 2011, p. 1, http://www.crisisgroup.org/en/regions/middle-east-north -africa/egypt-syria-lebanon/syria/109-popular-protest-in-north-africa-and-the -middle-east-vii-the-syrian-regimes-slow-motion-suicide.aspx.

12. Anthony Shadid, "Exiles shaping world's image of Syria's revolt," *New York Times*, April 21, 2011.

13. Radwan Ziyadeh, "Why Syria Will Be Next," *Foreign Policy*, April 6, 2011, http://mideast.foreignpolicy.com/posts/2011/04/06/why_syria_will_be_next.

14. Salwa Ismail, "Syria's Cultural Revolution," *The Guardian*, June 21, 2011, http://www.guardian.co.uk/commentisfree/2011/jun/21/syria-cultural -revolution-art-comedy.

15. http://critique-sociale.blogspot.com/2011/06/blog-post_23.html.

16. Riyadh Agha, "Syria at the crossroads," *Al-Ittihad*, August 12, 2011, http://www.alittihad.ae/wajhatdetails.php?id=60770.

17. http://www.jadaliyya.com/pages/index/2203/the-syrian-people-will -determine-the-fate-of-syria.

18. Fahmi Howeydi, "Syria to where?" *al-Shorouk*, June 16, 2011, http://www .shorouknews.com/Columns/Column.aspx?id=480622.

19. http://international.daralhayat.com/internationalarticle/290766.

20. Salamah Kaylah, "The Syrian Intifada," *al-Akhbar*, August 10, 2011, http:// www.al-akhbar.com/node/18696.

21. http://critique-sociale.blogspot.com/2011/06/blog-post_23.html.

22. Anthony Shadid, "Disparate Factions From the Streets Fuel New Opposition in Syria," *New York Times*, June 30, 2011.

23. Sulayman Nimr, "The opponents to the Syrian regime abroad," *Al-Ghad*, July 5, 2011.

24. http://thecable.foreignpolicy.com/posts/2011/11/07/daalder_we_re_not _even_thinking_about_intervening_in_syria

25. http://www.reuters.com/article/2011/10/31/us-syria-nato-newspro -idUSTRE79U52Z20111031

26. Tareq Elhomayed, "Syria. no benefit to Resistance!" *al-Sharq al-Awsat*, April 23, 2011.

27. Fahmy Howeydi, al-Jazeera, August 21, 2011, http://aljazeera.net/NR/exeres /92528629-2ACB-44C5-8841-99761A3546B8.htm.

CHAPTER 8

1. Michael Slackman, "Arab Unrest Propels Iran as Saudi Influence Declines," *New York Times*, February 23, 2011, http://www.nytimes.com/2011/02/24/world /middleeast/24saudis.html.

2. Personal interview with retired Iranian diplomat, March 2011. Also see Seyed Mohammad Marandi, "The Islamic Republic of Iran, the United States and the Balance of Power in the Middle East," Conflicts Forum, January 14, 2011, http://conflictsforum.org/2011/the-islamic-republic-of-iran-the-united-states-and-the-balance-of-power-in-the-middle-east/; Mehrun Etebari, "How Tehran Sees Tunis," *Foreign Policy*, January 28, 2011; "The View from Iran: The New Middle East Emboldens Iran," *The Daily Star*, March 5, 2011, http://www .dailystar.com.lb/article.asp?edition_id=10&categ_id=2&article_id =125647#axzz1HZbD1SV0.

3. Farideh Farhi, "Managing Arab Spring's Fallout in Iran," CFR.org interview, April 7, 2011, http://www.cfr.org/iran/managing-arab-springs-fallout-iran /p24617.

4. Mohammed Abass Naji, "Iranian views of the Egyptian revolution (in Arabic)," al-Jazeera, March 6, 2011.

5. Abdullah Iskandir, "Iran going against the tide," *al-Hayat*, March 9, 2011.

6. Ahmed Othman, "Iran tries to enlist Egypt in confrontation with Israel," *al-Sharq al-Awsat*, February 27, 2011.

7. Kayhan Barzegar, "Balance of Power in the Persian Gulf: An Iranian View," *Middle East Policy* 17, no. 3 (2010): 74–87; F. Gregory Gause III, *The International Relations of the Persian Gulf* (Cambridge University Press, 2010).

8. Elias Harfoush, "Iran playing with fire," *al-Hayat*, April 5, 2011.

9. Barbara Slavin, "Strategically Lonely Iran," *Atlantic Council*, March 2011.

10. Admiral Michael Mullen and Defense Secretary Robert Gates, press briefing, The Pentagon, March 1, 2011.

11. Marc Lynch, "Young Brothers in Cyberspace," Middle East Report 245 (2007), http://www.merip.org/mer/mer245/young-brothers-cyberspace.

12. http://www.whitehouse.gov/the-press-office/remarks-president-cairo -university-6-04-09.

13. See discussion in Ryan Lizza, "The Consequentialist," *The New Yorker*, May 2, 2011.

14. Aaron David Miller, *The Much Too Promised Land* (Bantam, 2008).

15. Ibrahim Houdabyi, "The January 25 revolution broke the bonds of foreign occupation," *Al-Shorouq*, July 22, 2011.

16. Graham Fuller, "The Hezballah-Iran Connection: Model for Sunni Resistance," *The Washington Quarterly* 30, no.1 (2006–2007): 139–150.

17. http://blogs.cfr.org/zenko/2011/08/11/what-does-libya-cost-the-united-states/.

INDEX

Abbas, Mahmoud, 118, 233
Abdulemam, Ali, 109–110
Abdullah (King of Saudi Arabia), 116
Abdullah (King of Jordan), 119, 145
Abu Aardvark (blog), 3
Abu Ghraib prison, Baghdad, 61, 224
Adly, Habib el-, 92
Ahmadinejad, Mahmoud, 204–205
Ajami, Fouad, 14
al-Adl wa al-Ihsan, 114, 213
al-Akhbar, 176
al-Aqsa Intifada, 57, 117
al-Arabiya, 80
al-Haq, 109
al-Hayat, 185
al-Islah, Islamist party of Yemen, 15
al-Jazeera
    Arab uprising and, 56, 58, 68–69
    Egyptian uprising and, 90–91
    election reporting, 12
    Green Movement coverage, 205
    Libyan uprising and, 112, 167–169,
        173–176
    Open Dialogue program, 77
    power of in uprisings, 82, 125–126
    Qatar media, role in public
        discourse, 20–21
    Tunisia, essays on, 79
    Tunisian uprising and, 76–79
    Yemeni coverage, 154–156

al-Qaeda
    Egyptian uprising and, 95
    as secular fringe, 207–213
al-Sharq al Awsat, 146
al-Wasat, 139
al-Wefaq society, 136, 137
Algeria
    #FEB12, hashtag protest, 107–109
    Islamic Salvation Front (ISF), 211
    Islamists in, 51–52
    protest in, 51–53
    riots in, 46
Alternative Homeland, 120
America
    anti-American sentiments, 61
    Arab distrust of policy, 196, 197
    declining influence of, 24–25
    failure of neoconservative politics,
        215–220
    invasion of Iraq, 163
    military intervention, in Iran, 206
    new Middle East challenges and,
        231–235
    position on Bahrain, 228
    response to Arab Spring, 193–197
    See also United States
Amin, Ibrahim al-, 176
Ammar, Rachid, 79
Anti-Islamist trends, in U.S., 234–235
Aoun, Michel, 123

April 6 Youth Movement, 87, 134, 230
Arab Cold War
    about, 16–17
    as battle of ideas, 34
    causes of, 32–33
    communism and, 33, 47–48
    defensive democratization after,
        47–55
    defined, 29–32
    Jordan, 120–121
    lessons of, 40–42
    military coups and, 35–37
    Obama and, 18
    pan-Arab revolution, 39
Arab Cold War, The (Kerr), 16
Arab Dictators Survival Manual, 104
Arab Federation, 39
Arab League, on Syrian
        bloodshed, 191
Arab Left, 133
Arab politics, post-uprising, 197–206
Arab Spring, defined, 9.
        See also Arab uprising
Arab uprising
    Arab cold war and, 17, 33, 47–48
    causes of, 67–73
    intervention in Libya,
        demand for, 172
    as Islamic awakening, 204–205
    Islamist and, 27
    labor strikes and, 13–14
    media and, 13
    Obama administration, response to,
        220–224
    peace process, Arab-Israeli, 202
    short-term results, 226
    slogans of, 69
    status quo destabilized, 225
    in Tunisia (see Tunisia)
    unity among, 101–102
Araby, Nabil al-, 19
Artists, role of in Tunisian
        uprising, 77–78

Assad, Bashar al-, 17, 103, 134
    attempts to save regime, 178–179
    clinging to power, 192
    initial support for, 190
    offering amnesty, 179–180
    reform failure, 180
    use of repression, 182–192
Assad, Hafez al-, 12
    military coup of, 35

Ba'ath Party, 29, 35, 184
Badran, Mudar, 50
Baghdad Pact, 33, 37
Bahrain
    American position on, 228
    direct intervention in, 135–141
    effects of Tunisia on, 83–84
    #FEB14, hashtag protest,
        109–112
    Saudi Arabia, intervention,
        135, 137–139
    social media war, 138–140
Bahrain Online, 109–110
Bakhit, Marouf al-, 143
Baradei, Mohamed el-, 80, 86, 87, 213
Barghouti, Mustafa, 117
Battle of the Camels, 96
Bayat, Asef, 54–55
Beirut, Lebanon, landing of
        U.S. Marines in, 37
Belhadj, Ali, 51, 53
Ben Ali, Zine el-Abidine, 8, 47, 53
    fall of, 68
    fleeing to Saudi Arabia, 80
    regime of, 73–80
Bendjedid, Chadli, 51, 52
Berlin Wall, fall of, 47
Bishri, Tariq al-, 150
Bizri, Afif, 35–36
Black September crisis, 30
Blogs, role in uprising, 56.
        See also Social media

Bouazizi, Mohammed
  self-immolation of, 70, 73
  as symbol of uprising, 2, 7, 15,
    75, 226
Bourghiba, Habib, 45, 47
Bread riots, 43, 45
Bush, George W. (administration),
    94, 207, 216–217, 223, 227

Camp David Accords, 45, 94, 202
Carapico, Sheila, 106
Carvin, Andy, 194–195
Ceauşescu, Nicolae, 47
Cedar Revolution, of Lebanon, 13, 31,
    62, 124
Censorship
  of media, 12, 13
  in uprising, 74
    See also Repression; Media;
  Social media
CFR. See Council on Foreign Relations
Chalabi, Ahmed, 162
Charter of the League of
    Arab States, 25
Cheney, Dick, 58
Christian Free Patriotic
    Movement, 123
Clinton, Bill, 223
Colonialism, Western,
    in Middle East, 32
Communism, Arab Cold War and,
    33, 47–48
Communist Party, 35
Constituent Assembly, Tunisia, 149
Constitutional Democratic Rally,
    Tunisia, 146
Constitutional reforms
  Egypt, 150–152
  Jordan, 145
  lack of, Syria, 180
  Morocco, 142
  Yemen, 155–157

Cook, Steven, 79
Corruption, role in uprising, 67–68
  Jordan, 119–120, 121–122
  Tunisia, 73–74
Council on Foreign Relations (CFR),
    79, 229
Counterrevolution, 72
  Bahrain, direct intervention,
    135–141
  defined, 131–132
  violent repression, 131–134
Crown Prince Sultan,
    Saudi Arabia, 116
Culture, role of popular in
    Tunisian uprising, 77

Daalder, Ivo, 191
Daily Motion, censorship of, 74
Dann, Uriel, 38
Day of rage, 81, 91
  Jordan, 121
Decentralized movement.
    See Leaderless movement
Democracy
  defensive, post–Arab Cold War,
    47–55
  growth of in Arab world,
    198–200
  uprisings as opportunity for, 226
  U.S. credibility on, 223–224
Demonstration effect, Syria, 180
Dictator's dilemma, 69
Djaout, Tahar, 114–115
Doha Summit, 172
Dream TV, 97

Economic power, role in
    democratization, 200
Economic troubles, role in uprising, 67
  Jordan, 119–120
Effendi, Abd el-Wahhab el-, 79

Egypt
    al-Jazeera role in, 90–91
    April 6 Youth Movement, 87
    attack on Coptic church, 70–71
    Battle of the Camels, 96
    campaign against World Bank/IMF
        loans, 229–230
    communication shutdown, 89–90
    constitutional reform in, 150–152
    elections in, 53, 153–154
    Freedom and Justice Party, 208
    independence of, 32
    Kefaya movement, 13, 56
    key moments, 98
    leaderless movement, success of, 97
    military, Obama influences, 92
    police violence, role of in
        uprising, 86
    postrevolutionary, 98–99, 201
    protest of Israeli killing of
        soldiers, 203
    revolution of 1952, 32
    role of Tunisian success in uprising,
        85–87
    security forces' response to
        uprising, 91–92
    soldiers killed, by Israel, 153
    stalled revolution, 149–154
    suppression of Islamists, 53
    Supreme Council of the Armed
        Forces (SCAF), 72
Eisenhower Doctrine, 33
Eissa, Ibrahim, 80
El General, Tunisian rapper, 77–78
el-Nahda Party, in Tunisia, 53, 75,
        147–149, 208, 210
Election fraud
    Egypt, 87–88
    Iran, 63, 205
    Jordan, 119
Elections, Islamist gains in, 208
Erdoğan, Recep, 19, 191–192
Ethnic polarization, 23, 144

Facebook
    about, 10–11. See also Social media
    Arab uprising, role in, 56
    Assad lifts ban on, 179
    Egypt shuts down, 89–90
    Jordan and, 121
    Oman protest, 113
    Tunisian uprising, role in, 74
    use in Syria, 181–182
    We Are All Khaled Said, 86, 97,
        213
Farhi, Garideh, 204–205
#FEB3, Yemen hashtag protest,
        105–107
#FEB12, Algeria hashtag protest,
        107–109
#FEB14, Bahrain hashtag protest,
        109–112, 136
#FEB17, Libya hashtag protest, 112
#FEB18, Oman hashtag protests,
        113–114
#FEB20, Morocco hashtag protest,
        114–115
#FEB25, Iraq hashtag protest, 115
Flickr, censorship of, 74
Ford, Robert, 166–167, 186, 190
Foreign policies, democratization and,
        200–201
Fotouh, Abd el-Moneim Aboul el-, 152,
        212, 213
Fotouh, Abou el-. See Fotouh, Abd
        el-Moneim Aboul el-
France, Tunisian uprising and,
        78–79
Free Egyptians Party, 152
Freedom Agenda, of Bush
        Administration, 216
Freedom and Justice Party (Egypt),
        151, 208
Friday of Cleaning (Egypt), 150
Friday of Determination (Egypt), 150
Front de Libération Nationale
        (FLN), 51

Gallup poll, Egypt, 99

Gama'a al-Islamiyya
  as Islamist party, 151
  new politics of, 206–213

Ganzoury, Kamal el-, 154

Gaza blockade, 14

GCC Peninsula Shield, military
      intervention forces,
      131–133, 156

Ghalyoun, Burhan, 56, 185, 187

Ghannouchi, Mohammed, 146

Ghannouchi, Rached, 75, 77,
      147–149, 210

Gheit, Ahmed Aboul, 81

Ghobashy, Mona el-, 89

Ghoneim, Wael, 86, 97

Globe Roundabout, 113

Glubb, John Bagot, 38

Golan Heights, 41, 189

Green March, Oman, 113

Green Movement, Iran, 17, 63, 205

Guardian, The, 105

Gulf Cooperation Council, 25, 60

Gulf War, 49, 54. *See also* Operation
      Desert Storm

Habib, Mohammed, 212

Habib, Randa, 144

Hamad (King of Bahrain), 135–140

Hariri, Rafik, 13, 56, 179, 188
  assassination of, 31

Hashtag Debates, 121, 122, 144

Hashtags, protests, Twitter
  about, 102–105
  #FEB3, Yemen, 105–107
  #FEB12, Algeria, 107–109
  #FEB14, Bahrain, 109–112
  #FEB17, Libya, 112
  #FEB18, Oman, 113–114
  #FEB20, Morocco, 114–115
  #FEB25, Iraq, 115
  #Lebanon, 123–124

#MAR11, Saudi Arabia, 115–117
#MAR15, Palestine/Syria, 117–118
#MAR24, Jordan, 119–123
#MESpeech, 194–195

Hassan, Bilal al-, 134, 146

Hezbollah
  Cedar Revolution and, 62
  #Lebanon, hashtag protests,
      123–124
  position on Syria, 189

Hijacked revolutions, 134

Hilterman, Joost, 48

Honecker, Erich, 47

Houdaiby, Ibrahim, 225–226

Howeydi, Fahmy, 128–130, 185, 192

Human Rights Watch, 138

Hussein, Saddam, 45

Hussein (King of Jordan), 119

Huthi movement, Yemen, 155

Ideology
  battle of, 34
  power, role in democratization,
      200
  See also Sectarianism

IMF. *See* International Monetary Fund

Independence, from colonial rule,
      Middle East and, 32

Independent Election Commission,
      Tunisia, 149

International Criminal Court, 25, 164,
      171, 177, 188

International Monetary Fund (IMF), 45
  Egypt and, 229–230
  funding cuts, Jordan, 49–50

Internet
  cutoff in Egypt, 89–90
  Hashtag Debates, 121
  Jordanian activism, 143
  Libya cuts off, 112
  Moammar Qaddafi mocks, 82
  online activists, post-Tunisia, 81

Internet (*continued*)
  online dialogue on Arab Spring, 195
  role in Tunisian uprising, 74
  role of in uprisings, 10–11, 13
  Syrian activists on, 180
  See also Social media
Intervention
  Arab states and, 164
  direct, Bahrain, 135–141
  in Libya, no-fly zone, motivations,
    170, 173–174
  neoconservative opposition to
    Libyan, 219–220
  online debate on, 195
  Saudi Arabia, in Bahrain, 135, 137
  Saudi Arabia, in Yemen, 156
  support for Western, 163
  Syrian opposition against, 186
  in uprisings, 161–176
  Western military, 162
Iran
  Arab/Israeli conflict and, 204–205
  Bahrain fear of, 138–139
  on Egypt uprising, 94
  Green Movement, crushing of, 17, 63
  military intervention in, 206
  support for Syria, 189
  war with Iraq, 45
Iraq
  American invasion of, 163, 215
  #FEB25, hashtag protest, 115
  Hashemite king, fall of, 34
  invasion of Kuwait, 49
  military coup in, 39
  opposition in exile, 162
  postrevolutionary role of, 201
  sectarianism in, 60
  U.S. war with, 43, 59–60
  war with Iran, 45
Iraqi National Congress (INC), 162
Islamic Action Front Party, 50, 121
Islamic Awakening, 94
Islamic Salvation Front (ISF), 51–53, 211

Islamist Party of Justice and Develop-
    ment, Morocco, 208
Islamists
  al-Adl wa al-Ihsan, Morocco,
    114, 213
  in Algeria, 51–52
  anti, in America, 234–235
  banning of political, in Tunisia, 75
  discord between groups of, 210–212
  in Egypt, 151–154
  fear of, uprisings and, 27
  Friday prayers, day of rage, 81, 91
  gains in elections, 208–210
  in Libya, 176
  new politics of, 206–213
  Saudi crackdown on Sahwa, 54
  suppression of, in Egypt, 53
  in Yemen, 154–157
Islamists, American diplomacy with,
    234–235
Ismail, Hazem Abu, 152
Israel
  America's relationship with,
    rethinking, 233
  Arab alignment with, against Iran,
    216
  death of Egyptian soldiers, 203
  embassy sacking, 153
  1967 war, 29–30, 40–41
  Palestinian Intifada and, 48–49
  post uprising, 202
  regional politics and, 23
  Turkish freedom flotilla and,
    202–203
  uprising, security fears, 225
  Western support for, 162

Jaliil, Mustafa Abdul, 176
Jeddo, Ghassan Ben, 77, 126
Joint Meeting Parties (JMPs), 106, 157
Jordan
  Baghdad Pact, 37–38

Gulf War/Intifada, effects of on, 49
IMF funding cuts, 49–50
labor strikes in, 13–14
#MAR24, hashtag protest, 119–123
monarchial reform in, 143–146
National Pact, 50
Palestinian issues in uprising,
        121–123
Qaba'at movement in, 56
riots in, 47–48, 70
Tunisia, effects of on, 83
Justice and Development Party
        (Turkey), 211

Karman, Tawakul, 14, 15, 106
Kefaya movement, of Egypt,
        13, 31, 87
    history lessons of, 64–65
    Kefaya wave, 56
    revolution and, 55–64
Kerr, Malcolm (*The Arab Cold War*),
        16–17, 36
Khalifa, Prime Minister, 137
Khamenei, Ali, 94, 204–205
Khanfar, Wadah, 174
Khasawnah, Awn al-, 145
Kilo, Michel, 180
King Abdullah (Saudi Arabia), 116
King Abdullah (Jordan), 119, 145
King Hamad (Bahrain), 135–140
King Hussein (Jordan), 119
King Mohammad VI (Morocco),
        141–142
Krishan, Mohamed, 77
Kurds, slaughter of, 45
Kuwait
    attack on Obaid al-Wasmi, 70–71
    Iraq invasion of, 11, 49
    labor strikes in, 13–14
    protests in, 84
    sectarianism in, 158
    war to liberate, 43

Labor strikes
    in Arab world, 13–14
    Tunisian General Labour Union
        (UGGT), 77
Laden, Osama bin, 15, 207–208, 218
Last Chance Friday, 156
Leaderless movement
    about, 97
    Tunisia, 146–147
Leading from behind, 25
Lebanon
    Cedar Revolution in, 13, 31, 62
        #Lebanon, hashtag protest,
            123–124
    U.S. Marine invasion of, 37
Libya
    crackdown/UN intervention in,
        167–176
    effects of Tunisia, 82
    #FEB17, hashtag protest, 112
    humanitarian intervention in, 25
    intervention in, 164–165, 228–229
    Saif al-Islam, speech, 169
    Transitional National Council
        (TNC), 175
    violence in, 21,170–176

Madani, Abassi, 51
Madrid Peace Conference, 224
Maliki, Nuri al-, 189
Mansour, Abdul Rahman, 86
#MAR11, hashtag protest, Saudi
        Arabia, 115–117
#MAR15, hashtag protest,
        Palestine/Syria, 117–118
#MAR24, hashtag protest, Jordan,
        119–123
Mavi Marmara, 202–203
Mayateh, Samih al-, 56
Media
    blackout in Tunisia, 76
    manipulation of, 10–12

Media (*continued*)
  power of, role in democratization,
      200
  role in uprisings, 13, 65
  shutdown, in Bahrain, 138
  shutdown, in Libya, 167–168
  in Syria protests, 118, 186
  Tunisian control of, 74
  Voice of the Arabs, radio, 33, 34,
      37–38
Meguid, Wahid Abdel, 140
Memorandum of Advice, 54
#MESpeech, 194–195
Middle East
  challenges for America, 231–235
  independence from colonial rule
      and, 32
  new U.S. strategy in, 213–220
  U.S. presence in, 223–224
Middle East Partnership Initiative, 62
Middle East studies, 219
Military coups
  in Algeria, 211
  Arab Cold War and, 35
  Iraq, 39
  in Sudan, 46
Military intervention forces
  about, 131–132
  in Bahrain, Saudi Arabia and,
      137–139
  in Libya, no-fly zones, 170,
      173–174
  in Yemen, Saudi Arabia
      and, 156
  Western, 162
Miller, Aaron, 224
Moderate axis, 17, 133, 188, 200,
      218–219
Mohammad VI (King of Morocco),
      141–142
Monarchy
  Bahrain, 135–141
  Jordan, reform, 143–145

Morocco reform, 141–142
Morocco
  constitutional reforms, 142–143
  #FEB20 hashtag protest,
      114–115
  monarchial reform, 141–142
Moumneh, Rasha, 76
Muasher, Marwan, 144
Mubarak, Gamal, 87–88
  as father's successor, 57
Mubarak, Hosni, 45
  blockade of Gaza, 14
  elections in, 53
  fall of, 68
  negotiations for power, 93
  refusal to step down, 97–98
Muhsin, Ali, 156
Mullen, Michael, 206
Muslim Brotherhood, 32, 35, 51
  condemns Syria bloodshed, 191
  gains in Egypt, 151–154
  Islamic Action Front Party of, 50
  joins Egypt protests, 91–92
  Jordan crackdown on, 119–120
  new politics of, 206–213
  revolutionary role, 72–73
  rise of, 71
  support, postrevolution, 98–99
  suppression of in Egypt, 87
  in Tunisia, 75

Nabulsi, Suleiman, 38
Nakhle, Rami, 181–182
Nammour, Joumana, 126
Nasser, Gamal Abdel, 14, 36
  Arab Cold War and, 29
  independence and, 32
Nasserist pan-Arabism, 214
National Action Charter, Bahrain, 135
National Agenda project, Jordan, 144
National Association for Change,
      86, 87

National Council for Freedom, 77
National Democratic Party (NDP),
    Egypt, 53, 87,149–150
National Dialogue Committee,
    Jordan, 121
National Islamic Front (NIF), 46
National Pact, Jordan, 50
National Transitional Council, 161
NATO interventions, 163
  in Libya, 170, 173–174, 175,
      228–229
Nawaat, Internet activist, 74
Neoconservatives
  broad ambitions of, 59
  challenge to, 4
  failures of politics, 215–220
  response to Obama on uprising,
      197, 227
  support of Syrian activists, 188
  on Syria's Assad regime, 230
Netanyahu, Benjamin, 233
New Arab public sphere, 10–12
New York Times, The, 156
New Yorker, The, 25
No-fly zone, Libyan 170, 173–174
Nobel Peace Prize, Tawakul Karman,
    14
North Africa, protests/coups in, 45–46
Numeiri, Jaafar, 46

Obama, Barack
  Arab allies angered, 94
  on the Arab Spring, 193–197
  Egyptian military and, 92
  leadership during uprisings,
      26–27
  Libya and, 171–172
  Mubarak negotiations, 93–94
  peace initiative, Arab-Israeli, 203
  response to Arab uprisings,
      220–224, 227–231
  support for uprisings, 18

  on Syrian intervention, 190–191
  Syria, position on, 184
  uprisings as opportunity for, 226
  urges Mubarak to step down,
      94, 95, 96
Oil, as motivation for Libya
    intervention, 171
Oman
  #FEB18, hashtag protest, 113–114
  protests in, 84
Open Dialogue, Al-Jazeera, 77
Operation Desert Storm, 54, 224
Organization of Petroleum Exporting
    Countries (OPEC), 41

Palestine
  conflict with Israel and, 23–24
  issues in Jordan, 121–123
  #MAR15, hashtag protest, 117–118
  statehood, UN and, 203–204
  See also Palestinian Intifada
Palestinian Intifada, 8, 9
  al-Jazeera's coverage of, 58–59
  first (1987), 21, 43, 47, 48–50, 54
  second (Al-Aqsa, 2000), 8, 31, 55,
      57–59, 202
  call for nonviolent, 117
Palestinian-Israeli war, 13
Palestinian Liberation Organization,
    30, 41
Pan-Arabism, 30, 33
Pearl Roundabout, 83–84, 110,
    111, 136
Pew survey, Egypt, 99
Politics
  banning of political Islam, 75
  Islamists' gains in, 208–213
  new Arab, post-uprising, 197–206
  postrevolutionary, 72
  regional, 23–26, 132–133,
      188–189, 206
  structure of international, 31–32

Power, Samantha, 164
Prism of pain, 58
Progressive Democratic Party, Tunisia,
      149
Protests of 1980s, 44–46
Public sphere, new Arab, 10–12

Qaba'at movement, 56
Qaddafi, Saif al-Islam, 169
Qaddafi, Moammar, 9, 161–162
   brutal crackdown, 167–176
   at Doha Summit, 172
   hashtag protests against, 112
   on Tunisia, 82
Qaradawi, Yusuf al-, 169, 209
Qassem, Faisal al-, 7
Qatar
   Libya and, 172, 175
   media in, 20
   postrevolutionary, 201
Queen Rania (Jordan), 122

Rashed, Abdul Rahman al-, 80
Rasheed, Madawi al-, 116
Rasmussen, Anders Fogh, 191
Realism, Middle East and, 214–216
Red lines, 12, 79
Reform. See Constitutional reforms;
      Monarchy
Regional demonstration effect, 132
Regional politics, 23–26, 166
Responsibility to Protect norms, 164
Repression
   in Bahrain, 137–138
   of communications, in Egypt,
      89–90
   in Egypt, 151
   in Jordan, 143–144
   in Syria, 179–192
   of Tunisian uprising, 75–76
   in Yemen, 154–157

Resistance bloc, 19, 133, 191
Revolution
   defensive democratization, 47–55
   episodic protests of 1980s, 44–46
   history lessons of, 64–65
   Kefaya, 55–64
   legitimacy of, 128–129
Rhodes, Benjamin, 194–195
Rice, Condoleezza, 62, 216
Rice, Susan, 157, 164
Rifai, Samir al-, 83, 121, 143
Roberts, Hugh, 108
Romdhani, Oussama, 76
Ross, Alec, 195
Ross, Dennis, 170
Rumman, Mohammed Abu, 145

Sadat, Anwar, 14, 45
   Arab Cold War and, 30–31
Saghieh, Hazem, 80
Sahwa, Islamists' group, 54
Said, Khaled (death of), 86.
            See also Facebook.
Salafi-jihadists
   Islamists' party, 61, 71, 151–152
   new politics of, 206–213
Saleh, Ahmed, 86
Saleh, Ali Abdullah, 83, 105–107, 134
   repression/refusal to step down,
      154–158
Sanctions, against Syria, 189
Sarkozy, Nicolas, 78
Satellite television, 13
Saudi Arabia
   in Bahrain, repression, 135,
      137–139
   #MAR11, hashtag protest, 115–117
   media campaign, 20
   as moderate state, 218–219
   Operation Desert Storm and, 54
   Yemen and, 156
Sawiris, Naguib, 152

SCAF. *See* Supreme Council of the
       Armed Forces, Egypt
Seale, Patrick (*The Struggle for Syria*),
       16–17
Second Day of Anger (Egypt), 150
Sectarianism
    Bahrain, 111, 137–138
    Egypt, 152
    Syria, 179
    Iran, 204–205
    Iraq, 60–61
    Kuwait, 158
    role in uprising, 67–73
    Sunni–Shi'a, 23, 60–61
    Tunisia, 148
Shabi, Abu Qasim al-, 77
Shafik, Ahmed, 149–150
Shalgam, Abd al-Rahman, 169
Sharaa, Farouq, 185
Sharaf, Essam, 149, 154
Sharek, video-sharing portal, 168
Shari'a law
    Egypt, 206–207
    Libya, 176
Sharon, Ariel, 57
Shi'a al-Wefaq, 109
Shi'a–Sunni sectarianism, 23, 60–61.
       See also Sectarianism
Shishakli, Adib, 35
Sidi Bouzid, Tunisia, 70, 71, 75
Sidris, Suham bin, 77
Sinai, 41
Siniora, Fouad, 62
SMS messages, in protest organizing,
       88
Snap referendum, Morocco, 142
Social media
    Bahrain, regime use of, 138–139
    in Libya, 169
    role in uprising, 10–11, 55–56, 68,
       74, 81–82
    secular representation on, 128
    shutdown, Bahrain, 135–136

    shutdown, Egypt, 89–90
    in uprising, 63
    use in Syria, 181–182
    See also Facebook; Twitter; YouTube
Soviet Union, fall of, 47
Special Tribunal for Lebanon, 189
Struggle for Syria, The, (Seale), 16–17
Sudan, military coup in, 46
Suez Canal, nationalization of, 36
Suez crisis, of 1956, 33
Suleiman, Omar, 96
Sunni–Shi'a sectarianism, 23, 60–61.
       See also Sectarianism
Supreme Council of the Armed
       Forces, Egypt (SCAF), 72, 88,
       92, 134, 149–154
Swing states, Middle East, 19, 201–202
Syria
    beginnings of uprising, 181–184
    conflict in, 24
    intervention, lack of, 165–166
    #MAR15, hashtag protest, 117–118
    military coup in, 35–37
    neocon response to, 230
    operation of state power in, 12
    pre-uprising conditions, 178–180
    role of exiles in uprising, 187–188
    sanctions, 189
    violence toward protesters, 181–192

Tahrir Square,
    core protestors, 127
    occupation of, 72
    seizure of, 91, 93
    See also Egypt
Technology, role in uprisings, 10–12.
       See also Media; Social
       media; Text messages
Telhami, Shibley, 58
Terrorism, Marrakesh, attack in, 141
Text messages, in protest
       organizing, 88

Transitional National Council (TNC),
        Libya, 175, 187
Transjordan, 120
Tunisia
   control of media, 74
   corruption in, 73–74
   el-Nahda party in, 53, 147–149,
        208, 210
   elections, 148–149
   fallout of uprising, 80–85
   Islamist Party of Justice and
        Development, 208
   isolation of, 84
   military coup in, 47
   military role in uprisings, 79–80
   political Islam banned, 75
   repression of uprising, 75–76, 78
   revolution in, causes of, 73–80
   riots in, 1983, 45–46
   self-immolation of Bouazizi, 70
   stalled revolution, 146–149
   uprising in, 7
Tunisian General Labour Union
        (UGGT), 77
Turkey, Justice and Development
        Party, 211
Turkish freedom flotilla, 202–203
Twitter, 10–11, 14, 16
   hashtag protests, 102–103,
        104–123
   #MESpeech, 194–195
   role in Tunisian uprising, 77
   role in Kefaya movement, 56
   sectarian feuding on,
        Bahrain, 111
   use of in uprising, 63
   See also Hashtags, protests, Twitter;
        Social media
Twitter time, 228

Umma Party, Sudan, 46
UN Special Tribunal, 178–179

United Arab Republic (UAR), 36
United Nations
   Goldstone Report, 202–203
   Human Rights Council, 172–172
   Palestinian statehood and, 203–204
   Security Council, 163
United States
   Bahrain and, 136–137, 140
   counterrevolution and, 134
   Egypt and, 153
   intervention, Syria/Libya, 166–167
   military presence, in Middle East,
        223–224
   no-fly zone, Libya, 170, 173–174
   response to Yemen, 156, 157
   strategy, for Middle East, 213–220
   Tunisian uprising and, 78
   See also America

Violent repression
   American condemnation of, 194
   counterrevolution, 131–134.
                See also Counterrevolution
   Egypt, 154
   Green Movement, 205
   Jordan, 143
   Libya, 165–166, 167–176
   regimes' fear of prosecution for, 177
   as self-defeating, 192
   Syria, 165–166, 181–192
   Yemen, 154–157
Vodaphone, shutdown in Egypt, 89
Voice of the Arabs, radio, 33, 34, 37–38

Wafd Party, 32
War
   Israeli (1967), 29–30, 40–41
   Iran-Iraq, 45
   Iraq, 59
   on terror, 215
   U.S. invasion of Iraq, 59–60

Wasmi, Obaid al-, 70–71
We Are All Khaled Said. *See* Facebook
Wedeen, Lisa, 12
West Bank, 41
    #MAR15 hashtag protest and, 118
Western imperialism, 12
Whitaker, Brian, 105
WikiLeaks, role in Tunisian
            uprising, 73
Wisner, Frank, 96
World Bank, 229–230

Yemen
    al-Islah, Islamist party, 15
    in Arab Cold War, 40

effects of Tunisia on, 83
#FEB3, hashtag protest, 105–107
Huthi movement in, 155
military defections, 156
repression and crackdowns, 155–157
unification of, 54
violence in, 156
YouTube
    censorship of, 74
    Syrian video, 182
    See also Social media

Zarqawi, Abu Musab al-, 184, 207
Zawahiri, Ayman al-, 95, 207–208
Zenko, Micah, 229

Marc Lynch (@abuaardvark) is associate professor of political science and international affairs at George Washington University, where he is the director of the Institute for Middle East Studies. He is also a non-resident senior fellow at the Center for a New American Security, and edits the Middle East Channel for ForeignPolicy.com. His most recent book, *Voices of the New Arab Public*, was selected as a Choice Outstanding Academic Book. He lives in Bethesda, Maryland. (Photo: Christopher Leaman)

PublicAffairs is a publishing house founded in 1997. It is a tribute to the standards, values, and flair of three persons who have served as mentors to countless reporters, writers, editors, and book people of all kinds, including me.

I. F. STONE, proprietor of *I. F. Stone's Weekly*, combined a commitment to the First Amendment with entrepreneurial zeal and reporting skill and became one of the great independent journalists in American history. At the age of eighty, Izzy published *The Trial of Socrates*, which was a national bestseller. He wrote the book after he taught himself ancient Greek.

BENJAMIN C. BRADLEE was for nearly thirty years the charismatic editorial leader of *The Washington Post*. It was Ben who gave the *Post* the range and courage to pursue such historic issues as Watergate. He supported his reporters with a tenacity that made them fearless and it is no accident that so many became authors of influential, best-selling books.

ROBERT L. BERNSTEIN, the chief executive of Random House for more than a quarter century, guided one of the nation's premier publishing houses. Bob was personally responsible for many books of political dissent and argument that challenged tyranny around the globe. He is also the founder and longtime chair of Human Rights Watch, one of the most respected human rights organizations in the world.

· · ·

For fifty years, the banner of Public Affairs Press was carried by its owner Morris B. Schnapper, who published Gandhi, Nasser, Toynbee, Truman, and about 1,500 other authors. In 1983, Schnapper was described by *The Washington Post* as "a redoubtable gadfly." His legacy will endure in the books to come.

Peter Osnos, *Founder and Editor-at-Large*